Praise for *The Commercial Real Estate Revolution*

New movements are transforming the building industry and there hasn't been a single place to find them represented together, until now. In a systematic and coherent way, current inefficient processes are identified. *The Commercial Real Estate Revolution* is an essential road map for organizations and owners that want to transform the industry.

—Kimon Onuma, FAIA, Onuma

This is a thoughtful and wonderful read that should interest architects, designers, and leaders in the construction industry. The research is solid and leads to important strategic understanding. I recommend it to you.

—James P. Cramer, President, Design Futures Council Chairman, CEO
for the Greenway Group, and Editor of *Design Intelligence*

The Commercial Real Estate Revolution does more than just provide us a clear view of a dysfunctional AEC industry. Rex and his Mindshift posse are leading the way for owners, design and construction professionals to develop new collaborative processes that will lead to better workplace environments that are on-time and on budget.

—Daniel Gonzales, Corporate Manager, Virtual Design & Construction Swinerton, Inc.

Anyone who has tried to manage a major construction project can readily attest to the fact that the current model fails to consistently deliver the desired results. But what could you do? An entire industry had been built, passed down from one generation to the next, around the concept of control. Yet in *The Commercial Real Estate Revolution*, we clearly see there is a better way, a way to run projects based not on control, but on trust. And it delivers every time.

—Randy Thompson, Area Leader, Client Solutions, Cushman & Wakefield, Inc.

The work of Mindshift is an industry innovation catalyst. *The Commercial Real Estate Revolution* identifies the glaring problems and lurking inefficiencies in the current process by which buildings are dreamed, planned, budgeted, designed, coordinated and built. Mindshift also advocates a common sense but revolutionary design and construction business model that is rapidly gaining supporters and will ultimately add tremendous value to clients. Architects, engineers, and contractors: take notice and prepare to mind shift.

—Bradley H. Thomas P.E., MBA, CEO, Progressive AE Grand Rapids, MI

Anyone involved in the construction industry needs to read and understand the ideas and principles presented in this important book to remain viable in the built environment. Business as usual will not work or be of value to owners and to society in the near future.

—Ray Lucchesi, Principal, Lucchesi Galati

The Boldt Company continues to lead the industry in helping develop transforming trends. *The Commercial Real Estate Revolution* does an excellent job of explaining these trends and their importance for all of the project stakeholders including the owner. The book provides a better understanding of the challenges associated with traditional project delivery and a deeper appreciation for the emerging trends within the industry. A must read for ALL stakeholders.

—Dave Kievet, Group President, California Operations, Boldt Construction

Owners want high design, speed to market, flexibility, and green initiatives—all at predetermined value. The current delivery model forces the industry to trade between these values. An adversarial and fragmented system will never be able to pull these together. It is time to change the rules to allow and support trust-based teams who can deliver on these demands. *The Commercial Real Estate Revolution* provides several examples of owners and project teams who have changed the rules—the results will make you sit up and take note. The book describes a growing movement delivering buildings that please the owners and are rewarding to all involved. It's a true Win/Win model.

—Ric Nelson, Vice President, Development Services, Transwestern
Commercial Services Central Region-Dallas

The Commercial Real Estate Revolution rings the bell, and it must be answered. The collision of this game-changing economy with the large, slow, inept construction industry machine offers a perfect backdrop for the basic Mindshift message—rebuild the entire system, now! I am listening.

—David Dillard, President, CSD Architects

The Commercial Real Estate Revolution sets the table for radical improvements within the world of real estate development. Change is hard, but by exploring the principles outlined in this book, I believe we'll find better solutions in these rapidly changing times—more collaborative, more cost-effective, more integrated, and more innovative.

—Dean Strombom, Principal, Gensler

Finally, someone has actually taken the time to think about how we build things—or rather how we should be creating the buildings of the future. Every project needs to be examined in the light of many of the ideas and experiences in this *The Commercial Real Estate Revolution*. It is the work of experienced and thought provoking professionals. The only remaining question is, "Will we listen?"

—Larry Fees, President, former VP Real Estate, Compuware
Great Lakes Renaissance Group

The *Commercial Real Estate Revolution* is a great introduction to the project delivery process that is based on trust. The industry is calling it Integrated Project Delivery. This book outlines the concepts that must be in place for this new delivery process to achieve its maximum potential.

—Greg Wilkinson, LEED AP; CEO, Hill & Wilkinson General Contractors

THE COMMERCIAL REAL ESTATE REVOLUTION

THE COMMERCIAL REAL ESTATE REVOLUTION

NINE TRANSFORMING KEYS TO LOWERING COSTS, CUTTING WASTE, AND DRIVING CHANGE IN A BROKEN INDUSTRY

**REX MILLER,
DEAN STROMBOM,
MARK IAMMARINO, AND
BILL BLACK**

WILEY

John Wiley & Sons, Inc.

Contents

Acknowledgments

Writing is a solitary endeavor, but *The Commercial Real Estate Revolution* is a true collective effort. More than 50 individuals played important roles putting together a book that covers such a wide range of trends and disciplines. I will do my best to name those who deserve credit but will likely overlook some simply due to the scale of the project.

The Mindshift experiment begins with Dick Haworth's willingness to invite a group of respected leaders together to discuss the current and future state of the industry. Art Gensler offered to host that first meeting in their Houston offices, and through those two leaders the dialogue began. Christine McEntee (executive director for the American Institute of Architects) affirmed the value of our effort and joined us in Chicago and allowed us to tap into Markku Allison for coaching and guidance throughout the process. Peter Davoren added Turner Construction's weight behind the initiative and from there the interest and momentum grew.

The hard work took place during our retreats in Houston, Chicago, Calgary, Dallas, and Denver. Kyle Davy led some of those sessions that took us through the difficult process of layering away preconceptions about how the industry really works, how we think it should work, and what we thought of each other. That process opened us to discovering a new way to think about our industry and future. The greatest thanks go to those who invested time and resources to attend the retreats, not hold back, ask hard questions, hold each person accountable, and push beyond readymade solutions. They include Mark Iammarino, Dean Strombom, Bill Black, Craig Janssen, Mabel Casey, Ray Lucchesi, Mark Charette, Les Shepherd, Marilyn Archer, Susan Szenasy, Ric Nelson, Ben Weeks, and Lydia Knowles.

Our discovery led us to several experts, advisors, and coaches who helped us understand the scope of this revolution and just how fundamental the mindshift is. I would like to thank George Zettle, Kurt Young, Gary Hamor, Dan Gonzales, Will Lichtig, Vince Chapman, Andy Fuhrman, Tim Springer, Tim McGinn, Andrew Fisher, John Paul Beitler III, Mike Wolff, Stephen Jones, and James Timberlake.

I want to thank several who shared the details of their breakthrough projects and how those lessons tested our assumptions and revealed common themes for successfully transforming future projects and the industry. Those include David Thurm, Dean Reed, Bob Mauck, Scott Simpson, David Kievet, and Larry Fees.

I also want to thank many who followed our blog and got into the act by reading and commenting on our early drafts or shared a cup of coffee to offer their insights. They include Larry Canfield, Tyler Adams, Monte Chapin, Kevin Kamschroer, Carl Chinn, Bob Theodore, Wes Garwood, Peter Paesch, Steve Fridsma, Cathy Hutchison, Raymond Kahl, and Cliff Bourland.

I would like to thank my three co-authors: Mark Iammarino, Dean Strombom, and Bill Black. They were venturesome enough to take the message on the road, speaking at conferences and at several other venues. The feedback they received showed us important gaps or questions we needed to address. Their expertise and ongoing consultation through the book has shaped its content and tone.

All of these people have been very generous and open with their time— sending articles, providing interviews, proofing draft chapters, taking spur-of-the-moment calls and answering questions, and tolerating (and responding to) a barrage of requests. All who participated expressed a common interest in producing a well-written, well-documented account and map of the revolution transforming the commercial real estate industry.

I also want to thank some good friends who patiently listened to these ideas take shape for the last three years, and helped probe and test them over many breakfasts. They include David Dillard, Greg Wilkinson, Doug Harden, and Randy Thompson.

I turned to Naomi Lucks, the editor for my first book, *The Millennium Matrix,* to help me complete this on time and to provide the wonderful developmental editing work she is so gifted with. She coached me through the process and kept me on track.

I would like to thank my wife, Lisa, and our three children, Michelle, Tyler, and Nathan, for allowing me to hide away in my office for three months to compile and write the book. Their support and interest provided encouragement to put in the hours needed in the short timeframe.

Richard Narramore, with John Wiley & Sons, provided the strategy and framework for writing the book. He very quickly found the meat of the book and provided clear direction on what to eliminate. I enjoyed his coaching and his economy to conveying strong content.

Finally, I want to thank Haworth for supporting my efforts and allowing me to focus on the Mindshift project and on writing this book. They provided the ideal context for support. They are genuinely interested in seeing our industry transform and to realize its potential—for the benefit of building owners and for everyone who works in the industry. Haworth's leadership recognizes how dramatically the world and business are changing, and how important it is that we adapt. There is nothing more fulfilling than to wake up to a meaningful mission and do so for a company and people who appreciate your contribution.

—Rex Miller
Southlake, Texas

Foreword

Imagine work relationships built on trust, supported by technology, and aided by collaboration. In the twentieth century this seemed like an idealist's dream. But for those of us who like to envision better ways of getting things done, this dream was always alive. It was just hard to find really good examples of it. Now—as this book proves—we are seeing the realization of our dreams.

We are also witnessing a momentous shift into the new century. The timing for this shift is urgent. Our systems, based on the old industrial model that has served us well for more than a century, are facing calamitous post-industrial stresses. They are becoming increasingly unworkable in our networked world. Our beleaguered economy, dangerously polluted environment, and worldwide competition for limited materials spell out the urgent need for a new approach.

The building industry may present the best case study for how the twenty-first century can work. With its potential for productive collaborations between architects, designers, engineers, developers, construction companies, subcontractors, furnishers, and others, it can unite hitherto adversarial professionals around a common goal.

Today, these groups have access to mature electronic software and hardware systems designed to work for teams who solve problems across time and space, and streamline the way buildings are made and furnished. These bring us a good distance toward changing the way we work. But our industry needs more than a tech fix.

It's the human element that needs our full attention today. How can an array of strong personalities, all used to working self-protectively, become members of a smoothly functioning integrated team based on trust? How, for instance, can an architect who sees her design as being compromised by the developer, the engineer, and the sub-contractor learn to work productively with these specialists? How can an owner used to seeing project after project come in over budget, over schedule, and in danger of litigation believe that a trust-based team can even exist?

The teams whose stories are told in this book—and the successful projects they brought in on (or under) budget and on schedule—are the outriders of the building industry. Like those brave scouts who galloped ahead of the westward-moving wagon trains, the individuals on these teams had the interest of the group in mind. They learned to put aside differences because they wanted to learn how to make better, sustainable buildings—ones that are resource- and energy-efficient as well as healthy for their users. Along the way, they learned how to put together a realistic budget, work flexibly together to make adjustments in real time, and meet deadlines without budget overruns. Their experience shows that building on trust is the foundation of design and construction for the twenty-first century: better, more efficient, higher-performing structures that fit the financial, social, environmental, material, and cultural conditions of the twenty-first century. It really can be done.

The groundbreaking book you hold in your hands right now gives you everything you need—the understanding, the principles, the tools, and the encouragement—to change your mind about what's possible, and to begin changing the world.

—**Susan S. Szenasy**
Editor in Chief, *Metropolis Magazine*

Construction plays a vital role in the nation's economy. Owners have growing demands to manage real estate cost, improve quality, and deliver sustainable buildings. However, we are an industry divided by disciplines, traditions, contracts, and old habits. This fragmentation produces lower trust and increased conflict that gets in the way of all of our efforts. Owners want more and they deserve more.

Turner accepted the invitation with an open mind to participate in the first Mindshift meeting in Houston. We knew there would be a broad cross section of leaders that we normally do not have a chance to sit across the table from. We also heard that the leaders attending shared similar concerns and interests for improving how our industry works together. The candor and insight reached during those two days produced a mutual interest to dig deeper into some of the problems that we commonly face and explore promising trends.

The Commercial Real Estate Revolution is an important contribution to the current dialogue about the future direction for the industry. The book offers two years of our collective effort to deal with the questions raised during that first meeting. In our work together we identified nine trends that are reshaping our industry. We also discovered common themes that offer an organizing framework for a future that can replace fragmentation with integrated team efforts and high performance results.

—**Peter Davoren**
President and CEO, Turner Construction

I think we can all agree that everyone associated with the building industry wants to create great spaces. We crave beautiful design. We ache to create buildings that reach their potential. We love it when a space comes together on time and delights the customer with its aesthetics, its function, its furnishings, its sustainability, and its price tag.

So if everybody working on buildings has essentially this same commitment to excellence, why does the process so often go horribly wrong? Why do customers end up with bad spaces that don't function well and cost far more than they should?

As the leader of a global company that designs and manufactures commercial building interiors—including raised floors, moveable walls, systems furniture, seating, wood and steel casegoods—I've asked myself that question countless times. I'd venture to say that Haworth has created more than our fair share of great spaces. But it's rarely easy. It's characteristically painful. And the process often leaves me thinking, "There's got to be a better way."

Enter Rex Miller and his revolutionary ideas about commercial real estate. When he approached us with the concept, I was excited about the possibilities it offered to literally change a basic paradigm in the building industry and give us a decent chance to do a better job for our customers, ourselves, the broader economy, and the environment. This book contains that essence: a blueprint of new and better ways of working together as an industry.

In working with our customers to create world-class buildings, Haworth has had the privilege of partnering with many of the world's most outstanding architects, contractors, interior designers, real estate developers, dealers, facility managers, and owners. But what would happen if instead of functioning as a loose coalition of quasi-competitors, we truly collaborated on projects from beginning to end, with the customer as a full partner? Here's what would happen: Better projects. Lower costs. Happier customers.

Achieving such a seismic shift will require trust, collaboration, and effort. For a start, the executive leaders of all the players must set the right vision for the project team. As leaders, we are the only ones who can break the destructive bid environment that lurks at the heart of conventional thinking. We must agree upon a clear set of project objectives to help our employees become more effective. Those objectives should include achieving strategic alignment with the owner/occupant, developing realistic budget parameters, agreeing on the project's sustainability, and setting a clear expectation that partnerships will begin early and carry through to completion.

As an early adopter of lean thinking and total quality management, Haworth has been in sync with these forward-looking ideas since at least the 1970s. Rex has now articulated them in a way that could benefit our entire industry. We look forward to partnering with organizations who embrace this collaborative approach to improving our industry.

Haworth is excited to be a supporter of this much-needed shift in thinking. After you read the book, we hope you are, too. We know that this new way of working will help create better, more sustainable and pain-free projects that wow our customers and make us proud to be a part of them.

—**Richard G. Haworth**
Chairman Emeritus, Haworth, Inc.

Introduction: The Money Pit

We are proposing a radical change in the way we build.

—Rethinking Construction: The Egan Report

In the 1986 movie *The Money Pit,* Tom Hanks' and Shelly Long's characters pour buckets of money into a disastrous and never-ending home remodel. Back in 1948, the Cary Grant comedy *Mr. Blandings Builds His Dream House* told a similar tale of high hopes that are quickly dashed by real estate renovations. But it's not only homeowners who laugh through their tears at these films: The familiar story of unforeseen building nightmares touches a well of deep emotions with anyone who has ever been involved in a construction project. The conditions of poor quality, cost overruns, and late projects are just the obvious symptoms of an increasingly dysfunctional industry. Randy

Thompson, a construction manager for the global real estate firm Cushman Wakefield, summarizes this situation well: "The current system causes good people to do bad things."

Jokes reveal another symptom and insight into a dysfunctional system. Here are some fun definitions for many of the key stakeholders in construction.

- Contractor: A gambler who never gets to shuffle, cut, or deal
- Bid Opening: A poker game in which the losing hand wins
- Bid: A wild guess carried out to two decimal places
- Low Bidder: A contractor who is wondering what he left out
- Engineer's Estimate: The cost of construction in heaven
- Project Manager: The conductor of an orchestra in which every musician is in a different union
- Critical Path Method: A management technique for losing your shirt under perfect control
- Completion Date: The point at which liquidated damages begin
- Liquidated Damages: A penalty for failing to achieve the impossible
- Auditor: A person who goes in after the war is lost and bayonets the wounded
- Lawyer: A person who goes in after the auditors to strip the bodies

In the real world, however, these jokes are not a laughing matter. Recently, a large southeastern U.S. hospital awarded their project to a reputable national contractor. The plumbing subcontractor who won the job quoted $1 million. Several months later when it was time to begin work that price suddenly increased to $5 million and would require an additional six months. The job quickly spiraled out of control. The domino effect of delays and the ensuing conflict resulted in disaster for all parties. The hospital finished a year late, costing the owner an additional $13 million. The contractor paid a year's worth of liquidated damages and quickly tainted their good reputation in the region. The subcontractor made a mistake on the initial bid that no one caught until it was too late. Even an honest mistake in a system of mistrust backs everyone into a corner with only one way to go—down.

Even worse are the systematic attempts to overcharge clients, a topic that is the underlying theme of Barry LePatner's book *Broken Buildings, Busted Budgets*. And during my own interview with leading construction auditor Vince Chapman, I heard stories that were so outrageous that I had to laugh in disbelief. Vince said this bad behavior was common.

"How do firms get away with these kinds of tricks?" I wondered out loud.

Vince's answer was simple: "If you don't think there's something there to look for, you won't find it." Fortunately, a growing number of clients know that something isn't right, but they still need a pro like Vince to sniff out the hidden tricks.

Owners are at a marked disadvantage. The design and construction process is complicated and opaque, and blame is easy to shift. LaPatner describes this disadvantage as "asymmetrical." Even hiring third-party intermediaries is not enough, and can often add another unnecessary layer of opacity and cost. Building—the way it is currently done—is indeed a money pit. In fact, the buildingSMART alliance™ estimates that more than 50 percent of the cost of a building is waste.[1] That's more than *half*! Every organization that builds a facility pays a hidden tax comprised of delays, cost overruns, poor quality, rework— and *not* building what was really needed. Why is this? Because our current system of deciding, designing, and delivering these buildings is fundamentally broken.

It was this realization that prompted several organizations to come together to begin talking about a solution to this ever-growing problem. Their gatherings became known as the Mindshift consortium. This group of 23 top commercial real estate and construction leaders— fed up with a system that "makes good people do bad things"—aimed at achieving nothing short of transforming an industry.

MINDSHIFT FACES THE CHALLENGE FOR TRANSFORMATION

The Mindshift consortium pulled from the industry the most promising initiatives and went one step further: They completely changed the rules by moving their concepts from a think-tank to a "do-tank." The result was a *mindshift:* a change of perspective and understanding that allowed the group to see the problems from a vastly different perspective. In the process, they discovered a beginning-to-end, trust-based integrated paradigm that proved it is indeed possible to not just fix the process but to *transform* it, and to create less expensive, higher-quality, and sustainable green buildings that meet the needs of builders and users.

Mindshift members are practical business leaders governed by a bottom line. We know, after all, that there has to be a compelling business case if one company—let alone an entire industry—is going to be compelled to change its fundamental behavior. Still, innovation takes a long time to adapt and adopt. So Mindshift focused on the three biggest hurdles when introducing disruptive innovation: the fragmented variety of new solutions; the lack of live or well-documented examples; and the lag time that exists before the larger companies feel that it is safe to join in the effort.

We sorted through a wide range of experiments and innovations, considered which were worth pursuing and where the potential payoff was. The diverse configuration of the team meant that we could move quickly to find the unifying principles and a common framework for a new innovative system of delivery.

We drilled down into the struggles and challenges that each member—and the industry as a whole—faces. We also drilled up, in order to imagine what the industry could look like if we started with a blank sheet of paper. We imagined our best work, delighted clients, projects that connected with and restored communities—and a legacy that we would all be proud to look back on. And although we all recognized bottom-line justification as our first order of business, these visions created a stronger pull than we realized. No member was intrested in getting sidetracked by feel-good management or nice talk with no walk to back it up. We indulged just enough to find the common ground that we agreed could make a positive difference to our businesses, our industry, and the world around us.

Interesting serendipities take place when a strong team embarks into uncharted territory in search for the better mousetrap. We met some of the early innovators and began to learn about some fascinating work from among our own members. We found that the higher calling in which we had momentarily indulged was not only alive, but fundamental to the effectiveness of these groups and projects. These efforts had the following in common: a new set of assumptions, a commitment to change, highly engaged team members, deep trust, delighted clients, and profit margins that exceeded industry averages by several multiples. We began to believe that it just might be possible to combine our best work within a new context that also produced the best possible results: lower costs, earlier completion, sustainable building, and virtually no change orders.

Right now our industry's traditional way of doing business forces undesirable and unacceptable trade-offs that compromise our best work. Conventional construction has three components that live in constant conflict: cost, quality, and schedule. The rule of thumb is that you can pick any two, but you must forgo the third. In other words, if you want a project completed quickly, you either have to pay more or sacrifice quality. If you want a low-cost project, you must give up quality or extend the schedule. If you want a high-quality project, it will either cost more or take longer—or both. Yet the new model projects that Mindshfit examined accomplished all three of these, and included several non-monetary benefits as well. The reduced conflict, added reliability, and retained learning are some of those additional benefits. More important, the traditional dynamic of conflict was transformed into high collaboration, which resulted in improvements and solutions that couldn't possibly surface within the current construction model.

The last challenge for transformation is the fear of being on the bleeding edge of change. Smaller firms tend to be more comfortable with risk and are typically the source of innovation. However, because these trailblazers are not nationally known, larger firms often hold off until enough industry leaders consider the conditions tested enough to enter.[2] Unfortunately, many innovators crash and burn along the way. Once a few prove that it can be done, a new wave of early adopters—who either believe in some of the ideas or seek a competitive advantage—tend to step up. Mindshift made a conscious decision to create a team that combined these marquee firms with smaller innovators. It provided an ideal mix of creative tension, a depth of resources, and a focus on practical application.

We immediately recognized two things. First, marquee firms would not participate without that focus on practical application and a well developed business case; second, their credibilty could act as a catalyst to accelerate broader industry change. When organizations like Gensler, Turner, Haworth, American Institute of Architecture, Walter P. Moore, the General Services Administration, *Metropolis Magazine*, and KPMG join forces along with other industry leaders, it is worth taking note.

THE COMMERCIAL REAL ESTATE REVOLUTION

The Commercial Real Estate Revolution came as a result of Mindshift's gathering and deliberation, and it is a bold manifesto. Unlike similar collective efforts, it is not a bland, high-level executive summary with generalized initiatives and recommendations. Nor is it an academic exercise, a tradebook for insiders, or one person's rant. It is a stinging critique of current industry practices along with a well-developed alternative: a reliable, trust-based model that provides specific examples and a roadmap on how to achieve these objectives.

Our model is by no means monolithic; it is certainly open to critique. But the principles of beginning-to-end thinking and trust-based teaming form the core of the model and challenge the industry status quo. Those who wish to continue to participate in an outdated model will be increasingly forced to defend their poor results. Patrick MacLeamy, CEO of HOK, made the choice very clear when addressing the 2004 Construction Specifications Institute's annual conference in Chicago: "People are paying too much for their buildings, and the buildings are just not that good."

We're all familiar with the saying that "Insanity is doing the same thing over and over again and expecting different results." The building industry is more than overdue for new, saner results. Whether readers wear a hard hat or a suit, create the renderings, submit the permits, design the building, finance the venture, manage the project, inspect the work, or sit in the C-suite evaluating the business case for their next project, *The Commercial Real Estate Revolution* offers a map to a new and better way of building with benefits that extend far beyond the project itself. *The Commercial Real Estate Revolution* is more than a theory; it is an industry case that provides real-life projects, a business model, and simulations that serve as a guide for colleagues, peers, and clients.

Here's the bottom line: Conventional design and construction consistently produce bad results, and that will continue to be the case if we continue doing business as usual. This book is aimed at helping every player in the construction industry, and all who deal with it, understand that a new trust-based integrated paradigm can transform the process and create less expensive, higher quality, and sustainable buildings.

The Commercial Real Estate Revolution is a call for change. It prepares corporate leaders to tell the commercial real estate world, "I'm mad as hell, and I'm not going to take it anymore!" It outlines a strategy that leaders can use to position themselves to take advantage of this new mind shift built on trust, flexibility, and tightly integrated work teams focused on delivering *value*—not just a building. The stories of early adopters will guide a new core of leaders through the process of "mind shifting" their real estate. Leaders will learn how to implement practical ways for improving environmental efforts—embracing and achieving sustainability without committing balance sheet suicide.

In Part One, we'll take a hard look at our dying system, based on mistrust and fragmentation, and why it's so difficult to leave the old paradigm behind. In Part Two, we'll look at what it takes to make the mind shift to the new paradigm—based on trust and integration—and explore some projects that are doing it right now. In Part Three, we'll show you the commercial real estate revolution in action: four principles, four tools, and one hidden revolution that together comprise the nine transforming keys to lowering cost, cutting waste, and driving change in a broken industry (see Figure I.1):

Figure I.1   Mindshift Target

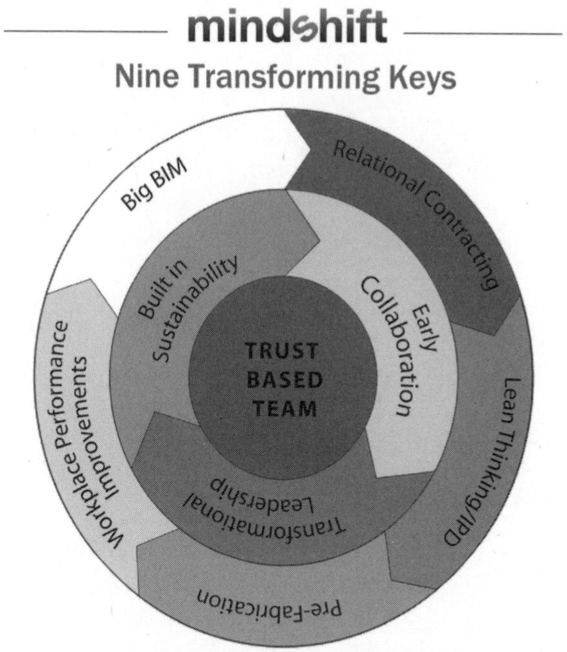

Mindshift Nine Transforming Keys to lowering cost, cutting waste, and driving change in a broken industry.

Key 1: Trust-Based Team Formation (Principle 1)

Key 2: Early Collaboration (Principle 2)

Key 3: Built-In Sustainability (Principle 3)

Key 4: Transformational Leadership (Principle 4)

Key 5: "Big" BIM (Tool 1)

Key 6: Integrating Project Delivery (Tool 2)

Key 7: Trust-Based Agreements and Client-Centered Incentives (Tool 3)

Key 8: Offsite Construction (Tool 4)

Key 9: Workplace Productivity (The Hidden Revolution)

This future world of the built environment is well worth venturing to discover: savings of 25 percent and more, LEED® Platinum buildings at the same cost as conventional constrution, substantially improved schedules, and conflict-free projects. Yet *The Commercial Real Estate Revolution* is about more than innovative project delivery; it is about transformation of behavior and relationships, as well as projects. This transformation represents the true revolution.

Part One The Commercial Real Estate Money Pit

"Executives of major U.S. corporations, the leaders of public institutions, and millions of American homeowners are routinely held hostage by the construction industry to pay or face greater costs and delays."

—Barry B. Lepatner

Chapter 1 The $500 Billion Black Hole

About 60 percent of the office space that companies pay so dearly for is now a dead zone of darkened doorways and wasting cubes.

—Mark Golan, vice president of real estate, Cisco Systems

In 2007, U.S. construction was estimated at $1.288 trillion—with more than 50 percent of that cost attributed to waste.[1] If you're skeptical, join the club. Some Mindshift members initially expressed the same skepticism. "There's no way half the cost of building is waste!" But under the skepticism of owners and builders and contractors lies a real concern: I have no clue how to cut out 50 percent of my cost for a building.

The numbers are consistent, available to anyone who wants to take a close look,[2] as we did. Because the first step to unlocking the mystery is to take a systematic look at the categories of waste. On virtually every construction project in the United States, we can trace this $500 billion black hole in the American economy back to two root causes: simple inefficiency and not-so-simple bad behavior.

WHY THE DESIGN-BUILD MODEL IS DEAD

The industry's traditional model for building—"design-bid-build (DBB)," solidified in the 1950s with the American Institute of Architects (AIA's) establishment of distinct phases for a project: schematic (concept), design development, construction documentation, and construction administration. The process follows a logical linear progression: design a building, assemble a team to build it, and implement the plans. Sounds like a reasonable idea, and for many years it was. The DBB delivery method began to falter in the 1960s with serious cracks by the 1970s. These cracks are evidenced by the introduction of alternative delivery models each attempting to remedy one of DBB's shortcomings.

Construction paralleled manufacturing gains in productivity right up until 1964, when it hit a roadblock. From that date forward manufacturing consistently improves, but construction productivity slowly declines. By 2003, the Bureau of Labor Statistics measured a 275 percent gap between manufacturing gains and construction declines (Figure 1.1). What happened?

Figure 1.1 Department of Labor Productivity Gap Between Construction and Manufacturing

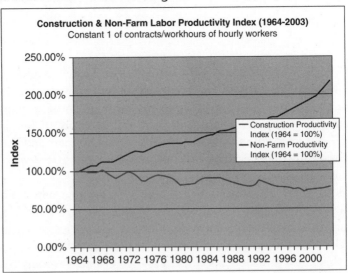

Source: US Dept. of Commerce, Bureau of Labor Statistics

A number of factors explain the divergence, including fundamental changes in the economy.[3] The post-World War II expansion and baby boom peaked, and the information economy began to surpass manufacturing. Beginning in 1973, the recession pushed architects and engineers to move from a craft practice model to a professional services model, adopting fee structures similar to lawyers and accountants. Emphasis shifted away from the master-builder role, where the architect not only designed but supervised construction, to a specialist mentality that focused on the architect's unique business capability in design.[4] Contractors also began to deal with shrinking margins and higher risk by migrating away from performing the work with their own employees to becoming labor brokers.

Way back in the 1970s, Alvin Toffler's *Future Shock* was prescient in identifying the factor most responsible for the decline of the design-bid-build delivery method: a need for speed. Back in the days before cell phones and personal computers, Toffler described a new world that would be qualitatively different from past eras. This new economy would be based on information and driven by change. It would require speed and flexibility. This way of doing things would be like a Ferrari, hugging the road and taking the turns with ease. Unfortunately, the design-bid-build process was a Lincoln Town Car—built for quality and a comfortable ride, but not much good on the hairpin turns and switchbacks of the brave new world that we live in today.

The paradigm has changed, and the building industry is scrambling to catch up. The speed-to-market business driver has forced a conflicting trade-off between quality, cost, and time.[5] During the last 30 years or so, we have experimented with several variations of the design-bid-build model, looking for better ways to address the speed-to-market demand without sacrificing quality, compromising the owner's intent, inflating costs, or putting the project or a key stakeholder at undue risk. Owners have a choice of the first two variables, but they must allow the construction team to control the third. In addition to process waste there is waste in the end product. According to Mark Golan, vice president of worldwide real estate, Cisco Systems,[6] "About 60 percent of the office space that companies pay so dearly for is now a dead zone of darkened doorways and wasting cubes." This is not the result we want.

Mindshift took a close look at all of the different delivery models and concluded that most are variations of DBB that seek to bring harmony to the three variables of cost, schedule, and quality. They take the same familiar approach—assembling fragmented collections of companies, selected independently and most often based on low bids. These solutions not only do not solve the problem, they compound it, resulting in more of what we don't want: waste.

WHERE THE WASTE COMES FROM

A very visible form of waste comes from inaccurate information that creeps into projects with multiple specialties gathering and regathering the same data during a project.[7] But less visible and much more ingrained sources of waste come from the structural components that govern our industry:

- lack of time
- silos (vertically organized departments or organizations that work without consideration of other interdependent entities)
- boilerplate planning
- sub-trade coordination
- hierarchical dilution
- phase-induced ignorance
- problems that come with fielding a new team with every project

Robert A. Humphrey said, "An undefined problem has an infinite number of solutions." Before we go any further, then, let's see if we can define the problem.

LACK OF TIME

"Haste makes waste" in a system designed to function as a sequence of distinct phases. DBB no longer reflects the fluid reality of a project. Most buildings commence construction before architectural plans are completed. One colleague attributes the majority of the problems he has experienced with projects using this phased approach to the lack of time invested in the design phase. We will see in the third section of the book the need for owners to bring their team on board even prior to design to assist with the business plan for the project. Architect Paul Adams sums it up: "All the big mistakes are made in the first day."[8]

Rushed implementation ranks as the next most common complaint after the bid process itself. Brokers are key contributors to the lack of planning time given to the design and construction process. They are trained to get the best deal on a new building or a lease, and often they do not appreciate the details and time necessary to plan and coordinate construction and the move. The commission brokers are paid for the transaction has no tie to the success of the transition. Some brokers see their role in the larger context. Those brokers are often essential team makers and team leaders. These are individuals who rise above the industry's fragmentation and go against a compensation structure that narrowly rewards completing the lease transaction.

The owner of one national project management firm noted that the narrow role and incentive of the broker affects more than single-transaction accounts. His firm works side-by-side with a brokerage firm on a multi-year, multi-site account. The project management firm has documented the need for five weeks to design and deliver a space once the lease is signed. Despite several mutual meetings with the client and broker, the average time allowed is three weeks. Contributing to this lack of coordination are the different departments that the broker and project management firm reports to. The results are predictable. Each project requires more time, experiences errors and cost overruns, and creates a high level of conflict. When projects run into problems, the broker is long gone working on the next transaction, and the project management firm is front and center taking the criticism. Fragmentation is the true culprit and reason the client has yet to make the connection that the handoff from the broker determines if the project is successful or problematic.

A general contractor noted another common omission: Capital equipment and long lead-time items are commonly overlooked by the owner and not factored in to the bid schedule. In one case, the contractor won a project requiring several chillers. The owner expected and counted on a four-month construction schedule based on the architect's estimated timeline. What they did not consider was the five-month lead-time to purchase and produce the chillers, and the additional month to connect the piping and make them operational. The general contractor commented that had they used the five-week bid process for intense pre-construction analysis and planning the owner could have achieved the desired outcome and saved several million dollars due to delays and fixing errors on the job.

SILOS

If you've ever been to the Midwest, you know what a silo is: a vertical storage facility dedicated to protect one product and one product only, with only one way in or out, and with no connection to any of the other silos that dot the land. Sadly, this also describes the building industry (see Figure 1.2).

Planning a new facility involves many stakeholders, all narrowly focused on their different interests. In general, the user groups focus on how much space they need and their budget, the real estate group focuses on optimizing the capital they have allocated and on ways to lower operational costs. Other departments—including information technology, tax department, human resources, and marketing—also have an interest in the new facility, and may contribute to the final solution. Unfortunately, few companies have a defined process for sorting through all of these different and, usually, competing interests; and few consultants have the expertise to sort through this complexity in a rapid or cost-effective way.[9] The result is an awkward analysis

Figure 1.2   Silos

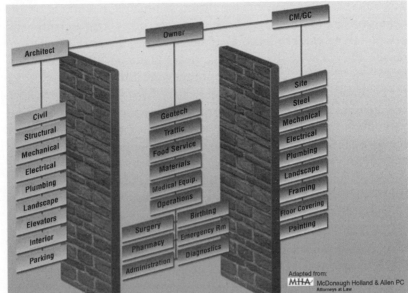

and business planning process that ends up with little more than a head count, a wish list of desired features, a capital budget, and a timeline.

Now it's the architect's turn. He or she must reconcile a broad wish list with an inadequate fee for the services required to provide a thorough assessment, an insufficient capital budget to fulfill the wish list, and a project that is already behind schedule.

If the silos inside the owner's company produce a plan based on speculative assumptions, unreconciled conflicting demands, floating priorities, and wishful expectations, it must then augur through additional silos—including the interests of the owner, the architect, the general contractor, and their agents. Those interests are separated by walls governed by legal and insurance concerns and filtered through different business cultures, methodologies, and missions.

The owner's mission is to get a facility that meets their needs as close to the budget and schedule as possible. The architect's mission is to get the most bang for the buck with the budget and parameters the owner sets. The general contractor will attempt to build what the architect and owner design, while managing the many variables that impact construction and increasing their fee to cover potential unknowns.

There is a built-in tension between the three parties. The owner will adjust as much as they can to take into account changing business needs. The architect will wait as long as they can to lock into a final plan responding to owner adjustments or contractor suggestions to lower cost or improve constructability. The general contractor will attempt to secure earlier decisions or increase their contingency fee. These separations restrict the flow of information, delay decisions, create conflict, end in adversarial relationships, and turn natural allies into enemies.

This adversarial behavior is better understood by looking at the larger system.[10] When teams work well, each member works toward the success of the other. That success, however, is the result of more than good rapport. Reinforcing positive behavior is a feature of a well-designed system. Members first understand the different processes others use to get their work accomplished and therefore understand how their actions can aid or detract from that work.[11] Secondly, members have a clear understanding that the benefits of team success outweigh individual success. In fact, members see clearly that a narrow focus on individual success not only limits but also can derail team success. Even casual sports observers see how this dynamic plays out.

The term for this among systems theorists is "accidental adversaries." Kyle Davy explains, "When our mutual success depends on one another we unwittingly work against each other and become adversaries further eroding our mutual chances for success." One contractor described this as "three ticks and no dog."

During a Mindshift retreat, our facilitator, Kyle Davy, walked us through a common scenario of accidental adversaries. Architects and mechanical, electrical, and plumbing engineers (MEPs) should be natural allies. Their mutual work should lead to tighter alignment and cooperation. Instead, if you ask MEPs which entity creates their greatest turmoil, they point immediately to architects. If you ask an architect the same question they immediately point to the MEP.

The problem occurs when each follows an internal success logic creating unintended impacts on their partner. The architect, for example, sees design as a constant search integrating new information to improve the design. Constant change and searching for a better solution becomes an exercise in futile rework for the MEP. The MEP views change not as an improvement in design but as a partner who can't make up their mind or control their client.

MEPs are impacted because they have to scrap their work and start over. The internal logic for the MEP is to protect the time quoted and their profit margin. To do so they respond with a strategy to hold off with estimates as long as possible until the architect has finished making changes.

This strategy creates an unintended impact on the architect. They now view their partner as continually late with work, uncooperative, and creating last-minute fire drills for the architect to complete their work. This creates a feedback loop that reinforces this vicious cycle. These loops are common in complex systems that are not well integrated or are dramatically fragmented like the construction industry.

Several forward-thinking architectural and engineering firms seek regular training in system dynamics through organizations like the Senior Executive Institute and Peter Senge's Society of Organizational Learning. As good as this training is, however, leaders still have to swim against the tide of a much larger dysfunctional system. Our education has trained us to be more competent as compartmental thinkers rather than systems thinkers. (In Part Two, we'll look at the move toward whole system thinking from those who recognize this root problem as a natural byproduct of sustainable practices and the use of technologies like Building Informational Modeling.)[12]

Liability concerns further make the external silos harder to cross. "Architects and engineers are guided by their lawyers and insurance companies to back away from responsibility in the name of risk management and avoiding lawsuits," one architect told us. "Example: Providing an owner a 'Cost Estimate' is now an 'Opinion of Probable Cost.'

"Architects cannot walk onto a job-site and point out conditions that appear to be unsafe, because if it is and someone gets hurt, they have just become liable.

"The construction industry has also responded to the fear of liability," he continued. "Many contractors appear to be unable or unwilling to fulfill the coordination role and lead the project through the means and methods of getting the work built. They hold back their input on implementation expressing frustration that the drawings are not complete enough for them to plan their work adequately. In my opinion, they are mistaking coordination for design. This can result in poorly scheduled and staged efforts across job categories, requiring costly tear-outs that lengthen the project schedule.

"I believe both industries are at fault here and need to do better at meeting in the middle to close the responsibility gap," he said.[13] I heard the same general complaints from owners and builders.

The siloed mindset works against cooperation and coordination and usually prevents parties from meeting each other halfway. The remedy for silos is a structure of collaboration with tools promoting collaboration.

BOILERPLATE PLANNING

Lack of time and lack of collaboration leads to finding the easiest solution when setting parameters: boilerplate planning that relies on industry standards or rules of thumb rather than innovative, custom solutions that actually fit the needs of the project.

Each entity creates its own spreadsheet to plug in parameters that set the size and budget for their portion of the job. It results in large amounts of underused space or dead zones and projects that too often miss the mark, perhaps this too should be called into question.

The broker takes their portion and translates head count into a square foot requirement and then a lease rate. The landlord provides an allowance to build out the space based on factors used to amortize that cost over the life of the lease. Architects calculate a fee based on the square footage of the lease. Relocation is estimated at a cost per head, technology at a cost per drop, dry wall at a cost per lineal feet, cabling based on how many pulls and connections, and the list goes on. When all of these are added up they become the sum total of the cost of a job. The problem with this math is that it reinforces superficial problem solving and maintains a process where, as Patrick MacLeamy earlier stated, "People are paying too much for their buildings, and the buildings are just not that good."

When a company wants to consider a sustainable solution and the numbers are plugged into these boilerplates, the results say it will cost a premium. When a company wants to consider a non-standard but more efficient underfloor air solution that also houses data and electrical cabling, the boilerplate calculates that it will cost more. When a company wants to consider a more natural lighting solution conventional wisdom says it will cost too much. When a company wants to use a prefabricated interior wall solution, the standard planning process presents a higher front-end cost for the product. In each case and others these better solutions don't have to cost more—unless they are run through the gauntlet of boilerplate spreadsheets.

A Fortune 50 company planned a new regional headquarters. Their business model projected uncertainty and the need for a flexible solution. One company proposed a raised floor solution for their data and electrical wiring and a prefabricated interior wall to accommodate that change. The CFO and Vice President of Real Estate requested a site visit to another large company using the solution to address possible concerns for how it might look. They came away from the trip both comfortable and impressed with how the space looked. The next issue was cost. The CFO made it clear that if the solution cost more the company was not interested. The fact, however, is that these solutions are traditionally more expensive because they are priced and planned within a conventional construction boilerplate. The construction manager for the developer had prior experience with this approach during the telecom boom. He had the confidence to challenge conventional wisdom. He did so by forming a team commissioning the general contractor to pull the key subs together along with the floor and wall supplier and invest three weeks in preplanning. They learned that the subs, unfamiliar with the solution, were pricing their labor the same way they would for standard construction. The front-end coordination reduced the initial cost estimates by more than 15 percent, and the final cost was almost one dollar a square foot less than conventional dry wall construction including installing the data and electrical under a raised floor for the 130,000-square-foot first phase. The client expressed enthusiasm with the result, and the team that developed the pricing recognized the value that could be brought to future jobs through early coordination.[14]

The first hurdle had been overcome, but a second would almost scrap this unconventional approach. This time the landlord weighed in when they realized the extent of the raised floor on the project. Even though the raised floor was part of the signed lease, the landlord claimed they had the right to require the tenant to leave the space in its original condition when they moved out—the boilerplate requirement. Everyone knows what a typical lease space looks like; the electrical and data are installed above the ceiling and the carpet sits on a slab, not a raised floor. That meant that the raised floor would need to be removed and the electrical and data placed back into the ceiling. The cost to do that was estimated at $500,000. This curve ball created a series of stressful negotiations. Again, the landlord was operating out of unfamiliarity and boilerplate thinking.

Then a curious thing happened. The landlord made an unannounced visit to the manufacturer's showroom to see the floor and research their case. When the negotiations reconvened, the landlord had a 180-degree reversal. Instead of resisting the solution, they now saw the raised floor as an asset and negotiated to have the floor left in place when the lease was up. Without key people willing to risk their positions and challenge the system, a project like this would never have happened.

Companies eager to build sustainable buildings typically participate in a process called LEED® certification. LEED stands for Leadership in Energy and Environmental Design through the United States Green Building Council (USGBC). LEED provides a checklist (boilerplate) to guide companies in their efforts to achieve different rungs of recognition. The conventional wisdom is that to receive a Gold or Platinum level of recognition a building will cost more. Depending on who you talk to and in what part of the country it is built, that front-end premium can range from 10 percent to 30 percent.

Aardex, a developer in Golden, Colorado, took a different approach. They designed a 190,000-square-foot speculative office building (it was not built for a particular client) with a philosophy of "doing the right thing." They were 75 percent through working out the design details when their director of marketing commented that it might be worth comparing the plan of the building against the LEED criteria. Anyone LEED certified would immediately cringe anticipating a costly and difficult effort to convert a standard design this far along in the process. However, when Aardex made the comparison they discovered the design was only three points away from the highest rating, Platinum. Achieving those additional three points required no design changes, simply a reformatting of how the information was submitted.

In addition, with the Platinum LEED rating, Aardex fully pre-leased the building at a 21 percent higher lease rate than neighboring buildings. They also used a raised floor to handle their HVAC, electrical, and data, which lowered the operational costs by 45 percent compared to neighboring buildings. Their prefabricated interior walls improved the build-out schedule and now allowed them to reconfigure office space in days compared to weeks if they had used conventional drywall. In this case it took a developer who ignored conventional wisdom and was willing to take on the risk of breaking the rules.

SUB–TRADE COORDINATION

"Leaks happen at the intersection of contracts" according to Will Lichtig with McDonough, Holland, and Allen PC (see Figure 1.3). Scope-based contracting reinforces silos—and in fact creates *more* silos—and provides a disincentive for cooperation and coordination. It further produces an intricate dance of risk-shifting. Each trade responds to the explicit requirements within their contract and disclaims any responsibility if they are unable to integrate their work with adjoining trades.

Canned specs and scope-based contracts create coordination problems in the actual construction that end up in change orders or quality problems. One example is the coordination between the structural steel and the curtain wall (outside wall). Standard specification for the structural steel allows for a ½-inch tolerance, whereas the curtain wall may require a ¼-inch tolerance. To resolve the possible gap, either the structural contractor will issue a change order to add splice plates (wall anchors) to attach the curtain wall or the curtain wall contractor will have to add attachments back to the structure.

These kinds of tolerance disconnects can also create problems with insulation. Common coordination problems occur between the foundation and the structural contractor, the concrete slab and the floor

Figure 1.3   Leaks at the Intersection of Contracts

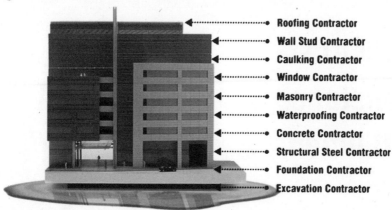

Adapted from: Todd Zadelle, Strategic Project Solutions.

laid on top of the slab, and the exterior caulking that seals creases between trades: the list includes any two trades that intersect. Drawings and specifications do not typically detail the means for trades to coordinate, but expect that the trades will work that out. However, the result of tightly defined contracts means that each intersection can turn into a jump ball that the owner must decide and pay for.

HIERARCHICAL DILUTION

- Construction is a hierarchical structure with the client at the top and the vendors at the bottom (see Figure 1.4). This separates the primary source of knowledge and cost from those making the initial important decisions that set the course for the entire project. Eighty percent of a project's cost lies within the specialty sub-trades who are only brought into the project once all of the design decisions are made.[15]
- In a typical bid process a general contractor will compete against a dozen or more other general contractors. The architect sends them a large set of blueprints; a bid document that explains the requirements of the project; the expectations of the owner along with the rules for the bid submissions. The general contractor assigns an estimator to assemble a bid quote. The architect will then hold a meeting with the bidders to answer questions and address any omissions that are in the document. The owner may or may not be present at this meeting.

Figure 1.4 House of Cards

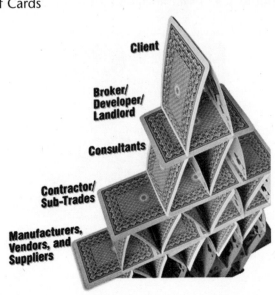

Distrust
Distance
Dilution

Adapted from Haworth.

One contractor noted that those meetings are often a game to make sure each contractor keeps the other honest.

- The estimator then determines which sub-trades are required and sends invitations to review the plans and submit pricing. There can be 100 or more sub-trades required for a project. Each sub-trade is then bid against a half-dozen subcontractors. That means the estimator will compile several hundred quotes and sift through those to assemble his final estimate.

- Typically what the estimator receives is a price with little or no explanation of how it was arrived at. If one party submits a number that deviates widely from the others, they might get a call to double-check the submission. The bid response is more like a mechanical assembly of price quotes than an examination of the design of the architect's proposed solution for the owner. The subcontractors have little incentive to invest much effort thinking through how best to perform their scope of the project. If the general contractor has a one in twelve chance of winning the project, the subcontractor must then factor that their chances of winning are further reduced by the number of firms they are competing with (see Figure 1.5).

Figure 1.5   Vendor Dilution of Interest

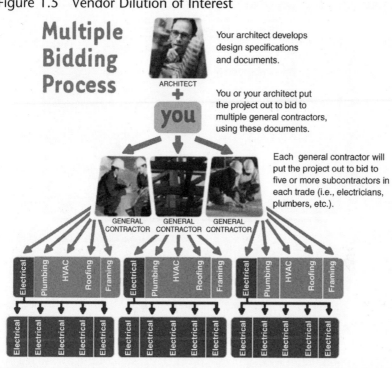

Courtesy of Solidus.

- The general contractor and subs know that most of the assumptions used to bid the job will change as the design proceeds and more clearly defines the scope and conditions for each trade. That fact provides another disincentive to spend a lot of time working through the details and to submit a proposal with rule-of-thumb costs.[16]

PHASE-INDUCED IGNORANCE

- As Figure 1.6 illustrates, the current model engages the major stakeholders, leaving out input from those who actually do the work. Every sub-trade and vendor we talked to says they walk away from construction meetings shaking their heads. And they all say the same thing: "If only I was brought in when they were considering this solution, I could have saved them a bundle." The waste is twofold: unnecessary costs due to poor or uninformed decisions and lost opportunities for innovation.

Figure 1.6   The Lag of Intelligence Curve

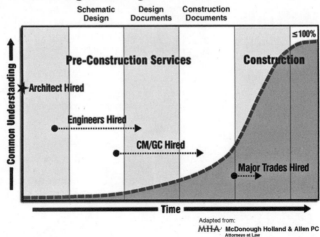

Adapted from:
MHA· McDonough Holland & Allen PC
Attorneys at Law

NEW TEAMS FOR EVERY PROJECT

Construction teams—designers, contractors, subcontractors—are put together anew every time a building goes up. Different actors bid on the design, the general contracting, and the subcontracting—from pouring the concrete to installing window glass to carpeting the floors. Final choices are generally made on the basis of lowest cost. This process virtually ensures that no matter how sound the original vision, it will become fragmented almost as soon as the building process begins.

Often these players are working together on a project for the first time. With no history together, lack of communication is built in to every project.

Worse, each firm signs a contract with the building owner or other key stakeholders containing clauses aimed at protecting both parties from liability and litigation. So, from the beginning, the construction process is based on distrust.

The bottom line? Instead of playing toward a common goal, each party is playing to finish their part and get out unscathed. Imagine the chaos that would result if any sports team had to put together a new set of players every time they wanted to play a game!

IT'S TIME TO CONNECT THE DOTS

The cumulative effect of the current model produces buildings that cost almost twice as much as they should, and more than half of that space is considered a dead zone. The current model is wasteful in other ways: constructing buildings that create 48 percent of carbon dioxide emissions, the highest single contributor to green house gases.[17] Business owners cannot rely on promised results laid out in their contracts when more than 72 percent[18] of projects are completed over budget and 70 percent[19] run beyond schedule. In one study, 75 percent of those late projects were 50 percent over the initial contract price (see Figure 1.7).[20]

So it should come as no surprise that construction continues to decline in productivity while other industries show dramatic gains.[21] That loss of productivity is further reflected in an 8 percent to 12 percent annual cost escalation. Both architecture and construction professionals express an inability to attract new talent to their spheres.[22]

Construction workers are 2.5 times as likely to die compared to other occupations.[23] Some have estimated that 50 percent of a construction project is comprised of labor, with average labor efficiency measured at 30 percent.

Figure 1.7   Projects Over Budget and Late

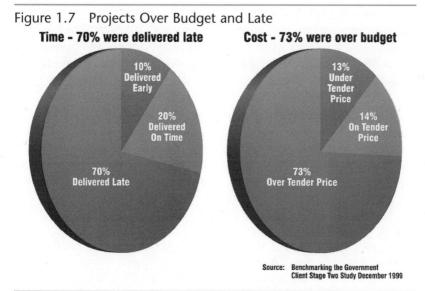

Source: Benchmarking the Government
Client Stage Two Study December 1999

Source: Adapted from Cain, Clive Thomas. *Profitable Partnering for Lean Construction*. Malden, MA: Wiley-Blackwell, 2004.

Materials are estimated at approximately 40 percent of the cost of a job. Material waste is estimated at 30 percent.[24]

Arol Wolford, founder of Construction Market Data, says that 10 percent or more of the cost of a project is consumed with counting, measuring, pricing and transporting documents. These are almost all avoidable costs.

Poor planning misses 3 percent to 7 percent (and often more) in project cost reduction because construction tax planning is either overlooked or not brought into a project early enough.[25] Up to 10 percent of the cost of a project is lost because of rework and avoidable collisions between trades in the field with plans that show both trades building in the same place. When taken as a whole, and taking out overlap, these exceed 50 percent.

These numbers do not fully account for inflated costs that firms price into their quotes to cover the unknowns and anticipated inefficiencies. It also does not include overcharging by those who take advantage of the current system.[26]

A system that does not fit current business realities first produces high levels of inefficiencies. Attempts to resolve those inefficiencies within the same system produce convoluted solutions that spiral downward into dysfunctions. Ultimately they lead to incentives for each player to game the system, hedge their positions, and/or engage in adversarial practices. Stephen Covey quotes in his book *The Speed of Trust* that mistrust increases the cost of doing business by 50 percent.[27] The industry has reached the same crossroad that others have over the past 40 years.

- Emerging industry trends include Integrated Project Delivery, Lean practices,[28] sustainability, virtual design and simulation, and inter-operability between software platforms, methods, and regulations.[29] At the center of these solutions are teams of trust. Yet, as the rest of the business world is heading toward tightly integrated organizations that are increasingly flatter, the construction industry imposes one that is vertically and horizontally rigid, fragmented, and inherently distrustful.

- The current conventional model is structured to pull apart both the team and its trust. This chapter explored those forces. Part Two examines the industry's current crossroad where the pressure to change has reached a breaking point and the new opportunities and tools for change represent great promise and potential if we can collectively release our current mindset and shift to one that puts the focus once again on the interests of the owner with strategic teams formed and enabled by principles of trust.

The industry is attempting to reform itself, but it is hampered by a piecemeal approach based on years of fragmentation and sharply honed adversarial instincts. The nature of the reform at this point is highly tribal. Each tribe has coalesced around one of many trade silos: technology, sustainability, methodology, standards, legislation, contracting, liability, and conflict, to list a few.[30] Although a real insurgency and effectiveness underlies each effort, fragmentation makes it difficult for them to coalesce. Dan Gonzales, corporate manager of virtual design construction at Swinerton commented, "If we can just connect all of these efforts into one project, the results could be incredible."

Connecting the dots—synthesizing common elements, making the business case, and enlisting cooperation—represents the challenge. This is where owners wield the power as catalysts for industry transformation. Owners have the potential to bring together the tribal leaders. They can focus these leaders to coordinate efforts that bring immediate business value, while still allowing the innovators to continue pushing the boundaries of transformation. Institutional, cultural, and legal barriers within the building industry resist integrated supply chain approaches, collaborative design, and collective versus individual contracting tools. Owners who want to act as catalysts for change will need conviction and information.

Chapter 2 What Every Executive Needs to Know About Low-Bid Contracting

All too often projects suffer because the design and construction team are cobbled together for the first time and have no expectation of ever being together in the future. Worse still, most of them will have been selected on a lowest price basis, where profit margins have been squeezed to the bone and the only way of making a decent profit may well be through claims against other team members, or against the client.

—Clive Thomas Cain, *Profitable Partnering for Lean Construction*

The 2004 U.S. Olympic men's basketball team should have won the gold medal. They were the best players on the planet. They all wanted to win gold; they had strong incentives and the pride of representing their country. Yet the team failed. In 2008, the U.S. team—great players with strong incentives and the pride of representing their country on the world stage—did bring home the gold. The difference wasn't in the varying skills of the individual team members, but in the specific kind of leadership provided by Coach Mike Krzyzewski. In picking players for his team, he invested a great deal of time considering not only individual talents, but how well the players interacted with other team members: chemistry and complementary talents. The winning difference is seldom the aggregate of talent but how well players act as a team, making the most of the talent they have.[1]

The 2008 team's success was crafted and assured before they ever assembled as a team.[2] This winning approach would seem tailor-made for the building projects, which require teams of architects, designers, engineers, and contractors to get the job done. As one building owner says, "If you have the right team, you don't need to bid." Unfortunately, our bidding system virtually ensures that a winning team—one that brings in a well-designed building on time and on budget—will only be formed by accident. This behavior is sometimes described by the ironic acronym CATNAP: Cheapest Available Technique Narrowly Avoiding Prosecution.[3]

When owners go to the market for new space, they want answers to a few basic questions: What do I want and need? How much will it cost? When will it be completed?

But once they get into the bidding process, they find themselves with a whole new set of questions that are not easy to answer: Where will I most likely get screwed? How late could the project be and how much extra will I end up paying? How many compromises will I end up making?

The primary cause of this shift to uncertainty and suspicion lies in the nature of the bidding process itself: design-bid-build (DBB) the most common project delivery approach.

WHAT'S WRONG WITH DBB?

DBB is easy to define. It simply means "the owner develops the parameters of the project, the architect prepares the design, the owner invites contractors to bid on the design, and the selected contractor then builds the project."[4]

As we saw in the last chapter, it worked well for a few decades but ran into problems beginning in the 1960s. It was also during the 1960s that we also begin to see new delivery models, like fast-track and design-build. We now have a multitude of models, including multi-prime, construction manager agency, construction manager at risk, bridging, alliance teaming, and integrated project delivery. It's easy to get lost among the selections and understand fully the nuances and trade-offs for each model, so we'll briefly review just the four dominant strategies.[5] The first three basically follow an RFP (Request for Proposal) or bid approach:

1. **Design-bid-build (DBB)** gives separate power to two main players. The architect is responsible for design, coordination of trades, and quality. The general contractor is responsible for hiring the sub-contractors and building the structure (including cost control and schedule) according to the plans.
2. **Multi-prime** makes the owner responsible for contracting work to the architect, structural engineer, HVAC, and other trades. Each of these players bids individually.
3. **Construction manager at risk** makes the individual or firm that acts for the owner liable for selecting the construction team, holding the contracts, and coordinating the design and construction. The construction manager typically follows a DBB approach.
4. **Design-build** lets the owner give accountability to either the general contractor or the architect, and the other trades essentially work for that person.

According to a top industry publication, *Outlook 09, Industry Forecast and Trends* (McGraw-Hill), 82 percent of projects follow one of the first three approaches, with 52 percent using a straight DBB model and 18 percent utilizing the design-build approach (see Figure 2.1). Each of

Figure 2.1   Project Delivery by Percent

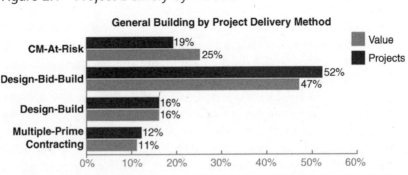

Source: McGraw-Hill Construction, 2008.

these strategies describes a method of assembling a team to work on a project through bidding: an adversarial system in which each player submits an estimate of how much it will cost to do the job and how long it will take, wherein decisions are made on who the owner or contractor thinks can do the best job, the most quickly, for the least amount of money. But if the initial team selection process creates a fragmented collection of companies that are introduced to the project *after* the big planning decisions have been made, then the delivery model selected will make little improvement in the outcome. Let's take a closer look.

PREQUALIFICATION

Most owners should understand that projects either succeed or fail due to the team dynamic and the complementary sets of skills and expertise that each participant brings to the job. So before requesting pricing proposals, owners usually try to pre-select companies that they think perform well as a group. This prequalification phase takes into account a company's size, their work on similar projects, financial strength, and a presentation that some refer to as a "beauty pageant." If no glaring weaknesses show up, and the presentation demonstrates some thought and effort, the short list of qualifiers can range from four to a half-dozen. Elimination from consideration is often due to nothing more than a need to limit the bidders to a manageable number, or a poor showing at the beauty pageant (typically a presentation to show off a firm's capabilities and best projects and find a way to create a hook or some distinctive trait that sets the firm apart).

The threshold and investment of time for prequalification is pretty low, and the list of necessary credentials is fairly predictable. The pre-selection process typically reaches out to what the industry calls "the usual suspects" frequently firms the owner already knows through a prior relationship or a nationally or regionally known company— which reflects an industry with few clear choices. Prequalification is therefore unfortunately based on a limited knowledge of the choices and a glaringly false assumption: that starting with the best known players available will lead to a successful project. But if team selection were that easy, then successful teams would simply be a collection of best-known companies.

INVITATION TO BID

The short list of suppliers that have been pre-selected by the owner then compete in a system that serves only to turn every participant into looking out for their own interests. Bid documents essentially strip away each company's unique value and experience so that all bidders can fit into a common box of qualifications and requirements. Bidding assumes that once the requirements are defined in a Request for Proposal (RFP), each firm can be compared side-by-side (apples-to-apples) to the other bid submissions. The translation: All other things being equal, the low price wins.

The goal and assumption for the bid document is that it creates a context where all things are equal. This linear breakdown of a project allows decision makers, who may or may not know anything about construction, to collect bid submissions and enter each quote on a spreadsheet for comparison. The owner is looking for the lowest total cost/price from the "bid tab" and for their consultants to point out any glaring omissions or possible mistakes.

For their part, bidders comb through the bid documents and identify errors, ambiguities, and loopholes—anything that might poke a hole in the box. These holes also allow bidders to lower the cost of their bid (even below acceptable profit levels) knowing they have these discrepancies to fall back on to recoup—and, in some cases, enhance—their profit.

AN EXPENSIVE PROPOSITION

Traditional bidding is clearly an expensive proposition. One vendor in particular created a spreadsheet to help owners better see the time and cost that goes into this procurement model, in the hope that they would re-channel the effort into better preconstruction analysis and planning. The spreadsheet used the example of a 200,000-square-foot building. At a cost of $200 per square feet, it represented a $40 million project. The owner may consider four developers, and the selected developer sends a bid request to six architects. The chosen architect then sends a bid request to five contractors and several consultants. Each general contractor will have anywhere from 25 to 50 sub-trades on a project, and bid each trade to four or more sub-contractors. In the end, the selection process alone will have involved more than 300 organizations, more than 800 individuals, and more than 30,000 man hours at a total cost to these organizations of $2 million—5 percent of the cost of the project.[6] And the owner doesn't realize that the contractor will need to recoup this cost somewhere once the contract is awarded, or in a future project with another owner if they did not win.[7]

BIDDING IS A WASTE OF THE SUPPLIERS' TIME AND RESOURCES

Another point of frustration is the time that is invested—rather, wasted—to respond to bid requests. One contractor said that a project in the range of $30 million can easily take five people four to five weeks to complete. Hard costs for blueprints, proposal documents, and props can cost $20,000. The salaries for the five people are in the range of $50,000—a fact of which many owners are unaware.

Another contractor I know expressed his frustration with a process that ignores the work and effort that he and his colleagues invest to demonstrate why their approach to successful projects matters. He called a particular owner's representative "Bottom-right-hand Bob," referring to this consultant's narrow interest in the bottom-line price.

THE WINNING TEAM

The owner has to create a team overnight, essentially performing a shotgun wedding among all of the successful companies. They may already know each other and have established relationships; however, it's more likely that they've either never worked together before or have some reason to distrust each other.

The winning contractor starts off the project with a "bid-deep" understanding. They are hardly ready to switch gears and begin building immediately after winning the job. First, it will take a few weeks to buy-out the sub-contractors—in other words, to make the final selection between subs and lock in their contracts.[8] The contractor also has to analyze the plans from a whole different paradigm— from winning a bid to building. He will send the architect a list of errors and omissions required to correct the plans and documentation, and those amendments become the first round of change orders.

Once the team is assembled, the project is officially underway. Unfortunately, the collection of winners only behaves as a team for the duration of the initial kick-off meeting. The adversarial outlines of their relationships, which are established in the bidding process, are soon cemented into place. The bid process produces low-priced winners whose motive is to protect and restore the margins they cut in order to win the job. They have no natural loyalty or reason to work as a team. The commodity approach to procurement, the reality of working with different players on every project, the normal cynicism and distrust between trades, and an industry that supplies little training in team formation or healthy team dynamics leaves owners with a raw collection of companies who are now expected to behave as a cohesive, collaborative group and successfully deliver a complex project.

Even when the architect and general contractor are selected based on qualifications rather than bids, the sub-trades are not. This is bad for the project and bad for the long-term survival of the subcontractors. According to Clive Thomas Cain, author of *Profitable Partnering for Lean Construction*:

"In the case of the construction industry, 80 percent of the team members are drawn from the specialist suppliers' sectors of the industry . . . they are generally selected on a project-by-project basis by the lowest price they can tender for the individual project. Consequently, their long-term security and profitability is at risk, the rate of bankruptcy is far higher than in other industries, their entry level is dangerously low and the valuable skill and experience of the specialist suppliers is hardly ever harnessed to drive out unnecessary costs and drive up quality."[9]

Clearly, these circumstances produce a system that rarely results in a positive or constructive outcome. It simply begets further distrust and heightened divisions between teammates and serves only to impede the project's development.

THE WINNER'S CURSE

The bid process sets up a common—and predictable—behavior pattern: Bid low to win. If successful, find justifiable ways to recoup and protect profit. And make sure there is someone else to blame as the cause for additional fees. In the industry, this built-in tension is called "the winner's curse." It goes like this: "The good news is, we won. The bad news is, we won." Or, as the construction industry joke goes, "The low bidder is the one wondering what they left out of the bid."

Contractors and consultants have a reputation for devising elaborate schemes to overcharge unsuspecting owners. The system certainly encourages and allows an element of bad behavior, and a cup of coffee with a construction auditor could lead one to see opportunism around every corner. The reality, however, is quite the opposite. Most contractors and consultants *do* play by the rules. One contractor even made this shrewd observation: "Contractors don't make money on change orders; they simply make up for what they should have charged." If contractors should have charged more for the project in the beginning, then why don't they? Because the object of the game isn't delivering the building, it's winning the bid.

An executive for a large contractor recently expressed frustration over a tense meeting with an architect. The architect complained that this contractor used a grade-one wall finish, instead of the grade-five that the contractor typically includes. The contractor told the architect bluntly that had they bid the normal grade five the additional $500,000 would have cost them the project. "If you wanted a grade five finish," he said, "then it should have been made clear in the bid." Now the architect's choice was to approve a change order for $500,000 worth of finish or resell the owner on the lower quality finish. Even though the contractor and architect had worked together many times in the past, this conflict at the very outset of the project immediately put them at odds with each other and eroded the architect's credibility with the owner.

This very typical situation illustrates just one of the many built-in problems with a bid document that attempts to specify a complex interconnected set of requirements. Under the current circumstances, this conflict is unavoidable. With new thinking, however, the players would be free to lay their cards openly on the table and work to avoid such oversights.

Architects and contractors don't like the existing process, and do not believe it serves their clients. They know that designing and delivering a building is a complex process whose success depends upon good communication, integration, and tight coordination. If owners began their projects by asking themselves what it takes to create a high-performance team, the rules and process for selection would dramatically change. Instead, they tend to see architects and consultants as interchangeable commodities. Using that framework, a bid among four or five equals defaults to the lowest price. A principal from one of the largest U.S. architectural firms lamented that clients always begin by saying that their decision will not be based on price, "so we go into the effort hoping and preparing like our experience and expertise will make some difference. But at the end of the process, it always gets down to price."

Is improving the system an impossible dream? No, not by a long shot. In fact, the projects reviewed in Part Three bring to light success stories of owners who made this mind shift: viewing success as a matter of team formation, not a collection of low numbers on a bid tab.

VALUE ENGINEERING

At the fall 2008 CoreNet Global Summit, a meeting of the world's leading professional groups for corporate real estate, we heard story after story on this common theme: projects that go out for bid return with prices higher than the budget. Given the current, fragmented structure, the ability to get a project back on track once initial costs come in too high can often become a losing proposition for everyone. The name of this process is a nice little euphemism: value engineering or VE. VE essentially means that the size, quality, or features of the job are reduced in order to lower the price.

Despite valiant attempts, value engineering has *not* proven effective at bringing projects back into budget.[10] More often, it produces a series of unintended new problems of coordination and quality issues raising cost and negatively impacting the schedule. A VE project quite often returns to its original costs or higher, but now with lower quality or reduced scope or both.

WHAT EXACTLY DOES THE WINNING BIDDER *WIN*?

The winning bidder earns the right to reprice the project without any competition. Adjustable (or mutable) contracts and the contractor's superior knowledge over the owner ensure the contractor comes out on top. Leading construction attorney Barry LePatner compares this asymmetrical relationship to practices employed by lawyers, accountants, and doctors: No matter what, they will make their fee and, in the case of the contractor, their profit.[11]

Once the contract is signed, control of the costs, schedule, and quality shifts disproportionately to the contractor. LaPatner explains in detail the dramatic monopolistic power shift that takes place once a contract is awarded. That power increases as the project progresses and the owner's investment grows. The contractor knows—and the owner soon discovers—that challenging the contractor is a game of chicken, which the owner is sure to lose. If the owner raises issues or points out problems, the contractor can easily find reasons to justify his charges for any added costs. One architect remarked that a contractor on a recent project suggested a different method for an area to simplify the job. They then tried to submit a change order for additional fees, because they claimed the architect had altered the scope of work.

To level the playing field once again, LaPatner recommends using true fixed-price contracts based on completed detailed drawings, strong and punitive contracts, and highly competent and forceful construction managers. This forces owners to carve out more time for planning and shift budget dollars forward in the process.[12] However, we do think many owners will need stronger outcome assurances before they'll be willing to make this shift in thinking and front load their planning. If owners were to make the adjustments that LaPatner suggests, it would certainly put a dent in the 70 percent of budget-busting projects with runaway schedules. Yet the reality is that few owners will do this. We think there is a better chance for large-scale shift to early planning by changing the rules altogether. The system is ripe for overhaul, and Part Three provides examples of owners who have not given up speed-to-market and quality and are not paying a premium to reign in schedule overruns. They are actually reducing costs. By doing so, they have additionally reduced the remaining 50 percent waste, improved the quality and life performance of their buildings, and made sustainable construction the norm rather than the exception. "When you improve things by an order of magnitude," says Steven Levy author of the article in *Wired*, "you haven't made something better—you've made something new."[13]

DISPELLING MYTHS AND MISCONCEPTIONS

Almost everyone in the building industry is operating under the burden of one or more of the common misconceptions and myths about the bidding process. They are worth looking at (and dispelling) here.

Myth #1: Line Item Bids Provide Apples-to-Apples Comparisons

In truth, they simply compare numbers and offer no insight about how the supplier will perform or contribute to the success of the project.

Picking a vendor based primarily on a number is like picking players for a team based strictly on their statistics.

Myth #2: The Process Will Help Me Arrive at the Best Value

This may indeed be the intent, but it is seldom the reality. Even evaluations that go through a prequalification phase end up with a short list of suppliers that give each competitor equal status. Every team has unique qualifications, processes, values, and track record. Owners have not yet devised consistent methods for comparing individual firms let alone project teams, and the industry has provided little support for establishing guidelines of standards of practice to aid owners.[14]

Myth #3: Once We Get the Bid Prices, We Can Select a Contractor and Finalize Our Costs

Most owners are prepared for the reality that the final project cost will be higher than the awarded contract price. However, they are typically unprepared for just how much deviation there will be and the many reasons why. One report cites 75 percent as the amount of projects that came in over budget—at as high as 50 percent over than the contracted price.[15]

Requests for bids often take place when plans are less than 50 percent complete, and bidders will always interpret incomplete plans on the low side of the cost. One contractor told us that he creates a two-column price sheet: one column responds to the letter of the bid, and the second column includes all of the identified errors and omissions that will need to be added as the plan details develop. The contractor bids the first column, and uses the second column for his change orders.

Myth #4: As an Owner, I Have Different Delivery Models that Help Me Control Cost and Risk

The owner begins with all of the risk and creates a structure (delivery model and contract) whereby he selects a team to distribute that risk, which includes financial (final cost), safety, performance (quality and schedule), and design (concept and function) components. The level of undefined but anticipated possibilities determines risk. An experienced owner may take more responsibility to manage that risk or pay the architect, contractor, and consultants for their expertise and time to reduce it. Spending more money and taking the time to define details reduces the chances for error, but there are no industry formulas for working this out. A Mindshift member and developer recognized and described the reality: "At the end of the day, we carry all of the risk, like any owner." Assessing and assigning risk and proper compensation comes down to the level of trust and confidence one has with their partners.

The bid process is, at its core, all about risk and who feels its effects. Documents attempt to tightly identify a supplier's scope and responsibilities (shifting risk). The supplier then works hard to narrowly define scope and responsibilities, while adding disclaimers and qualifications (shifting risk back). Written accounts and partially completed drawings fail to convey the complex coordination and real world variables that suppliers face and must work out. The bid process sets the stage for the finger-pointing and blame-shifting process—leaving no one accountable and the owner footing the bill.

Myth #5: The Competitive Bid Process Ensures We Get the Best Price

The upfront bidding process looks competitive, but what, exactly, are entrants competing *for*? Firms are not competing to see who can deliver the best building for the best value; they are vying to win a fierce, margin-eroding contest. Once they've won, their focus shifts to recouping and protecting that margin. As we've seen, contractors compete for the right to re-price the project with no competition. Only when this aspect is satisfied does the focus shift to the success of the building.

Myth #6: Our Process Will Help Us Find the Best Team

When the owner selects a contractor, they really don't know who will be working on their job. Sub-trades handle 80 percent of the work, and the owner will not even know the names of the companies let alone their lead people. The scenario is similar to picking a team based on its coaches, without ever seeing the players.

Myth #7: I'm Dealing with Well-Qualified Companies

Many firms are reputable firms, but some are not, and the industry does not make it easy to tell the difference. There are no established standards of practice for an industry mostly made up of firms under 20 employees. As cited in the previous paragraph, owners often do not even know who is performing four-fifths of the work they commission.

The threshold to become a subcontractor is fairly low. The story of "Joe the Plumber" during the 2008 presidential election illustrates the point.[16] Samuel Joseph Wurzelbacher was videotaped asking then-presidential candidate Barack Obama a question about small-business tax policy. His simple inquiry propelled him to immediate celebrity status, and he became a symbol for the challenges facing small businesses. Additional research into Mr. Wurzelbacher's background revealed that he was not actually a licensed plumber, although the company he worked for is. Joe had not finished the union apprentice program he began several years earlier, and the company he works for is reported to have somewhere between two and eight employees. If Joe's amateur status remained unknown to the nation at large, then it isn't hard to believe that other unlicensed professionals can have a similarly easy time obtaining jobs.

Myth #8: The Winning Contractor Gave Us Their Best Price

For the bid, perhaps, but the contract award was just the first step for the contractor to recover everything they may have given up on the bid and more. The process begins with the general contractor (GC) buying out the subcontracts, which is a hidden, second-round bid exercise. The GC has two points of leverage for renegotiating original bid submissions. First, they have a real project. Second, they have more information and better-defined scope and can compel the subcontractor to take a second, more realistic and more detailed, look at their bid. LePatner says this can reduce the GC's cost another 15 to 20 percent. This second-round bid exercise represents a hidden profit center that often equals more than the contractor's general conditions.[17] The next round of recovering is about change orders. There is actually a $268.20 book subtitled *The Art of Finding, Pricing, and Getting Paid for Contract Change*. It is obviously well worth the price; there's at least one boat out there lovingly named *Change Order*. Again, most contractors seek a fair profit for the work and risk they manage. Buying out and change orders are two tools contractors have at their disposal, and mostly invisible to owners, that stack the cards in favor of the contractor.

Myth #9: We Will Buy Our Equipment and Materials Through the Sub-Trades Performing the Work

This is a widely held, general assumption. However, sub-trades are hired for their labor expertise, not their buying clout. A good project manager or larger general contractor can usually buy direct from the manufacturer and cut out several layers of markup.

In one example, a national project management firm secured a higher-grade lighting solution that cost $55 per lineal foot. This price was the result of layers of mark-up that began with the manufacturer, the distributor, the subcontractor, and continued with the general contractors before it even gets to the client. Once these layers were removed, however, the client ended up paying $22 per lineal foot.[18] In addition, this lighting system had a quick connect feature that reduced the necessary labor. The initial fee reflected a traditional lighting system. The project manager spotted the discrepancy, which brought the labor cost down by 15 percent. Since materials make up 40 percent of the cost of the project and labor approximately 50 percent, it is worth the owner's time and effort to take a closer look at these expenses.

Myth #10: If We Hire a Third Party, They Will Protect Our Interest

Well, that's the theory. In the 1980s architects moved away from their traditional role overseeing construction to lessen risk. Contractors also began to shed overhead and risk by moving away from self-performing the construction to hiring subcontractors and independent contractors. These shifts created a gap in coordination and accountability. Third parties emerged as a new layer that was meant to advocate for the client and oversee the coordination between the architect and contractor.

The skills and qualifications provided by project managers and construction managers vary greatly, which makes it hard for owners to discern or compare. What further complicates the process is that brokers who provide this service may bundle the cost into their fee—again shifting the owner's focus to price instead of outcome.

There are many excellent project managers, but there are many more who are not so good, and owners need *exceptional*—not just good—project managers to stand in the gap. Many experienced and professional project managers voice a general lack of respect for their less effective counterparts. It's too easy for someone to claim to be a project manager, and there are too many clients who can't tell the difference. Some criticisms of project managers are that they:

- Are nothing but expensive checklist makers, spreadsheet managers, and schedule maintainers.
- Have an incentive to actually *add* conflict and *find* problems, because it supports their value.
- Are after-the-fact reporters and do little to anticipate problems or develop solutions when they arise.[19]

Project managers are a necessary bridge in a broken system. Principal of Construction Audits and Consulting (CCM) Vince Chapman[20] describes their role bluntly: "If you have outlaws, you need a sheriff."

BOTTOM LINE

After a while, the stories begin to sound similar: a lot of time invested in a selection process that fails to account for the team formation, creating links of accountability, and early coordination and planning needed to make the job successful. The process also frustrates suppliers who have to play one game to win a project, find ways to recoup the sunk cost, and then invest new time—if they win—to revise plans on how to implement the project.

Even this brief review makes it hard to miss the obvious: The system is broken. Bidding leads to cutting corners, so-called teammates who work against each other, and buildings that come in over budget, over schedule, and under quality. Clearly, we need to look at construction through a different frame, one that discourages fragmentation and adversarial relations in favor of a cohesive building and design team whose members are all working together to bring in sustainable projects in the best—and most cost-effective—way possible. And that requires a mind shift. In the next chapter, we'll begin to see how that might look.

Chapter 3 From Fragmentation to Integration

"Business and human endeavors are systems . . . we tend to focus on snapshots of isolated parts of the system, and wonder why our deepest problems never get solved."

—Peter Senge

Recently, a developer selected a new modular curtain wall solution for a 200,000-square-foot office building. Several subcontractors bid on the project, and the winning firm's offer was significantly lower than the competition. The developer was experienced at running projects. He chose the lowest bid and used its in-house personnel to manage the subcontractor. It soon became obvious, however, that the installer of the modular curtain wall had no prior experience with the particular structural frame used in this building. When it came time to install the exterior panels, the project screeched to a halt. The owner and developer were horrified when they found out that extensive modification of the panels was required to make them work at all and that a lot of experimentation would be necessary to find a way to securely attach the panels to the frame. After several grueling weeks of uncertainty, stress, and escalating conflict, a solution was finally reached. In the meantime, however, the job remained at a standstill. Nothing could be done until the exterior was completed, protecting the interior from weather damage. The owner had many sleepless nights, and the developer invested hundreds of man-hours scrabbling for contingencies in case the manufacturer could not solve the problem. Eventually, the job was completed—albeit over schedule and over budget—and everyone breathed a sigh of relief. No one outside the project would ever know the jeopardy the project faced. But the price of a beer with the developer, architect, contractor, or sub will buy you a tale worthy of any epic drama.

What happened to this building project was not an aberration; skirting disaster at some time in a project is close to the norm. It's the face of a dysfunctional system spawned by a faulty methodology in the middle of a dying paradigm.

Here's how the *American Heritage Dictionary* describes a paradigm: "A set of assumptions, concepts, values, and practices that constitutes a way of viewing reality for the community that shares them. . . ." Sound familiar? Fish spend their whole lives swimming in water—they live in it, they breathe it, and as far as they know that's all there is or ever will be. Similarly, the commercial real estate industry has spent the last half century living and breathing Design-Bid-Build and its variations. Most people in the industry don't even have to think about it, because despite their many frustrations they simply *know* that there's no other way to do business.

But no paradigm lasts forever. Just when we think nothing could ever replace ancient tales told and retold over a campfire, *boom!* Here come monks in a scriptorium, laboriously committing precious information to hand-inked manuscripts to be treasured and read by privileged elites. And just when their illuminated art had reached its zenith, *boom!* Here comes Gutenberg and his printing press, distributing the words of the few to the masses. And just when books and bookstores are everywhere to be found, *boom!* Here comes cyberspace and a whole raft of undreamed of possibilities. In the words of Kurt Vonnegut: and so it goes.

Design-Bid-Build is an old paradigm that is crumbling at the edges and springing leaks in the middle. And it's not going to get any better.

DRAINING THE SWAMP

In the words of some of our Texas buddies, we are just too busy fighting alligators to drain the swamp. So part of what the Mindshift group did was to go a little deeper into the swamp, take a look around, and see what we could come up with. We found several recurring negative patterns that commonly play out during a project: accidental adversaries, vicious cycles, fixes that fail, and tragedy of the commons. To begin to change these for the better, we must first understand their root dynamics.

Accidental Adversaries

Even though everyone knows that a project's success depends on mutual cooperation, team members end up working against each other and turning into adversaries. It's not on purpose, but it happens almost every time. As we saw in the previous chapter, architects and MEPs (Mechanical, Electrical, Plumbing) are a common example of this.

Accidental adversaries are created when parties focus on internal parameters of success, such as an architect's tendency to revise plans to reflect the latest understanding of the client's needs without seeing or considering the external impact on other stakeholders (like eating up the fee quoted by their subs to respond to those revisions). MEPs respond by holding off on revision requests until the last moment, putting pressure on the architect to finalize their changes without seeing that the delays create tension between the owner, who is waiting for those changes, and the architect.

Vicious Cycles

The basic dynamic at work is *escalation*. This occurs when one party perceives the other's actions as threatening or harmful and becomes defensive. The opposite party then sees *these* actions as threatening or harmful and responds in kind.

This can happen right at the beginning of a project. For example, an owner who creates a tight and punitive contract will drive suppliers to insert disclaimers and look for any loophole they can find. This kind of power imbalance naturally leads the less-powerful party to find overt or covert means to regain balance or control. Contractors respond to explicit contracts with opaque cost structures and methods. In the end, it takes experts and specialists like contract auditors to penetrate that kind of opacity.

On one project, a contract auditor was asked to examine the furniture supplier's bill of materials. Auditing furniture invoices does not typically fall under the scope of a high-cost construction auditor. Furniture suppliers have a tight box they work within. For furniture manufacturers a master contract is the box that sets a sale price based on a percentage of the published list price. This provides limited opportunities for additional profits. The same restrictions exist with all of the providers in that industry, so there is pressure to find creative ways to break out of the box.

The client had a furniture purchase order that included a quote with a line item breakout of every piece of furniture ordered, a bill of material with the physical product to compare against the quote, and a reference to the Master Contract that set the discount off of list price. The request looked tedious, but not complicated or opaque.

Then the auditor began comparing the bill of material with the product installed. He found it to be just as it was listed, with only a few noted exceptions that the vendor quickly took care of. The bill of material also matched the purchase order. Next, he checked the purchase order and invoice against the price book and Master Contract discount. Oops. Several quoted items were not listed in the price book. They were new. When the auditor asked for a price book, the furniture dealer said that these items were from the new line and there was no price book yet. The next question was obvious: "How did you arrive at the price?" When a few different answers were given, the auditor set the criteria for arriving at the price. The dealer was instructed to use the factory cost and mark that up in line with the same percentages as the older products in the price book.

This process yielded two results. The first was a check for several hundred thousand dollars returned to the client. The second was a closer reading of the contract, which revealed that the discounted price was tied to a particular catalogue edition. When the auditor checked the date of the price book against the contract, he found that the pricing came from a different and more recent catalogue edition. The dealer was told to recalculate the entire project using the listed prices in the contracted price book. This resulted in a second check for several hundred thousand dollars returned to the client.

But wait, there's more! The contract also indicated that there were different discounts for different product categories—seating, cubicles, filing, accessories, freestanding desks, wood, and so on. Based on the contract, some products carried a different discount than others. The deepest discount was given to items purchased out of the cubicle price book. So a file priced out of the cubicle price book carried a different discount than one purchased out of the freestanding desk price book, *even though it was the same file.* When the auditor asked the dealer to re-price every item based on the price book that would yield the deepest discount, *another* substantial check was returned to the client. The project represented a multimillion-dollar purchase. When the audit was complete, the client received a repayment close to $1 million in overcharges.

Product suppliers go through an equally rigorous bidding process that drives down their profit on the front end and leaves them to operate with very slim margins. These professionals are part of that 80 percent knowledge base excluded from the early planning and decision process. They invariably look for, and find, ways to protect and recoup the profit they gave away in their bid.

FIXES THAT FAIL

When we look for a quick fix to address a symptom, rather than try to adjust the root of the problem, that fix is usually doomed to fail. Although it may buy some time, it invariably sets the stage for a future larger problem.

Architects are often pressed by owner time constraints to issue drawings before they're ready. When they rush plans in this way, a lot of detail is left open for interpretation. Even if the architect and contractor meet and review the intent of the drawings, they must pass that understanding down the line—to the foreman, supervisors, and sub-trades. If you've ever played the gossip game Telephone, you know that the story told in the beginning is never the same one that the last person in the circle hears.

It's not surprising that fixing the time crunch problem by rushing the drawings often leads to field problems in construction. At that point, the time and cost to fix the new problem exceed by a multiple the time and cost it would have taken to make sure the drawings were complete.

Here's a familiar story: A supplier for a large project developed a custom solution for their client. There were significant problems throughout the prototype phase, but in each case, the field sub-contractor was able to make the prototypes work using a lot of field engineering and several trips to the local hardware store. The finished prototypes looked great because the subcontractor was able to use their top supervisors to make sure it was right. The representatives from the fabricator were under the impression that the product only needed a few minor adjustments prior to full production because of how well the prototypes turned out.

The fabricator promised to cover additional costs from the sub-contractor to make the production product work. When the job began, however, the leisurely pace of building a few prototypes turned into a pressured project schedule to erect several hundred offices. This time, the supervisors were no longer hands-on; they were overseeing less-skilled work crews who were completely unfamiliar with the product. To compound the problem, the fabricator had trouble getting the completed product out the door, so shipments arrived piecemeal. The project outstripped the fabricator and the sub-contractor. To make the job work, the subcontractor had five times the labor expense than originally estimated. The quality suffered, and the process took its toll on the client and all of the relationships.

TRAGEDY OF THE COMMONS

The phrase "tragedy of the commons" describes the overuse of a limited common resource. Instead of prioritizing demand on the resource, it is simply used until it is depleted. At this point, everybody suffers.

In commercial real estate, *time* is the common resource everyone competes for. We've all heard the common wisdom: If you don't have time to do it right, when are you going to have time to do it over? Most of the time, however, we forget what we know. Planning is typically shortchanged to respond to other pressures, such as interim financing and the felt need to start moving dirt or to put bodies to work.

Even though we can graph the fact that the biggest impact on success with the least cost happens in the planning phase, we still succumb to the pressure to *do* something. This pressure, however, is partly the result of eroding confidence in architectural plan details and the over-the-wall process of handing off drawings to the contractor and their subs, leaving them to work out the details. In turn, contractors push back by demanding more time to determine means and methods. At the same time, they send back requests for information on any question for whose interpretation they do not want to be held liable. These sequential handoffs ensure there will not be enough time for everyone. Managers end up playing a revolving game of robbing Peter to pay Paul. Once schedule problems creep into a project, it flows downhill and gets bigger.

HOW DID WE GET INTO THIS MESS?

As we've seen, the rapid transition of the economy during the 1960s and 1970s changed the rules—not just of commercial real estate, but of countless other industries. The new information-driven economy required companies to move with speed. But when you take a linear process like DBB, further fragment it with specialization, and add a layer of technological complexity, you need *more* time to process and coordinate—not less. These changes threw the DBB model into its current crisis, resulting in a high percentage of over-budget, late, and poor-quality projects.

Within this linear, siloed paradigm, the industry introduced several different delivery models aimed at rebalancing cost, speed, and quality. In addition to the four delivery models described in the last chapter, there are some lesser-known approaches—like fast-tracking, multi-prime, bridging, job order contracting, and design-assist. They can all work with guidance that is able to overcome the system's built-in drive toward fragmentation and conflict as well as inadequate time. However, without superior leadership, each model's tendency to focus on optimizing one of the three values can lead to disastrous outcomes with the other values.

For example, fast-tracking was created to greatly compress the schedule by designing and building simultaneously. But attempting to fast-track within a fragmented framework threatens the quality of a project. According to George Elvin, "Many . . . architects express concern that fast-track production prevents them from delivering the level of quality they and their clients demand."[1]

The current paradigm forces a choice; the new paradigm realigns the process using trust-based teams to create a circular approach to planning and design. This allows teams to design faster, have the right knowledge readily available to work out details and coordination, and execute with greater precision. These new projects deliver all three components without compromise. They also deliver additional benefits: diminished conflict, continually improved processes, high levels of commitment, and increased profits among the suppliers.

WHEN SYSTEMS ARE OUT OF SYNCH

When the environment undergoes fundamental change, supporting systems attempt to adapt: They can protect themselves, become defensive, attack perceived threats, and draw a tighter circle. Or they can seek to open up and better integrate into a larger circle of relationships. The first approach may provide short-term survivability, but it causes the larger system to degrade further, creating the vicious cycle described earlier. On the surface, the second approach looks riskier and is definitely longer term. Yet it naturally leads to connections with other players who are opening up their organizations to a larger circle of relationships—a rising tide that floats all ships.

When Dick Haworth and Art Gensler first collaborated on the concept that became the foundation for Mindshift, they felt that the best way to improve their organization's future was to try to better the industry as a whole. They committed to share Mindshift's findings with the industry—including competitors. If they had approached Mindshift as a way to create a proprietary product for competitive advantage, they would not have attracted the numerous experts from around the country who freely gave their time and secrets for a greater good. It would be hard to sell the idea of trust-based supply teams otherwise. Ray Anderson, founder of Interface Carpet, makes a similar comparison when it comes to companies promoting sustainability by explaining, "You can't be a brown company and create a green product." His story is another case in point.

Anderson changed the direction of his company and industry beginning with an internal speech presented in 1994, when he experienced what he later called his "Mid-Course Correction." The carpet industry, in fact, is one of the more toxic and environmentally damaging industries; yet Anderson has led the company on an ascent to reach zero carbon emissions by the year 2020. By choosing to integrate into a larger system of relationships and focusing on their impact on the planet, he was forced to make radical changes to Interface's business model. This required a paradigm shift and changed everything about the company. The result has proven to be highly successful, and Ray Anderson is just one example of doing well by doing good.

Systems also evolve through incremental adaptations. Architects, for example, slowly adopted Computer Aided Drawings (CAD) in the early 1980s, allowing them to respond more quickly and deal with greater levels of complexity. CAD did not change the fundamental linear nature of the practice but simply provided a tool to temporarily deal with the growing complexity of projects. While it gave additional life to an approach that was becoming increasingly out of synch with the need for integration CAD further reinforced a sequential approach to projects.

If a system does not address its imbalance and seek to integrate into the larger environment (and its stakeholders), it may withdraw and become internally focused. We use phrases like "circling the wagons" or "becoming insular" to describe a system or organization that is out of touch with surrounding realities. Each entity within the system will begin to redefine itself independently from the whole. The whole disintegrates. A system can survive a long time in this condition. Eventually, however, it reaches a crossroad that leads one of two paths: die or innovate. The commercial real estate industry has reached that crossroad.

In fact, the whole paradigm could soon collapse.

THE OLD PARADIGM GIVES WAY

Watching a paradigm give way is like watching a retaining wall crumble under the pressure of a relentless tide. It seems to hold firm, even with an increasing number of cracks and leaks. But suddenly, the wall is gone, washed away by the surging sea.

For those who see the new paradigm coming, the wait can seem interminable. But for paradigms to dissolve and common wisdom to lose its hold, there must be anomalies that confront the myth of the current paradigm and challenge its sense of entitlement. It was assumed that the human heart could not stand the pace of running a mile in under four minutes—until Roger Bannister proved this fact wrong. It was also assumed that the human body could not withstand the gravitational forces of reaching Mach 1, the speed of sound, until Chuck Yeager broke the sound barrier and eradicated this assumption. Once a barrier is breached, it can be more easily breached again, and eventually, the barrier gives way.

Ray Anderson's quest with Interface is easily underestimated as one small piece in a trillion dollar puzzle. Of course, "That's just carpeting." Not surprisingly, those invested in the current DBB construction model rightly challenge the plausibility of emergent claims. Breaking the "trust barrier" in the construction world seems impossible to many. It has certainly been a topic of discussion for many years. Until recently, including the concepts of trust and construction in the same conversation felt more like an exploration of why men are from Mars and women are from Venus.

Some companies are ready to put the ideas into practice right now; some are open but just don't yet see their circumstances allowing such a change; some can see the opportunity but not how to operate with what they see as two separate business models; and others simply can't be bothered.

An office furniture supplier with whom we worked was immediately attracted to the promise offered by trust-based strategic partnering, and the owner began exploring how they might form strategic partnerships. This firm was a key supplier in their projects and a critical component to a project's success. We showed how a furniture supplier on the East Coast was generating a net profit more than two times this owner's earnings through a trust-based turnkey approach. After a few months of internal discussion, the owner decided not to pursue the model. His reason? "I just don't see us sitting at the table with a contractor and architect and being viewed with respect or seen as bringing value to the table."

Sadly, his response reflects the effect of the current hierarchical paradigm. Even with strong evidence to the contrary—a live example of a firm earning enviable profits and the recognition that their current business model projected continued decline—the owner still backed away. He simply could not make the mind shift and see his company as an equal and respected partner in the process.

During a presentation to several regional general contractors, there was unanimous recognition of the acute problem in the current model and interest in the new paradigm. The benefits seemed straightforward, and the examples were compelling. One of the contractors then raised his hand and asked, "What if you select a sub that sandbags?" We responded with questions of our own: "Why were they selected to be part of the team in the first place? What criteria would you use for team selection?" This contractor was filtering the selection of team members through the current model of "beat subs down on price and then watch them like a hawk to make sure they don't pull any tricks." Once the mind shift takes place, team selection shifts to looking for long-term partners, respecting and helping one another earn a fair profit, and developing a level of trust and transparency.

SHIFTING PARADIGMS

Business is losing confidence in the current fragmented adversarial paradigm that governs commercial real estate and construction. Companies within the industry are grappling with decreasing profit margins and looking at expanding their services to provide greater value to clients and control over their fate. Construction firms are adding architects, architects are expanding into construction services, brokers are adding project and facility management services, and still other firms are creating one-stop-shop capabilities. When the lines blur like this, it is a sure sign of more fundamental shifts taking place.

The last 40 years have brought the rise of the current dominant players in each sector of the industry: development, brokerage, architecture, construction, and furniture, fixtures, and equipment (FF&E). Over the last few years, many of these marquee names have merged as the industry attempts to sort out shifting market needs.[2] Consolidating a fragmented and dysfunctional model marginally removes the inefficiencies of external coordination by bringing them into one entity. However, consolidation brings with it its own set of inefficiencies: different cultures, processes, technology platforms, and unique factors of success.

Wharton Business School Professor Robert Holthausen says, "Various studies have shown that mergers have failure rates of more than 50 percent. One recent study found that 83 percent of all mergers fail to create value and half actually destroy value. This is an abysmal record. What is particularly amazing is that in polling the boards of the companies involved in those same mergers, over 80 percent of the board members thought their acquisitions had created value. We are beginning to understand some of the reasons why these mergers fail."[3] It's clear to see that navigating sea change successfully requires a flexible and ambidextrous approach.

THE AMBIDEXTROUS APPROACH

Most firms concede that innovation holds the key to sustainable growth. In addition, innovation now extends beyond products and techniques. It seeks to change market rules—dramatically. It may be defining an emerging but amorphous new market. Offsite construction will likely be one of those new opportunities. Currently, offsite construction is a niche entity with a surprisingly broad range of solutions. Aligned with current BIM capabilities, fabrication provides a potential "Blue Ocean" opportunity.[4] In fact, this area may well be moving us from a product-based model to a service- and knowledge-centric approach, in the same way IBM remade itself in the 1980s. Using rich BIM data and other assessment tools, consulting firms will be able to tie facility performance to worker performance.

It may take the form of adopting a new delivery model, the way firms like DPR Construction, Swinerton, Turner, Linbeck or Mortenson have in implementing Lean Construction. Their enhanced efficiency has opened the door to additional levels of value as some clients look to espouse Lean practices for their own internal operations.

It might mean taking an innovator's leap with a disruptive technology like BIM, in the way that Gehry Technologies has applied it to projects like Bilbao and the Walt Disney Performance Hall. All of these provide lessons for the would-be innovator.

Few question the need, but many question *how* to innovate, especially in industries that produce very low returns. Charles O'Reilly and Michael Tushman published the results of a Harvard study that measures the success rate for different innovation strategies.[5] They noted that companies take one of four paths. The first is an innovation effort with teams integrated within the organizational management structure. The second is a cross-functional team within the company but outside the management structure. The third is a team outside the organization and outside the management structure. The fourth is structurally independent of the organization and culture but integrated into the hierarchy of the company.

Their results showed that only two of the approaches produced successful results. Efforts within the company and integrated with management experienced a 25 percent success ratio. These efforts found it hard to maintain outside thinking because of internal contamination. Management sponsored efforts independent of the organization experienced a 90 percent success factor. These organizations had the benefit of executive support, but did not have to compete or swim upstream against embedded mindsets, procedures, or internal justifications of value; in other words, there was no cross-contamination.

Mindshift adopted this fourth model, maintaining a separate identity as a coalition of equally committed and similarly minded leaders. Each member is either the owner of their company or an executive endorsed by the leadership of their organization. Companies that consider exploring this new model will do well to consider the benefits of taking this ambidextrous approach. (We'll share the Mindshift story and strategy in Chapter 4.)

CHANGING THE METAPHOR

In his book *The Power of Myth*, Joseph Campbell said something along these lines: If you want to change the world, you have to change the metaphor. Sustainable design represents a world-changing metaphor related to whole-system thinking. Ray Lucchesi of Lucchesi Galati (LG), a charter Mindshift member, told us about how his firm shifted into whole system thinking, transforming their business model from traditional architecture to designing from three integrated levels that bring a collective intelligence to the process that improves use and value of spaces they design.

For example, a financial client came to LG with what they thought they needed: a new building and an expanded parking lot. This organization had recently expanded from 15,000 members to more than 30,000, and it felt the current parking would not support the growth. LG stepped back and reviewed the big picture. They concluded that the real problem was not parking or a building. The solution lay in the organization's operations and how the scheduling of benefits was handled. LG asked what the cost would be to add two more benefit days a month. It turned out that it would cost the organization nothing, because the people could easily reorder their work flow to better distribute benefit work. The organization did not have to buy additional land, build a new parking structure, and spend $2.5 million for additional parking.

The value of stepping outside the conventional design process lies in exploring the transformational opportunities for the company's culture and organization. It focuses design thinking toward clarification of a client's culture and values and then links those values more directly to the other systems the company inhabits—the building, clients, industry, community, and environment. An example of this is an advertising client of LG's that was spread out between three locations. LG evaluated the current inefficiencies, frictions, and isolated subcultures in the organization. They developed what Ray calls "cultural stitching," moving from distinct subcultures to one facility in a larger community envelope using a town center model. After the first year, the firm saw a reduction in turnover from 40 percent to 10 percent!

Clearly, this depth of involvement produces greater dividends and returns. Changing the metaphor for LG meant adopting whole systems thinking; it also meant adding new capabilities, including sociology, cultural anthropology, and architectural biology. Not surprisingly, LG takes a different approach to the design process, using modeling and "serious play"[6] as a means of helping clients think through the discovery process and framing of the solution.

Moving from the current paradigm to trust-based partnerships will require several significant mind shifts, including those from:

- tolerance to respect
- exclusion to valued participation
- predetermined solutions to open-ended thinking
- quick technical fixes to holistic views
- narrow advocacy to broader integration
- individual perspectives to interconnected implications
- reaction to thoughtful leadership

Building, at its essence, is a relational practice. It is creative. And, when done well, it is restorative. Right now, we have an opportunity to think beyond simply minimizing our damage to the environment or seeking to limit initial capital outlay. There is a bigger, far more valuable picture.

Part Two Making the Mindshift

"Never doubt that a small group of thoughtful committed citizens can change the world. Indeed it is the only thing that ever has."

—Margaret Mead

Chapter 4 Working the Mindshift

*"Do you think the real estate and construction industry is
ready for a fundamental change?"*
"I sure hope so."

—Conversation between two Mindshift members, 2005

If you want an informative and unvarnished take on the real estate
and construction market, you'll want to show up at the Pancake
House in Dallas on the first Wednesday of each month at 7:30 A.M. to
observe the Pancake Roundtable—where Mindshift first began to
take form.

There really is a round table in the corner of the restaurant. On any
given month there will be four to six attending, and the group has gathered
as long as any of the members can recall. They include the owner of a large
regional contracting firm, president of a national architectural firm, the
managing principle of a national civil engineering firm, the owner of a
landscape firm, a principal for an international engineering firm, and a
sales representative and mascot from an interior's subcontractor. The
waiter knows each person's order by heart and loves to go around the
table reciting the specifics: "Two eggs over easy, sausage, hash browns
crispy, Tabasco sauce, and coffee . . ."

On a typical morning, the discussion covers topics all over the map—from upcoming projects and family news to the local and national economy and healthcare. This naturally leads into a longer and more detailed dialogue on a large healthcare project that's on the horizon. There's consensus that the politics of the project align nicely for one firm. When a second firm is mentioned, a few at the table nod with cup in hand, "They've got a shot." The third architect teamed up with an out of state firm. Everyone agreed it was an odd match. Another explained, "They're like the Buffalo Springfield of the architectural world—four other architects are now in the healthcare business because they inherited alumni from this firm." The conversation veered off again as he proceeded to offer everyone a six-degrees of separation chart linking Crosby, Stills, Nash, & Young, Poco, Loggins and Messina, the Byrds, Flying Burrito Brothers, Jackson Browne, and the Eagles back to Buffalo Springfield.

The roundtable group laughed, and some asked for charts. Then we drifted back to business, conducting postmortems on current project disasters circulating through the industry grapevine:

"The architect's drawings were terrible."
"The general contractor stuck it to the owner."
"The MEP couldn't keep up."
"The developer doomed the project with an unrealistic budget."

Suddenly, we all fell quiet. Every project had its scapegoat and innocent victim. They couldn't *all* be to blame.

We looked around the table, all sharing the same thought: After six years and week after week of talking about how dysfunctional the industry was, we were all pretty fed up.

A BRIEF HISTORY OF MINDSHIFT

During those six years, a lot of innovative ideas had come into general consciousness. Fresh technology—in the form of 3D Building Information Modeling (BIM) and sustainability—opened the door to the possibility of new ways of doing business. Yet no one seemed to be taking hold of all these original ideas and really running with them. In fact, instead of using some of these new wheels, most people in the industry were still trying to reinvent the old one. For the Pancake

Roundtable, frustration began to bubble over into action that would culminate in a new group: Mindshift.

At a 2005 regional industry trade show in Dallas, one roundtable member decided to test the waters in the open with a presentation called "The Next Design Revolution." After his lecture, a principal for Gensler's Houston office named Marilyn Archer told the speaker she was intrigued and wondered if he might be open to presenting his ideas to their office.

He replied cautiously: "Do you think the real estate and construction industry is ready for a fundamental change?"

She said, "I sure hope so."

Change was in the air. The following week, Dick Haworth, chairman of the board of Haworth, traveled to Dallas to meet with some key clients, and also with that same roundtable member. After a brief discussion about how challenging it was to promote new construction technologies to the local market, our Mindshift colleague asked the same question—"Do you think the industry is ready for change?"— and Dick Haworth gave the same answer: "I hope so." And then he made an offer. The Mindshift colleague suggested that Haworth sponsor a day for dialogue to see what other industry insiders were feeling about the current and future state of the industry.

Marilyn's conversation found its way to Art Gensler, founder and CEO of the largest architectural design firm in the world, who called Dick Haworth, striking the spark that would soon flame up into Mindshift. It took an entire year talking to industry leaders to determine who might be interested in attending this kind of gathering. Fifteen top leaders said, "Sign me up!" We were surprised at the interest from the many high-level leaders from such diverse sectors of the industry. Setting a date to accommodate as many as possible may have been the most challenging aspect of the venture.

In March 2007, a meeting was held at Gensler's Houston office. The group included leaders like Tom Gerlach, senior vice president at Turner Construction; Franco Bianchi, president for Haworth; Dean Strombom and Marilyn Archer, principals from Gensler; Craig Janssen, principal for Acoustic Dimension and current president for the Global Design Alliance; and yours truly, Rex Miller, futurist and lead author. The American Institute of Architects (AIA) and companies like Transwestern, KPMG, and Beitler LLP also participated.[1] Men and women who usually met as adversaries—and who rarely sat

Figure 4.1   Time to Change

Courtesy of Bill Black.

in the same room—began to come together, curious to see and hear from the others in attendance.

Nationally known facilitator Jim Oswald led this unlikely gathering of top executives through a day-and-a-half of engaging and sometimes intense discussions. The power of their dialogue, and Jim Oswald's powerful visual notes, is captured in this series of photographs (see Figures 4.1–4.6).

Figure 4.2   Drivers of Change

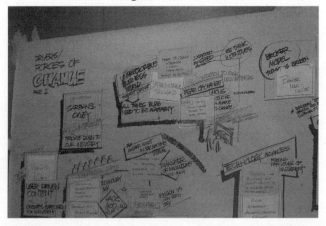

Courtesy of Bill Black.

Figure 4.3 Gensler's Jim Oswald Facilitating

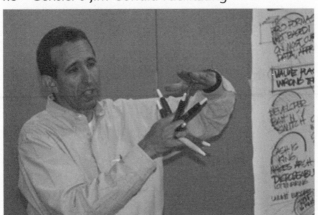

Courtesy of Bill Black.

By the end of the first morning, the participants were revved up. They summed up their feelings with statements like this:

- "All of our companies are very successful; we have happy clients and we're profitable. For some reason, however, when we try to work together our best intentions and talented people get sideways

Figure 4.4 Stakeholders

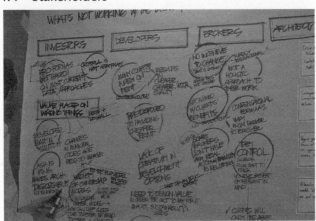

Courtesy of Bill Black.

Figure 4.5   Not Working Together

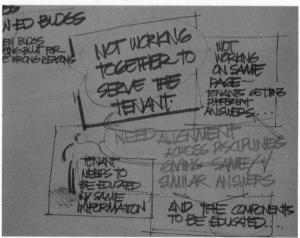

Courtesy of Bill Black.

somehow and the process becomes a battleground—and sometimes the client gets pulled into that war."

- "For some reason, the system causes good people to do bad things."
- "'What is it that is broken?' When I try to frame what this means to me, it came down to 'we' . . . the entire industry."

Figure 4.6   Yes, It's Broke

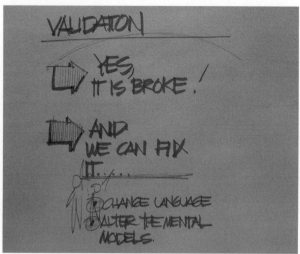

Courtesy of Bill Black.

There was complete consensus among the 15 leaders that the current system was fundamentally broken and that reform efforts—or reinventing the wheel—would at best produce only marginal results. We described the underlying foundation as distrust, driven by a system of fragmentation and conflict.

During the lunch break, we all reflected on this image of a broken industry. Jim Oswald's sketches and notes, scrawled across one of the walls, helped us begin to see the larger context of our common challenges. We had stepped out of our familiar roles and adversarial mindsets and had become unified in our belief that things had to change. We had no idea where the afternoon discussion might lead, but we did know that we had to move beyond checking off all the things that were wrong with the commercial real estate and construction world.

Jim Oswald started by having us explore what it might mean to achieve the goal of having no negative effect on the planet by 2030.[2] The AIA representative expressed, "Even if every building going forward was built at the USGBC's LEED Platinum level—that would only achieve 30 percent of that goal." The responses came quickly:

- "To even think in those terms requires a completely new approach!"
- "We've focused on the more than 50 percent waste in the way we currently do things? We haven't even begun to explore the potential for innovative ideas. Exponential returns and unexpected results are the kind of thing that happens with true innovation."

We went on to consider the kind of legacy our buildings would leave:

- "I'd like to leave something that my kids can be proud of."
- "I'd like to better align the work I do with the values I hold."

With a collective effort, what could we deliver? Bill Black, with Haworth summarized, "I believe if a collection of companies similar to those in this room combined their knowledge and capabilities we could accomplish far more than just a lower cost better constructed building. We could apply that knowledge so the building improves over its life. We could apply that knowledge to help those in the building perform at a higher level—and prove it."

Things were beginning to get interesting. And then we decided to make them even more so and completely flip the paradigm.

FLIPPING THE PARADIGM

We took the current problem, fragmentation, and conflict, and turned it upside down. In that powerful, shared Aha! moment, virtually every person in the room made what we could only describe later as a "mind shift" to a whole new way of doing business: Instead of continuing with our current dysfunctional model of distrust and fragmentation, we could base our future work on teams formed by unity and trust.

The dam of pent-up new ideas broke as we began to ask in earnest and with excitement: What would trust-based teams look like? How do they move from fragmentation to integration? How much waste could be reduced? What kinds of innovation might they develop? If this did create a higher value, how would it be delivered and then monetized? What does the business model look like for this new entity, product, or service? Who is currently providing trust-based integrated solutions? Are there other groups already doing this? Are there other industries that offer a good model? Who else in our industry do we need to include in this dialogue?

None of these questions were really answered that day. What did emerge, however, was deep curiosity, motivating discussion, and a framework for moving forward. Each person in the room felt the desire, need, and value of moving forward together. These leaders from all aspects of construction—from design to management to hands-on building—saw their industry from a new and challenging perspective. Instead of seeing and acting from a narrow spectrum, they could see the industry refracted through a full prism of possibilities. One even claimed, "I've never seen a group in our industry that had such diversity sitting at the same table. To have the contractor, the dealer, the manufacturer, a developer, an architect . . . that puts this group in a unique position to start to connect the dots around the problem we're trying to solve."

This group was not selected by accident; every member was a principal of change within his or her own organization. Having a room full of high-caliber, progressive leaders who were able to put their egos aside generated a kind of energy and exchange that many described as rejuvenating and unique. One participant said, "Our challenge will be to commit the time, to continue coming together and figure out how to finish what we've started."[3]

Another agreed, saying, "If someone discovers how to bring integration to the current mess and create a building culture of trust, then it will revolutionize the entire industry."

MAVENS AND PERSUADERS IN SEARCH OF CONNECTORS

Great innovations are big things that usually start small, and Mindshift's idea about building a culture of trust that would revolutionize the construction industry was just such an innovation. In his groundbreaking book *The Innovator's Dilemma*, Clayton Christensen describes a trap to which companies and industries often fall victim: They can't separate their future from their past success, and the models that led to that success. There is low tolerance for failure and high expectations for following the proven formula. But that doesn't lead to innovation, and that's the dilemma: There is no precedent for innovation. Transformation is not a linear path, but rather a breakthrough that occurs on a journey of discovery. Christensen advises that innovation needs a context for exploration, experiments, and some failures along the way.[4]

Mindshift had already taken the first step: We'd realized that our future could not be based on some variation of "business as usual." We truly were after innovation—a brand new path to walk. We knew that our challenge was going to be moving it out of the discussion room to the tipping point: an idea whose time has come, a concept that everyone is suddenly talking about with excitement and whose implementations are popping up everywhere. "We may be smart," said one, "but we're not all *that* smart. There has to be some group or forum that we can plug in to."

In his bestseller *The Tipping Point*, Malcolm Gladwell describes three key roles that help move ideas to the tipping point: *Mavens*, passionate experts who invent and talk about the idea; *Persuaders*, people who try to persuade others to implement the idea; and *Connectors*, who are able to synthesize the ideas of the Mavens and Persuaders and tie together key people who can influence their circle of relationships. Clearly, we needed to hook up with some Mavens, Persuaders, and Connectors who were already working on these ideas. Gut instinct told us we couldn't be the only ones who'd had this mind shift; so we began to look around to see who else might be traveling with us on a parallel—and hopefully converging—path.

DOTS WAITING TO BE CONNECTED

Right away, we found some compelling new ideas and technologies that just seemed to be waiting for someone to put them to good use: innovations like Lean Construction, integrated project delivery, shared risk shared reward contracting, and offsite construction. Along with sustainability and BIM, these would later turn out to be some of the major dots we would connect as we drew our big new picture of the future.

We didn't notice it at first, but almost everywhere we went we found ourselves in the company of people from the Virtual Builders Roundtable (VBR), who are innovators from Northern California's Silicon Valley. I met VBR's Dan Gonzales and Andy Fuhrman at the first event we attended. About six months later, we met people from the construction firm DPR and Sutter Health, including another innovator, attorney Will Lichtig. We stayed in contact with Dan, Andy, and Will, and they directed us to different resources, acting as mentors throughout our process.

But that's getting ahead of the story. First, let's look at the individual dots.

SUSTAINABILITY

The first event that the Mindshift group attended was the EcoBuild conference in San Diego in 2007. While we watched presentations about sustainability and about BIM, no presentations tied the two topics together. On the exhibit floor, software vendors like ECOTECT simulated energy use and improving building performance using BIM models. The sustainability presentations all explained the necessity for early collaboration. What better tool to facilitate that collaboration and actually test the design than BIM? The report back to Mindshift was that it was like attending two separate conferences—one on BIM and one on sustainability. We were finding lots of Mavens and Persuaders, but where were the Connectors?

We didn't know it at the time, but we'd already met a couple of them: Dan and Andy from VBR.

INTEGRATED PROJECT DELIVERY

The next conference we attended was the Construction User's Roundtable (CURT) in Orlando in November 2007. Once again, we met direct descendants from Virtual Building Roundtable, as well as from the Sutter team, including their attorney, and DPR (one of the construction firms on the Sutter team). Their presentation stood out from most of the others that dealt with the more traditional construction issues regarding safety, labor-management issues, labor shortages, work quality, and bringing key stakeholders to the table to work out conflict. Instead they focused on how they created long-term strategic alliances, reduced errors and change orders to just a handful, and brought their project in early and under budget.

We learned that CURT, too, was beginning to connect the dots between BIM and Lean, but had not addressed sustainability. We also learned that the collaboration initiated by CURT with the AIA and AGC would soon lead to the introduction of contract documents supporting project teaming. And it was at CURT that we connected with people from DPR, Sutter Health, and attorney Will Lichtig.

OFFSITE CONSTRUCTION

Most people think of Butler Buildings—those metal structures found around airports and in industrial parks—when they think about offsite construction. We learned, however, of a vast universe of exterior and interior fabricated solutions that was galaxies away from the old style. We saw hundreds of exhibitors at conferences like CURT, EcoBuild, AIA's national convention, Neocon, Metrocon, and the CoreNet Global Summit.

Currently, this field is comprised mostly of Mavens (passionate experts). There's no cohesive picture of how all of these solutions might collectively improve a building. We know that offsite construction lessens material waste, improves quality, reduces construction time, is often reusable, and can look beautiful. These solutions fit hand-in-hand with BIM and could make a significant contribution toward sustainability. Yet there are no conferences, no Persuaders making the case for offsite construction, and no Connectors linking this solution and its Mavens to other complementary components that, combined, have the potential to produce sustainable and highly adaptable buildings.

Mindshift has therefore taken on the role of Connector here. In fact, we feel that offsite construction is so important that we began making the case that it represents the future of construction (see Chapter 13, Offsite Construction, for all the details).

This brings us back to VBR. Who were those guys, anyway? And what were they doing on our journey?

THE VIRTUAL BUILDERS ROUNDTABLE

It should probably come as no surprise to discover that the Commercial Real Estate Revolution began in Silicon Valley. The dotcom boom (1995 to 2001) placed a premium on speed-to-market. The entrepreneurs launching these companies did not realize that their timelines were impossible. So what do people who have to fulfill impossible expectations do? They talk. In the end, they called it VBR, or the Virtual Builders Roundtable—sort of a Pancake Roundtable West.[5]

The very first participants were Dan Gonzales, now with Swinerton Builders; Dean Reed, with DPR Construction; Martin Fischer, with Stanford's Center for Integrated Facility Engineering (CIFE); and Chris Raftery, who, at the time, was a project executive for Magnusson Klemencic in Seattle. Dan describes their first meeting: "Dean got Martin, Chris, and I together for breakfast at Hobee's coffee shop in Palo Alto. Dean likes breakfast, and we did sit at a round table. We felt there was an obligation to get the idea of virtual building out to the industry and that we needed to get like-minded people who were actually doing this together in order to trade ideas. Dean's point was, 'You can't be good at baseball if you only throw the ball to yourself; you need to have someone throw the ball at you.' You had to be a practitioner—not a software vendor—to take part in VBR."

Jerry Laiserin,[6] an architect, Bell Labs researcher, and writer on design and construction, attended the first VBR public meeting in 2002 at DPR's office in Redwood City with around 75 other people. It was a watershed moment, as he described in his newsletter: "Several million aging baby boomers claim to have been among the 400,000 who attended the legendary Woodstock music festival during the 1960s. In hindsight, today's boomers recognize the cultural watershed that Woodstock represented: anybody who is (now) cool must have been there. Likewise, in just a few years from today, thousands of building industry folks will claim to have been among the 100 or so who attended the June 27 Virtual Builders Roundtable Workshop at DPR Construction and the June 28 executive seminar at Stanford/CIFE, 'Real Profits Through Virtual Building.' Just as Woodstock changed the course of popular music, the DPR and CIFE events promise to change the course of design and construction."[7]

Dean was also responsible for connecting with Glenn Ballard and Greg Howell at nearby UC Berkley, who recently formed the Lean Construction Institute. As Laiserin says, "Beginning in the late 1990s, DPR began exploring teaming and workflow methods that would move the assessment/resolution of 'coordination risk' earlier in the project, compared to traditional design-bid-build or 'conventional' design-build."[8]

These forces then came together with Sutter Health—a client that would rewrite the rules for all future projects, and was perhaps the first owner to connect some of the key dots and test these ideas over several projects on a multi-billion-dollar building campaign.

SUTTER HEALTH

Dave Pixley, Sutter Health's director for facility planning, was on a mission to reduce cost and improve quality. In 2003, he described the need to recapture the role of the master-builder to regain the coordination currently lacking in the construction process. In this reincarnation, he said, the master-builder would be a team acting with one mind. Sutter was planning a multi-billion-dollar, multi-location expansion, and they were determined to accomplish their mission by *not* doing business as usual.

In late 2003, Dave brought Glenn Ballard on as a consultant to implement Lean practices. DPR was invited to take part in this first experiment. In 2005, Sutter's attorney, Will Lichtig, provided the third leg to this stool: relational contracting. The contract was called an Integrated Form of Agreement (IFOA)—a method that, for the first time, shifted the contract focus on an incentive for the outcome of the project, not simply on each trade's specific scope. In other words, everyone swims together or sinks together.

In August 2004, people were talking about the new project. *East Bay Business Times* reported:

> Sutter Health, one of California's largest health-care providers, has embraced a new construction philosophy and management technique to execute an estimated $6 billion in capital projects over the next eight years.
>
> It is the largest company in the nation ever to adopt "Lean project management," which has the potential to revolutionize Northern California's construction industry, said Greg Howell, a founder of the nonprofit Lean Construction Institute, established to reform the way buildings are designed, engineered and constructed.
>
> Adherents of Lean Construction management call it a global movement with the potential to cut project costs by 10 percent to 40 percent. Those

savings spring from many sources, including eliminating work delays in the field and reducing inventory buildup on site.[9]

An article from the *Sacramento Business Journal* also covered the topic: "The idea dovetails with two other recent advances that have gripped the industry. Contractors and architects are embracing three-dimensional computer modeling, and builders have adapted 'Lean production' principles to reduce waste and down-time on construction projects by coordinating work teams and materials delivery. Sutter was one of the first to push for Lean Construction."[10]

As the project continued, Sutter reported dramatic improvements in both cost and schedule, and found that change orders had reduced dramatically. They also reported that relational trust and collaboration were transforming the entire project experience.[11]

If there is a ground zero for the current transformation, Mindshift felt like we found it in those connected to VBR. Interacting with this innovative group gave us an entirely new window into the potential of trust-based teams powered with Virtual Design and Construction tools, reducing waste and improving performance through Lean practices, and commonly aligned by relationally structured contracts.

Maybe it really *could* happen.

Chapter 5 What Does a Trust-Based Project Look Like?

"I've been waiting for 27 years to do a job like this. . . . No more finger-pointing. . . . It's about trusting your partners or it doesn't work. . . . We all sink or swim together. . . . Nobody cuts corners. . . . We are 'incentivized' to help each other. . . . There is no 'we' or 'they'. . . . It's one team. . . . Our goals are aligned. . . . We share risk and reward with the owner and contractor."

—Jay Halleran and David Swain, NBBJ[1]

How many stories begin with the hero stuck in circumstances that he knows just aren't right?

"There has got to be something more than this!"

"There has got to be a better way!"

"I can't believe this is the best we can do!"

Then, out of nowhere, a random encounter or a phone call changes everything. In Dave Pixley's[2] case, the game changer was a vendor presentation.

SUTTER HEALTH CHANGES THE GAME

In 2003, Sutter Health, one of the nation's leading not-for-profit networks of community-based health care providers, was moving forward with an $8 billion capital expansion to add several hospitals and medical office buildings in California. In the previous five years, construction costs had doubled to reach $2 million per bed. The weight of this responsibility coupled with Dave's deep frustration over a broken construction industry had put him on high alert for new ideas.

Then a building product's vendor demonstrated his solution using a 3D modeling software. Dave began asking questions about the software—even though he was pretty sure the vendor would have rather talked about his product. His slow-burning conviction that there must be a better way was stoked by what he heard. After the meeting, Dave did a little homework on what he learned was Building Information Modeling (BIM), and his conviction grew. Suddenly, he felt ready to take action.

"I laid down the challenge to our AEC[3] vendors: 'What's wrong with driving down costs? What's wrong with improving safety?' Well," he says, "we learned enough to be dangerous, and then we found some experts to show us how to really make these improvements."

Two years later, at the annual Lean Construction Congress, Dave spelled out what a trust-based approach looked liked for Sutter Health. He began by bringing Sutter's executive leadership into the process and gaining their support for this journey. He was able to make the case that at $1,000 per square foot for construction costs, the kinds of changes they were seeking were not going to happen without radical modifications to the status quo. In the end, eight shifts in how Sutter would do business effectively changed the game.

1. **Team selection:** Sutter would not pick each player independently through competitive bidding. Instead, they would choose the teams as a whole unit designed to work together.
2. **Contracts:** They jettisoned multiple sets of contracts with different allegiances, incentive structures, scope based and designed based on assumed conflict. Instead, all parties—including Sutter—would sign a single agreement.
3. **Full disclosure:** Traditionally, suppliers are only told the budget and their own scope: "Here's your piece of the puzzle. Tell me how much it will cost for you to build it." This time, key stakeholders

were brought into the process early on, even at the point of reviewing the business plan and the assumptions that went into creating the business plan.

4. **Outcome-based planning:** Sutter instituted a new process that collectively translates the business objectives into an outcome-based plan that answers key questions: What is Sutter really paying for? What do we want to accomplish? And, equally important, what is Sutter *not* paying for, and how can we eliminate that from our process?

5. **Collaborative design:** Sutter encouraged real collaboration around Virtual Design and Construction. Hospitals have complex mechanical, electrical, and plumbing requirements. All of the stakeholders were brought in to model their part of the project. The team was able to workout coordination and detect the kinds of trade conflicts that are typically missed using the old "over the wall" sequential planning process and looking at 2D drawings.

6. **Co-location:** Sutter co-located the project team and provided a common technology platform through which everyone could plan and communicate. This allowed real-time coordination and problem solving, and it changed the dynamic of how the team worked and how quickly decisions were made. Co-location created a level of understanding the whole project—and all of its interdependencies—that could have never happened on a traditionally run project.

7. **Lean:** Sutter adopted the Lean process of scheduling, coordination of handoffs, setting targets, establishing metrics, and ongoing course correction.

8. **Transparent and open:** They embraced an open and transparent culture and values that allowed stakeholders to voice their concerns, say no to requests without reprisals, make promises with confidence, and accept and provide corrective feedback without feeling the need to spin the situation.

Though these eight shifts were indeed radical, they only begin to touch the surface of what a trust-based integrated project and program can look like.

Dean Reed[4] of DPR Construction described the results of their first project with Sutter Health: the Camino Medical Project in Mountain View, California (see Figure 5.2). This project was originally planned under the old Sutter process, and the players had already been selected. Reed worked hard to adapt to this new approach, and the results were startling. The project—targeted to be $95 million—came in six months

Figure 5.1 A New Metaphor for Project Teams from Linear to Collective Centered on the Client

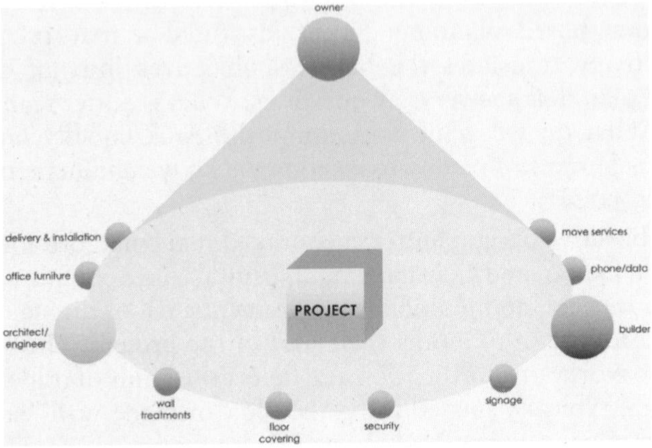

Adapted from the AIA.

early and $9 million under budget. According to Reed, Virtual Design and Construction eliminated *all* of the trade collisions between mechanical, electrical, and plumbing, which meant no change orders where there typically had been hundreds.

The Camino project provided proof of concept. As Dean himself claimed, "This stuff really works, but we had just scratched the surface."

Figure 5.2 Camino Medical Project—Virtual and Actual Building

Courtesy of DPR.

(We will cover Sutter's roll out of Lean Construction in more detail in Chapter 11, Integrating Project Delivery).

WORKING WITH THE SKEPTICS

A confident owner like Sutter Health—willing to defy conventional wisdom and engage their suppliers as partners—is admittedly rare in the commercial real estate industry. Self-assured suppliers who are willing to lead open minded clients to new ways are also rare, but their numbers are growing. It's easy to tell if a supplier has jumped into this new world with both feet, or is still waiting for someone to send them a personal invitation.

Every firm we spoke to that has implemented either Virtual Design and Construction or Lean for the last five to 10 years speaks with authority and ease. As one principal said, "This is now our standard operating procedure for every project." Yet, as accomplished as these firms are, they still work with skeptical owners or owners whose policies require traditional bidding. Suppliers can hope the owners they work with experience the mind shift, but in all likelihood, interested owners will need to ease into the model.

Scott Simpson, senior principal and managing director for the design firm KlingStubbins, explains, "The idea that a project will cost less if you *don't* bid is counterintuitive. Owners use bidding as a cost-management tool, but it inevitably ends up higher than managing that cost on the front end."

EAST RIVER SCIENCE PARK

Simpson described how KlingStubbins helped the owners of the East River Science Park project in New York City see the value of early collaboration. "The project included three towers with a glass curtain wall. The low bid came in at $125 per square foot, which was well over budget. We proposed to bring the fabricator into the studio to design the curtain wall and guarantee the work. The client accepted our proposal. By relying on the strength of our relationship and using our BIM capabilities, we dropped that cost to $104 per square feet— 20 percent."

Simpson goes on to explain, "Owners don't realize that bids have premiums for unknowns. If you can remove the unknowns, you can remove the premiums. Today, with the [use of] the Internet, any owner can check out any price on something within five minutes. There's nothing to hide anymore. Once a project goes out in bid form, suppliers have to guess at what the client really needs. That guesswork essentially turns into a bet and [the hope] that it comes true. The irony of bidding is that it guarantees a higher price, and for that higher price the client also buys a boatload of headaches. The point of this transformation and revolution is that we are moving away from contention to cooperation."

EMERSON COLLEGE

Some clients will remain skeptics. The solution? Propose a hybrid approach to conform to their procurement policies or to ease them into the idea. Boston's Emerson College liked the concept of trust-based teams, but like many clients, they were concerned that letting a team set the price without some outside auditing or competition was like letting the fox guard the henhouse.

Owners will often want a neutral third party to look over a supplier's shoulder, even if they are trusted. The hybrid model for Emerson College involved hiring a construction manager to oversee the budget process with KlingStubbins. The project was fully modeled by Kling-Stubbins, and the CM used the model to arrive at a $49 million price tag. Instead of the CM managing the bid process, they allowed KlingStubbins to hard-bid[5] the project to their prequalified sub-trades. KlingStubbins provided full 3D models to the sub-trades. The greater clarity regarding requirements and coordination removed uncertainty. The result? The bids came in at $44 million—9 percent lower. Why? According to Scott Simpson, "Clarity allowed the bids to be lower."

BIG 3 AUTO MANUFACTURER

Sometimes an owner's competition provides the pressure they need to be willing to think outside the box. A Big 3 United States auto manufacturer saw one of its competitors getting to market faster and taking away market share. Management determined that the size of improvement would not happen by tweaking the status quo. The mandate for double-digit improvement opened the company up to try a new approach for building a 1-million-square-foot manufacturing facility on the West Coast.

Ghafari, the firm that was brought in excelled in both BIM and Lean. The owner worked with the integrated design/build team to adopt Lean and BIM best practices across the project's design, fabrication, construction supply chain. Firms chosen had to be proficient in BIM and Lean, which made for a short shortlist initially.

All of the major players co-located so that any coordination needed happened in real time. The entire job was modeled. Instead of subtrades submitting shop drawings, they modeled their portion and inserted it into the master model. The co-location included a room set up to project the 3D BIM models along with walls to map out activity so teams could respond in real time to work out coordination or problems. They called this the Big Room.

The manufacturing complex was completed 20 percent faster than the owner's benchmark project and achieved LEED Gold certification. With this initial pilot project well up the learning curve, a second project was launched building upon these lessons learned and best practices and raising the bar to a 25 percent schedule acceleration and further reduction in first cost. Most impressive, however, is the fact that there were no change orders due to field coordination or interferences—none—earning the project an Engineering News Record (ENR) Cover slot.

FORTUNE 50 REGIONAL HEADQUARTERS

The project scope for a Fortune 50 company included consolidating five of its divisions into a regional headquarters. The first half of the project was more than 130,000 square feet. The business plan projected rapid growth, including a lot of unknowns in terms of the market, acquisitions, and new products. Some of those unknowns showed up in the middle of the project.

The owner's current facilities were a traditional mix of private offices and cubicles. Over a three-year period, they had spent close to $2 million in renovation work keeping up with just three of their divisions and almost 500 people. Each private office that was torn down and rebuilt somewhere else averaged about $18,000 and several weeks of disruption.

Ric Nelson, the construction manager for the developer, Transwestern, came from the telecom industry. He was used to companies that constantly reconfigure and who are constantly operating in a fast-track mode. Ric made the case to the client to consider a modular interior solution similar to what he had used in Telecom during the 1990s. Modular interior walls would allow the kind of flexibility they needed, and would drop the cost changing a private office from $18,000 to $2,000. It would also allow the work to be completed over a weekend instead of over several weeks.

The owner was willing to consider the concept, but was skeptical that a modular wall system would look adequate for a corporate headquarters. Ric took them to visit a supplier he had worked with in the past. Bill Black, one of Haworth's construction solution experts, provided a presentation to outline how the modular wall system worked and its benefits. He also introduced them to a solution to house the data and cabling under the floor. The theme was how to create a facility that adapts easily to change.

Jabir Hilali, from KPMG's construction tax planning group, covered the accelerated tax benefits, not only of this solution, but for the entire project. He advised that with the right up-front coordination with the architect, the depreciation benefit on an interior project like this could reduce project cost by up to 17 percent. The client liked what they saw, but the CFO made it clear that their business model required that whatever solution they chose, it had to be "first cost effective," which is just another way of saying low cost.

The procurement process for this client required bidding to several equally qualified contractors with a heavy bias toward taking the low bid. Ric Nelson reached out to Turner Construction and brought in two of their estimators, both of whom were familiar with modular walls and raised floors. The strategy was to allow the Turner team to provide a speculative prebid, preconstruction comparison between two different approaches. This would enhance the client's perspective by allowing them to see if they wanted to include the modular interior alternative solution when they bid it to the marketplace. The contractor and his team viewed this as an opportunity to show both the benefits of better coordination as an integrated team and the value of modular interior walls—along with a raised technology floor—as an alternative to building standard drywall with the technology distributed above the ceiling tile.

This team was given three weeks to develop a full scenario to see if this alternative solution was worth including in the bid process. After three weeks of working collectively with all of the sub-trades, the final comparison came in less than conventional construction. This simply won the Turner team the opportunity to bid again—this time, against four other general contractors. Turner Construction won the project along with Haworth because of the close coordination and reduction of waste achieved during those three weeks of planning.

Three weeks into the project, the client dropped a bomb during the weekly construction team meeting: "We purchased a company over the weekend, and they will occupy half of the third floor." That meant that the number of private offices they'd been working on would increase from four to nine and that *all* would have to be redesigned to fit the requirements of the new group. The existing offices would need to be moved, the planning would require figuring out how to handle the domino effect on the adjacent groups, and new product would need to be ordered for five more executive offices. The team asked, "How much additional time will we have to pull this off?"

The answer they received was not the one they were expecting: "We chose you and your solution because you said it would allow us to handle change—easily. I guess we're going to see if you were serious or not. We're keeping our original schedule of 12 weeks."

So the team had their work cut out for them. Turner, Haworth, the architect, the furniture dealer, the raised floor installation firm, and several subs began to develop different scenarios. The pre-construction time together created a cohesive dynamic that differed greatly from a typical project. Turner's team functioned like a cohesive unit: They knew how to work with one another. They had already practiced lines of communication, they knew who to bring in at different decision points, and they worked under the pressure of the pre-construction proposal deadline. Streamlined decisions allowed the wall dealer to quickly configure an order. Haworth shipped the additional product to still meet the original timeline. The project was re-phased and completed within the 12-week deadline. The construction manager told the client that had they used a conventional construction process with a standard drywall solution, the offices already built would have had to be torn down and carpet replaced, adding an additional $100,000 or more plus another eight weeks for completion.

After the project, the CFO said, "Handling the third floor changes and moving in on time more than justified the solution!" It required Transwestern's leadership to convince Turner and Haworth to take a calculated risk to help Transwestern's client see the value of a new solution and a more integrated approach.

As a sidebar, Ric Nelson also asked Gensler for some unpaid help to explain to the landlord how the raised floor solution[6] works and what its advantages were when the landlord nearly shut down the project over initial concerns that a raised floor might make future leasing more difficult. The project success gave each of these companies firsthand experience in the value of working as a trust-based team and early collaboration. Out of this project came five of the original Mindshift members: Turner, Haworth, Transwestern, KPMG, and Gensler.

All of them had seen the future.

AARDEX

A trust-based project can also look like the Aardex Signature Centre in Golden, Colorado. Aardex's developer design-build model places all of the suppliers under a common umbrella and contract. Aardex acted as both the owner and builder; they did not use BIM or Lean. The company selected long-time strategic partners for the key roles on the project. They brought their own expertise to the table with an in-house architect who worked closing with an architect partner, and an in-house construction manager working with the general contractor and all of the sub-trades. Aardex has cultivated a long-time philosophy of treating partners fairly and paying promptly. They also included

Figure 5.3   LEED® Platinum, Aardex's Signature Center

performance incentives, and their model focuses on trusted relationships and vertical integration. This resulted in a 190,000-square-foot LEED Platinum building constructed for a lower cost than conventional construction (see Figure 5.3).

A knowledgeable owner directly engaged in the day-to-day decisions of the project automatically removes a lot of assumptions and waste. In the future, Aardex intends to move toward adopting both BIM and Lean practices.

SUPPLY-SIDE ALLIANCES

In his book *Profitable Partnering for Lean Construction*, Clive Thomas Cain makes the case that significant improvement will come when suppliers take the initiative and self-organize into integrated teams—or supply-side alliances. The current model forces the owner or their representatives to configure and manage the team, or demand-side alliances.

Cain's extensive research confirms the problem that we describe in the first few chapters of this book: "Partnering should be about ending the selection of sub-contractors and suppliers by lowest price competition for each contract (which invariably causes the makeup of the design and construction team to constantly change from project to project and prevents any real and continuous improvement of the processor or of the constructed product)."[7] Highlighted here, however, is another element of the problem—the lack of continuity.

Cain points to industries like aerospace, electronics, and automotive—all of which rely on supply-side alliances. He notes the dramatic improvements that they have made as a result of the switch from demand-side mobilization to supply-side.

Perhaps the biggest hurdle for companies, says Cain, is this: "In the construction industry, demand-side customers have almost no experience of dealing with a single point of contact and have traditionally commissioned design separately from construction."[8] Owners have a procurement mindset and process, but they must throw it out if they want to get different and improved results.

Here is what setting up these trust-based alliances looks like from Cain's perspective: "The commercial core of supply chain integration [includes] setting up long-term relationships based on improving the value of what the supply chain delivers, improving quality and reducing underlying costs through taking out waste and inefficiency."

This is exactly what Dave Pixley did when he challenged his AEC suppliers to confront the conventional wisdom that costs will continue to escalate.

Cain further states that although owners may take initiative to mobilize suppliers into teams, the real leverage comes when the partnering becomes a supplier's strategy. When suppliers form integrated teams and stay together over multiple projects, they experience the full benefits of integration through tight coordination. That is the continuity quotient that pays exponential dividends. In *Rethinking Construction*, a study of teams using Lean construction over a series of projects found around a 5 percent improvement on the first project, but by the third project, these teams had reached a 30 percent level of improvement. The fact that teams that work and stay together significantly outperform an aggregate of players should be common sense. Suppliers can help their cause by helping owners see the benefits of common sense.

When supply teams form on their own, they bring together the players in which they have the most confidence, and who have a greater incentive to work as a team. There is a greater likelihood that teams formed by players who choose each other will develop more tightly and stay together longer than teams pulled together by an owner.

The marketplace, however, will dictate multiple strategies that self-formed teams will need to take. Some early adopter clients will see the model and benefits as common sense. Other clients will like the concept but want to insert their partners or go through a traditional bid decision process.

Rethinking Construction is a report issued by Sir John Egan's Construction Task Force in 1998. They identified the benefits of supply-side alliances more than a decade ago. The report tracked a variety of test projects. In one case, the town of St. Helen's in the United Kingdom tested two comparable school projects. The first was purchased through a traditional bid process. The second took an alliance team approach. The alliance team's price was 18 percent lower for the contracted price. More telling, however, were the outcomes. The alliance team came in 38 percent lower when the projects were completed.

The St. Helen's district issued a summary of the results using trust-based partnering: "Since this radical step the implementation of *Rethinking Construction* ideals is evidenced by the council's varied portfolio of partnering projects. From its pilot scheme at Bleak Hill

School, the change from traditional procurement has been applied to successful delivery of 600 housing refurbishments, the provision of secondary school technology facilities, the construction of two City Learning Centers, partnering a new school for children with Special Educational Needs and the *Rethinking Construction* principles have been applied to Civil Engineering contracts in highways and quarry reclamation works for Merseyside Waste Disposal Authority."[9]

The model and idea of self-selected supplier alliances is relatively new in the United States. There will be more efforts that look like the Sutter Health model, which is a hybrid of owner and self-selection at this point. However, we do project that firms will come together competing as single entities both against other single entity competitors, but also as alternative proposals within traditional bid processes. Owners will have a hard time passing up a proposal that is 18 percent lower in price, faster, and willing to offer guarantees on cost and schedule.

WHAT TRUST-BASED PROJECTS LOOK LIKE FOR SMALLER FIRMS

When Mindshift began its journey toward understanding a new way of doing business, we focused on large corporate projects and looked at what the marquee AEC firms were doing. We were surprised to read a McGraw-Hill survey that showed the majority of projects are handled

Figure 5.4   McGraw-Hill—Smaller Architects Make Up the Majority of the Market

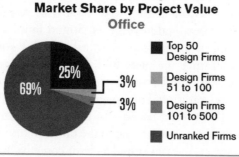

Source: McGraw-Hill Constuction, 2008.

Figure 5.5   McGraw-Hill—Smaller Contractors Make Up the Majority of the Market

Top ENR 400 Contractor
Market Share by Project Value
Office

- ■ Top 50 Contractors
- ■ Contractors Ranked 51 to 100
- ■ Contractors Ranked 101 to 400
- ■ Unranked Contractors

Source: McGraw-Hill Constuction, 2008.

by smaller firms, most of which you have probably never heard of. In fact, more than 65 percent of projects are handled by architectural firms that fall outside the top 400 architectural firms and the top 500 construction firms (see Figures 5.4 and 5.5). We were even more surprised to learn from industry pioneer Arol Wolford[10] that $6 million projects fall into the 80th percentile.[11] When we typically think of market leaders, we assume that they hold market share in the teens or larger. However, the largest construction firm in the world makes up less than 1 percent of the market.

What does trust-based construction look like for smaller firms?

Following the example of Solidus, a design-build-furnish firm located near Hartford, Connecticut, it looks good.

Mark Charette and his brother John are Solidus' second-generation owners. The company started out as an office furniture distributor but moved into construction in the early 1990s, in response to clients looking for better coordinated projects. Sound familiar?

Solidus specializes in projects that are 20,000 square feet and smaller. They guarantee the price and the move-in date, promise no change orders, and offer a two-year warranty on all work, and for all this, they use a non-traditional one-page contract. Mark explains, "We can use a one-page contract because of the trust we build with clients and the incredible partners we bring to the table. In more than 10 years of using this contract, I've never had a client come back to us with any problems."

Figure 5.6   Parade of Trades

The General Contractor Approach is combative, complex, and costly

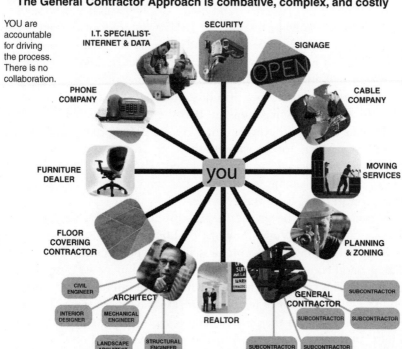

YOU are accountable for driving the process. There is no collaboration.

Throughout the process, there are many opportunities for miscommunication and misunderstanding.

Courtesy of Solidus.

When we visited their offices in late 2008, Mark mentioned that business was still strong despite the recent economic downturn. They had 38 projects in the pipeline, of those, 69 percent were negotiated instead of bid. The efficiency and quality of their work not only delivers a better product to clients, but also it returns a net profit distinctly higher than the industry average.

How did Solidus get to this level of trust and performance?

At first, construction projects were lessons in client pain. It seemed that one or more of the suppliers would drop the ball and mess up the whole project for everyone, and the client ended up the loser. Mark's strategy was to expand their scope of services and keep plugging client gaps, until Solidus eventually grew to become a turnkey supplier (see Figure 5.6). And he successfully did so through a project with Naugatuck Valley Savings & Loan.

NAUGATUCK VALLEY SAVINGS & LOAN

The executive vice president and board of Naugatuck Valley Savings & Loan had planned a two-story, 10,000-square-foot building. The bank would occupy the first floor and lease out the second floor. They had budgeted about $2 million for the project, including all of the furniture and equipment. Jill Carcia, marketing director for Solidus, called on the executive vice president and shared the Solidus concept. He said it sounded interesting but that they had made their selections and it was too late. Jill thought quickly, suggesting that that EVP still meet with Mark for consideration in their future buildings. The executive vice president was impressed with Mark's presentation. He said, "It's a shame we have already picked our team, but we'll keep you in mind for a future project."

But as soon as the project began, problems set in. The architect whom Naugatuck Valley Savings & Loan had chosen was having trouble developing an acceptable schematic plan (concept drawing). The general contractor was struggling to develop a cost range for the building. The two firms had been hired separately; there was little cooperation and a lot of miscommunication between them. The bank was frustrated with the process, and the project was just beginning. Eight weeks into construction, the executive vice president called Mark and asked to meet.

"I'd like to give you a shot," he said. "If you're interested, you have two weeks to get back with a plan."

Mark and his team conducted thorough programming, or needs assessment, and returned to Naugatuck with a complete schematic and a full estimate and schedule. "The executive vice president was floored by the detail, and the speed with which we turned this package around." The board had a similar reaction. They fired the original team and hired Solidus. The executive vice president turned to Mark with a challenge: "In 20 years, I've never worked with the same contractor twice. I hope you can get this done."

The project was already two months behind the original schedule when they started. But since the Solidus team had worked together over several projects, they used their tight coordination to make up the time. Their average timeline is in fact 25 to 30 percent faster than conventionally run projects (see Figure 5.7). Solidus brought and facilitated a collaborative project team, which included architecture, engineering, and consultants. This team worked in conjunction with

Figure 5.7   Reduced Schedule Through Integration

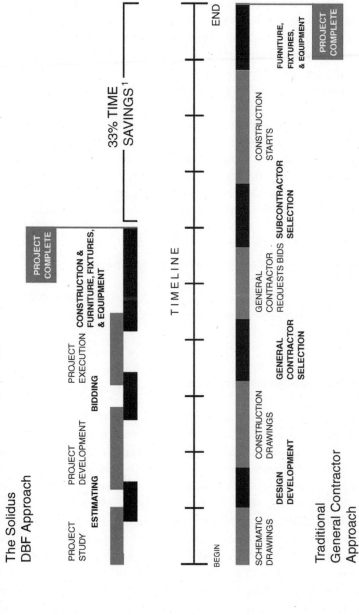

The Solidus
DBF Approach

PROJECT
STUDY

PROJECT
DEVELOPMENT

PROJECT
EXECUTION

ESTIMATING

BIDDING

**CONSTRUCTION &
FURNITURE, FIXTURES,
& EQUIPMENT**

PROJECT
COMPLETE

33% TIME
SAVINGS[1]

TIMELINE

BEGIN

END

Traditional
General Contractor
Approach

SCHEMATIC
DRAWINGS

CONSTRUCTION
DRAWINGS

GENERAL
CONTRACTOR
REQUESTS BIDS

CONSTRUCTION
STARTS

**DESIGN
DEVELOPMENT**

**GENERAL
CONTRACTOR
SELECTION**

**SUBCONTRACTOR
SELECTION**

FURNITURE,
FIXTURES,
& EQUIPMENT

PROJECT
COMPLETE

1 Construction Industry Institute: Findings, National Project Delivery System Study.

Courtesy of Solidus.

83

the client to define the project scope of work and coordination requirements. The fees incurred during this front-end work were passed through to the client without additional mark-up.

We asked Mark why he did not add a margin on top of their strategic partners pricing. Mark said, "It has to do with building trust and confidence. We show the client all costs up front, and the Solidus fees are negotiated separately. We also gain respect with our strategic partners, because they know we are not marking up their work. When we make the process transparent, the client better understands where we are adding value and what our role is worth." He went on to explain, "When you start marking up goods and services as part of your fee, it's complicated to explain and costs are hidden to the client. They'll naturally be suspicious, even if they don't come out and say so."

The bank project finished within budget. Naugatuck Valley Savings & Loan moved in on the promised date, and there were no change orders. The bank awarded the next two projects to Solidus without any negotiations.

HOW SOLIDUS CREATES A TRUST-BASED PROJECT

Solidus follows a proven three-step project development process. Each step clearly meets the client's business objectives building confidence and trust.

Step One. In-Depth Project Study

Solidus brings the client and key stakeholders together to review all of the requirements. Solidus takes a holistic view of each project, so they ask a lot of questions designed to discover anything that might be related to or triggered by a move and that the client may be overlooking: signage, move coordination, IT, electrical, phones, furniture, and even branding. That analysis is delivered in a full proposal that includes detailed concept drawings, an itemized budget, and schedule.

Mark explains, "We have tailored Step One to answer the three key questions a decision maker has: What is this going to cost? When will it be completed? How does this benefit my business?" Solidus charges for the analysis, enough to cover their costs. At this point, the client can choose to go forward, postpone, or cancel the project or use the information as a Request for Proposal to the open market.

"No client has opted to simply take the report and use it to bid to competitors," says Mark. "Occasionally clients have opted to either cancel or postpone the project once they see the full cost. In a typical project, the client is only getting a construction cost and schedule, which doesn't include move services, phones, and a variety of other requirements. They don't realize the full cost or time a project will take. The non-construction requirements can add substantially to the overall costs of the project."

Step Two: Design Development and Construction Documents

This phase answers some basic questions with certainty: What is the whole project going to cost? What is it going to look like? And when can I be certain to move in?

"In preparing the certain cost," says Mark, "our detailed scope review allows the subs to address any errors or omissions in the plan and make adjustments to their pricing. We will renegotiate the sub's fees on the spot, with the understanding that they are locked in—just as we guarantee pricing with no change orders to the client. Locking in the prices at the outset streamlines the process. It makes everything clean, easy to execute, quick to pay, and gives the client tremendous peace of mind. We don't have to go back and figure out why someone is charging an additional cost, explain it to the client, or deal with escalating costs."

Step Three: Execution

During the execution phase, Solidus coordinates all of the client's vendors, even if Solidus is not paid for it. "The client is not used to thinking about all of the little details that go into making the whole project go smoothly. Ninety-five percent of the project can flow without a single hitch, but if the last five percent has problems or creates last-minute fire drills, that is the experience the client will remember. Those last-minute fire drills also affect overall work too. We can chew up a lot of time in those last few weeks reacting to surprises or items the client forgot to consider. We have found it is in everyone's best interest to keep everything under one umbrella of accountability."

TOWARD A REAL CLASS A BUILDING

We all want to build Class A buildings, right? First, however, we have to agree on some ground rules. Here's the Urban Land Institute's criteria for a Class A building:

> Class A space can be characterized as buildings that have excellent location and access, attract high quality tenants, and are managed professionally. Building materials are high quality and rents are competitive with other new buildings. Class B buildings have good locations, management, and construction, and tenant standards are high. Buildings should have very little functional obsolescence and deterioration. Class C buildings are typically 15 to 25 years old but maintain steady occupancy."[12]

If these criteria are supposed to guide a client, they overlook several factors that now distinguish one building from another. First, lease rates are kept within a comparable range for each classification. A building that invests more to achieve lower operating costs, provide higher air quality, reduce its carbon footprint, or provide a facility that tangibly enhances worker performance must swim upstream and hope it can market a premium lease rate. Aardex, for example, was successful in doing so and secured a 21 percent premium over comparable properties. They achieved this by attracting a few large European tenants who valued and expected these features. The 45 percent lower operating costs more than make up for the higher lease rate. One of the firms has already commented at the lowered turnover rate of employees and improved performance over the last building they were in.

The industry has loosely used the term "high-performance" buildings. It is time for organizations like the Urban Land Institute, CoreNet, USGBC, and others to provide building classifications that are not only more meaningful, but also that provide an incentive for developers to build higher-performing buildings. These organizations would offer a great service too by developing tools for prospective owners to better compare how one building might perform over another. That performance can include an operational component (energy and maintenance), an adaptive reuse estimate (changing fixed construction vs. modular sub-components), a health rating (low pressure underfloor air), and even performance factors (lighting and acoustics). It is very likely that a building in an industrial park that included these features might garner a higher rental rate than a high-finish downtown high-rise.

HOW OWNERS CAN BE CATALYSTS FOR CHANGE

In the current model, the owner assembles their team by selecting and managing distinct components (architect, general contractor, third-party representative and consultants) using different contracts and holding competing agendas. In *Profitable Partnering for Lean Construction*, author Clive Thomas Cain recommends that owners begin to encourage and lead suppliers to organize as integrated organizations able to deliver a turnkey solution—supply-side partnerships. Cain goes on to say, "In all other sectors, the critical importance of measuring and eliminating unnecessary costs is well understood. The exception is the construction sector."

So, what steps can we take to walk down that path? Here are several of his recommendations plus a few more of our own.[13]

Owners Must *Stop*

- Going along with the current procurement process. They instead need to make "first cost" a smaller portion of the consideration (Cain recommends no more than 20 percent);
- Selecting individual key stakeholders with separate contracts, loyalties, and incentives;
- Buying based on lowest up-front capital outlay without looking at impact on life-cycle cost or asset value;
- Ignoring excessive waste in process, materials, and labor;
- Ignoring what other industries are doing for improvement, and claiming that those methods don't apply to construction;
- Interfering in alliance formation by piecemeal member or component selection;
- Delegating team selection to a technical and bureaucratic function.

Owners Must *Begin*

- Competitive selection based on integrated supply-side alliances;
- Approaching projects by anticipating the elimination of significant waste through improved communication and coordination;
- Looking deeper into how contractors pick their subs;
- Weighing how integrated teams secure and develop their subs;
- Benchmarking performance and demand evidence of improvement;

- Requiring evidence of involvement of key subs as core members to the team and consulting on best solutions;
- Providing incentives for firms to move in this direction;
- Using the experience from experts in BIM, Lean, and Alliance teaming;
- Setting criteria for team selection and team chemistry;
- Investing more time for preconstruction planning and simulation;
- Evaluating proposals based on outcome, and
- Establishing incentives for the project outcome and not individual performance.

It's obvious that the industry *wants* to change; owners, therefore, must be the catalysts and sponsors for this change. As long as owners go to market in a piecemeal fashion rather than through integrated teams, cost will continue to rise and quality will continue to decline. As we have seen in this chapter, many corporate leaders are already beginning to demand—and institute—change within their own firms. With additional insight, with the recognition of the many forces pushing for change, and with emerging capabilities pulling toward innovation, we will soon see a sea change toward trust-based teams that deliver turnkey solutions.

THE KEYS: AN OWNER'S ROADMAP TO GETTING STARTED WITH TRUST-BASED, TURNKEY CONSTRUCTION

If you are an owner, we hope that by this point in the book, you have begun to experience your own mind shift regarding trust-based, turnkey construction. Not surprisingly, the journey begins with forming trust-based partnerships and developing processes for tight integration. We've boiled these down to four key principles and four tools you can use to implement them. The rest of this book is devoted to exploring these principles and tools in depth. Before we start, here's a quick roadmap to the process.

The first four keys are four principles—the pillars that support every project:

Key 1: *Trust-Based Team Formation*: How you select your team, who you select, and the process you use to form them into a team is the most important component of a successful project. The owner can choose to bring the team together, or can choose to go to their lead AEC relationships and tell them to form teams.

Key 2: *Early Collaboration:* The clear channels of communication and efficient ways of working together that are established during this step virtually guarantee future success.

Key 3: *Built-In Sustainability:* Your team can deliver LEED Platinum results by focusing on removing the more than 50 percent waste generated by the current system. Beck's Betsy del Monte puts it bluntly: Making sustainability one of your best practices is the *only* route to significant cost-effective achievement.

Key 4: *Transformational Leadership:* Flexible leadership that trusts team members to work together to solve problems is key to seeing trust-based projects through to outstanding results. Don't be afraid to leave your comfort zone!

The second four keys are four tools that aid integration and achieve breakthrough results:

Key 5: *"Big" BIM:* Building Information Modeling is a game-changing, paradigm-busting technology. It facilitates early collaboration and allows the team to rehearse and resolve all of the issues in a virtual environment that carries over seamlessly to real construction.

Key 6: *Integrating Project Delivery:* This tool deals with the integration of the team's execution of the project. Teams will find and adapt many different ways to work on the same page, identify waste, and measure performance. We'll present Lean as one of the more promising and growing tools.

Key 7: *Trust-Based Agreements and Client-Centered Incentives:* Trust-based agreements align everyone's interests from the beginning. If the project succeeds, all do well. We will also review several different approaches to this challenge.

Key 8: *Offsite Manufacturing:* Fabricating materials off site beforehand provides an opportunity to change the nature, quality, and future of construction. Although this solution has been around for decades, it is just now finding broader acceptance.

The final key is a hidden revolution that lies beneath all the effort that goes into the design and construction of a building and its interior space:

Key 9: *Workplace Productivity:* When buildings are designed for the people who work and live in them, the building enhances the quality of life and work and ultimately earns money for the owner. It's a win-win for everyone.

In Part Three we'll explore these principles and tools in depth and answer some fundamental questions:

- How do you make trust a business proposition that suppliers and upper management buy into?
- How do you approach owners selling trust as part of your package?
- How do you take trust and establish a process to create, build, and restore it when broken?
- How do you turn trust into a hard skill and not simply a soft idea?

We'll share what we have learned on our Mindshift journey, and meet some successful firms who have learned the answers to these questions.

Part Three **Nine Transforming Keys to Lowering Cost, Cutting Waste, and Driving Change in a Broken Industry**

"The leaders who work most effectively, it seems to me, never say 'I.' And that's not because they have trained themselves not to say 'I.' They don't think 'I.' They think 'we'; they think 'team.' They understand their job to be to make the team function. They accept responsibility and don't sidestep it, but 'we' gets the credit. This is what creates trust, what enables you to get the task done."

—Peter Drucker

Chapter 6 Key 1: Trust-Based Team Formation

"In today's global marketplace speed is everything and in my experience one thing creates speed more effectively than anything else. That one thing is trust. It is the hidden variable that changes everything."

—Stephen R. Covey

Golf is a game where strong, talented individuals with healthy egos face each other down in competition. So what happens when the biennial Ryder Cup brings a team of European golfers and a team of American golfers together to play a team competition? Twelve of the best golfers from each team vie against one another in individual match-ups, with the winner of each round earning a point for their team. Traditionally, team captains offered slots to top-ranked players, and strategy involved little more than the trying to select the best match-ups against the other team's players. A *Wall Street Journal* story quotes Jack Nicklaus describing his past role as captain: "to deliver a few speeches" and make sure the players had "fresh towels, sunscreen and tees."[1] Prior to the 2008 Ryder Cup, the U.S. team had not won in nine years, including punishing losses by nine points in the last two contests. What's more, in this latest competition top U.S. player Tiger Woods was sidelined by injury.

But then Paul Azinger was chosen captain of the 2008 U.S. Ryder Cup team, and he decided to try something new: a trust-based team approach. First, he borrowed a team structure from the Navy SEALs: dividing players into three pods configured by the best psychological match. The *Wall Street Journal* quotes Azinger's assistant coach, Olin Browne: "Working together for the common good is not normally a function for us out on the PGA Tour. We play as individuals . . . But the pods allowed the players, without any formal training, to feed off each other and help each other and to manage all the different things that come up in a pressure-cooker situation like the Ryder Cup."[2]

In selecting team members, Azinger relied more on the team dynamic than individual talent or protocol. In fact, of the 12 members, four were rookies—making one-third of the team newbies. He also created a different context and path toward success. Azinger felt that establishing situations that would help each player perform at his best would actually give the team its greatest chance to win. It's a subtle but significant shift that made team commitment and support relational, rather than abstract.

In the end, Azinger's trust-based team gave the United States its first Ryder Cup victory in nine years. They won by five points.

Given this example of success based on trust and collaboration, you'd think that people would be jumping on the trust bandwagon. But it's harder to leave the old paradigm than you might think. In this chapter, we're going to try to dismantle the last bit of that resistance.

THE ROI OF TRUST

Trust is worth money. In fact, we've got figures to prove it.

The Trust Dividend

A 2004 study by LogicaCMG and Warwick Business School measured what is called a "trust dividend":

> Our research analyzed 1,200 case studies of outsourcing contracts from across the world since 1990. We found that contracts with well-managed relationships based on trust—rather than stringent SLAs (service level

agreements) and penalties—are more likely to lead to a 'trust dividend' for both parties.

Well managed outsourcing arrangements based on mutual trust can create a *20 per cent to 40 per cent difference* [emphasis added] on service, quality, cost and other performance indicators over outdated power-based relationships.[3]

Total return to shareholders in high trust organizations is almost *three times higher* [emphasis added] than the return in low trust organizations.[4]

According to Clive Thomas Cain, "Strategic partnering can deliver significant savings, of up to *30% in the cost of construction* [emphasis added] With this kind of arrangement a contract or framework agreement is awarded to an integrated supply team for a specified period of time; the team prices individual projects within the contractual arrangement."[5]

In his book *The Integrity Dividend*, leadership expert and author Tony Simons evaluated 275 companies and found companies that scored higher in trust among employees added *2.5 percent to a company's bottom line*. And according to Rebecca Merrill and Stephen Covey in *The Speed of Trust*, "The 2006 Annual Edelman Trust Barometer points out that 'trust is more than a bonus, it is a tangible asset that must be created, sustained, and built upon' . . . *Just as trust benefits companies, mistrust or lost trust has costs.*"[6] [emphasis added] The Great Place to Work Institute's annual "Best Places to Work for in America" report also made the following relevant analysis of this topic:

Great workplaces, with high levels of trust, cooperation, and commitment, outperform their peers and experience as a group:

- stronger long-term financial performance
- lower turnover relative to their industry peers
- more job applications than their peers
- an integrated workforce in which diverse groups of people create and contribute to a common workplace culture of benefit to all.[7]

In one comparison that the institute conducted, the 100 best companies were compared over a 10-year period against the Russell 3000 and the S&P 500, and *produced financial returns almost double*. They also showed trust and commitment levels that were almost 20 percent higher.

The Tax on Distrust

What does it cost a company and a project when people lack trust? You might be surprised at the answer.

Emory University Professor Christian Sarkara asked Stephen Covey where this distrust shows up. Covey responded by explaining, "On paper, you can have clarity around your objectives; but in a low-trust environment, your strategy won't be executed. We find the trust tax shows up in a variety of ways including fraud, bureaucracy, politics, turnover, and disengagement, where people quit mentally, but stay physically. The trust tax is real."[8] Covey has essentially developed a way to measure the dividend or tax that your current team is adding or taking away from a project. We'll review those different levels and provide a summary chart that makes it easier to compare your setting with Covey's assessment.

Covey was then asked what role leadership plays in building this competency within their organizations: "It is clear that relationships are now themselves strategic assets and demand on-going senior executive investment and attention commensurate with their importance. Ignoring the value of properly managed outsourcing relationships is tantamount to corporate negligence—simply because it has such a huge impact on return on investment and the potential value gained from outsourcing."[9]

Understanding the Trust Continuum

Covey provides a continuum to gauge what level of trust your organization currently operates at and the nature of the dividend or tax you are receiving. We've adapted that for projects and project teams.

EARNING A 20 PERCENT DIVIDEND: THE REASON I WAKE UP
IN THE MORNING

This is where team members show a high focus on the work and its quality, and engage in a high degree of collaboration. The partnering is positive, and each party actively seeks to improve the other's efforts. Support systems encourage positive interactions like co-locating the team, creating smaller pods around logical subdivided elements of a project, participating in regular social interaction, receiving shared risk and reward incentives, establishing a clear process for common understanding of the project and each stakeholder's role in its success, addressing problems and conflict in real time, using problems as opportunities to learn, creating a team charter to clearly explain the values and structure of relationships, generating a process for assessing and leveraging each member's strengths, and supporting positive can-do leadership. This kind of atmosphere might sound foreign to project teams, and it clearly calls upon a different skill set than we have required from traditional project leaders and foremen.

BREAKING EVEN: DOING MY JOB

Here, team members are cordial and the atmosphere is clear, with few politics. There is no looking over one another's shoulder, and the process and project are carried out with efficiency. And while there is nothing that gets directly in the way, there are no real incentives to look ahead or beyond one's scope of work. The break-even context removes the friction and CYA processes and behavior to allow each stakeholder to focus on their piece of the puzzle.

PAYING A 20 PERCENT TAX: AN EXERCISE IN FRUSTRATION

At this level, the rules are as important as the work itself. There is a clear chain of command, and approvals, corrections, and suggestions are slowed because of this rigid process. There is no incentive to streamline decisions, anticipate what may be needed next, or respond quickly to another stakeholder's need; in fact, doing so would break protocol and risk reprimand. The focus here is on compliance. Problems are more of an issue of disconnects, and incentives take the form of small carrots and big sticks.

PAYING A 40 PERCENT TAX: I BETTER COVER MY TAIL!

This is where bureaucracy, rules, and layers of redundancy often conflict. Each stakeholder invests a considerable amount of time crossing each "t" and dotting each "i." Substantial energy is diverted looking over each other's shoulders and finding ways to game the system. Distrust is a constant, and everyone behaves guardedly; no one puts their cards on the table. These projects play politics as an art and generate a high level of stress wherein stakeholders have to carefully watch both the stated and informal rules. Problems are covered over or shifted to someone else. There is a marked indifference toward the outcome of the project or the other players involved. This CYA category—and its 40 percent tax—seems to be the most common environment we come across in our interviews with those working in the old paradigm.

The construction manager for a developer on a 120,000-square-foot speculative building illustrated the point perfectly with two examples. There were some problems that needed to be worked out before the project could go further. The construction manager (CM) listed this roadblock on the agenda for the next weekly construction meeting, at which the architect, the general contractor (GC), the heating, ventilation and air conditioning (HVAC) sub, the plumbing sub, the electrician, and the data cabling sub were present. The CM was already irritated at the lack of coordination; so when he did not recognize any of the people at the table for this meeting, it set him off. "I went around the table and asked, 'Have you worked on any of the drawings? Are you involved in any way with this project? Have you reviewed the plans?' The answer from each person was 'no'—to each question! They were there to take notes and then bring back any instructions to their team. There was no one there who knew anything about the project or could make a decision. It was a complete [bleeping] waste of time. I told all of them that they better get their lead person back here at two this afternoon or I'll replace them by tomorrow. I also told them that I had better not see any of them back on this job!"

This same CM said that in one week, there was a parade of project managers on the job, all from different interests: the GC, the insurance company, the finance company, the architect, and for one of the tenants. "All they were there to do is to make sure the other person was doing what they were supposed to do, or not messing up what their team needed to do."

PAYING A 60 PERCENT TAX: I HATE THIS JOB!

At this stage, things turn openly hostile and adversarial. This is where people go in looking for traps and escapes. Overseeing the project turns into micromanagement. There is little or no buy-in on the schedule or any of the other objectives the owner puts forward; instead, suppliers develop well thought out contingencies and shift risk where they can. Honest oversights are viewed as incompetence or attempts to skimp on the project. Change orders are viewed as sticking it to the owner. Interaction and behavior crosses the line to open disrespect. Each player keeps score playing the "gotcha" game. "I hate this job" grows from passive resistance, inefficiency, and looking over everyone's shoulder to actively "taking care of number one." This level of dysfunction leads to all of the complex dynamics discussed in Chapter 3. Threats, spoken or perceived, generate responses like slowing down work, issuing numerous change orders, holding back on paying invoices, anonymous calls to inspectors, and the list goes on. At this point, bridges are burned, and relationships are left scarred.

PAYING AN 80 PERCENT TAX: GET ME A LAWYER!

Some jobs—like Boston's Big Dig, for example—deteriorate to the level that Barry LaPatner describes in *Broken Buildings, Busted Budgets*. The issue is well past passive resistance, change order wars, playing gotcha, or taking care of number one. It has shifted to taking down one's adversary, fighting back, and open warfare. Grievances and even lawsuits surface at this level. There is a clear us versus them, good guys and bad guys. There is open anger, offense, and retribution. There is little rational thought left in a project that reaches this point.

What Tax Are You Paying?

This chart will help provide an easier assessment on where you think some of your past projects have fallen in the Trust Tax categories and where you might like to take your next project.[10]

Trust Tax	−80%	−60%	−40%	−20%
Environment	Hated	Toxic	Stressful	Worry
Focus	Conflict	Escalation	Pre-emption	Process
Relationships	Anger	Hostile	Disrespect	Indifferent
Process	Open defeat	Sabotage	Hidden agendas	Chain of command
Behavior	Punish	Micromanage	CYA	Do my job
Outcomes	Grievance or Law-suit	Gotcha	Politics	Slow
Systems	Disintegrated	Dysfunctional	Distracting	Hassle
Ethics	Your ruin	Your harm	Self-interest	Compliance

(Continued)

Trust Dividends	Neutral	20%	40%
Environment	No worries	Positive	Uplifting
Focus	Scope	Outcome	Mutual success
Relationships	Cordial	Cooperative	Collaborative
Process	Task at hand	Keeping promises	Making others successful
Behavior	Respect	Partnering	Transparency
Outcomes	Efficient	Learn from mistakes	Improve
Systems	Does not get in the way	Supportive	Adaptive
Ethics	What is expected	What is right	What is good

THE MINDSHIFT BRIDGE

Let's contrast two statements by individuals following two different project paradigms:

1. "The industry is wrapped in a straitjacket of outdated contracts, competing interests, unequal levels of competency, uneven levels of power and influence, insulated sub-cultures, fear, and suspicion. The knowledge curve is upside down, constrained by low margins, off-balance because of unpredictable market cycles and a jungle of independent interests whose function is to look out for number one and operate in a CYA fashion."
2. "I've been waiting for 27 years to do a job like this. No more finger-pointing. It's about trusting your partners or it doesn't work—we all sink or swim together. Nobody cuts corners. We are 'incentivized' to help each other. There is no 'we' or 'they'; it's one team. Our goals are aligned. We share risk and reward with the owner and contractor."

Which of these more closely captures the project world in which *you* live?

If your team operates on the trust-based side—as described in the second statement—stakeholders are more highly engaged, even enthusiastic. However, if your team operates in the traditional contentious context described in the first statement, stakeholders more actively act out their suspicions and discontents. These two teams are worlds apart.

This simplified chart captures the gulf that owners and their teams need to bridge.

Distrust	Mindshift	Trust
Pro forma	→	People
Budget/Price	→	Value
Schedule	→	Commitments
Scope	→	Outcome
Process	→	Coordination
Paperwork	→	Shared knowledge
Over the wall	→	Collaboration
CYA	→	Transparent
Carrot and Stick	→	Team Success

The root of the divide seems clearer when we look at the contrasts in the chart. The current model of distrust focuses on paperwork. Trust-based teams focus on relationships between people.

The Construction User's Round Table (CURT) paints a picture of the trust-based world they see as possible for the industry. Their vision is surprisingly bold:

"The AE (architecture engineering) Productivity Committee envisions a building environment substantially changed in the future, where building projects are undertaken by deeply collaborative teams that include all disciplines that contribute to project fruition, and where better, faster, more capable buildings are the norm rather than the exception. This new building environment, where owners demand higher-performing AEC (architectural, engineering, and construction) teams, requires fundamental changes."[11] The fundamental change that CURT describes moves from a fragmented, sequential, hierarchical paradigm to one of long-term trust-based teams who play a strategic role for the owner. In this transformation, trust *is* the mind shift, and the first fundamental change for owners and suppliers to make is to accept the necessity to regain trust and build teams.

And here the clamor of voices raised against trust may suddenly become very loud.

HOW CONVENTIONAL THINKING GETS IN THE WAY OF COMMON SENSE

If supporting and acting with trust seems like common sense—and there are more and more studies that measure the positive effects of trust and the negative impact of distrust—then why is trust so uncommon and so difficult to reproduce?

The answer is that, unfortunately, conventional thinking (and sad experience) often gets in the way of common sense. We have all trusted and been burned, and we bring that prejudice forward. We talk teams, but in practice, we suspect collective efforts we can't pick apart, analyze, and evaluate on a piece-by-piece basis. Some want it both ways—trust, but verify. The premise behind this approach sabotages the outcome. We cut ourselves slack, but don't do the same for others.

Some people simply have not considered—there is a business case for trust. Here are some push back responses you might hear when you try to talk about trust to your peers and colleagues:

- Players come and go. It's easier to use a carrot-and-stick approach than to take the time to develop teams.
- Trust is too fuzzy a concept to manage as a business practice.
- People either have trust or they don't.
- The way we already do it is faster.
- Clear goals and the right incentives should be enough to encourage cooperation and good coordination!

These objections represent attitudes and behavior that are framed for a world of distrust, fragmentation, and conflict. They don't make sense in one where trust, integration, and collaboration are the major ways that team members interact. The paradigms are opposed in every respect. After one particular 90-minute presentation that we made to a large alliance of independent contractors, we ended by taking questions. In general, the group of owners said that they saw and believed in the value of the new approach. One owner, however, could not shift his paradigm regarding the character and competency of subcontractors; he still believed that they were all "incompetent crooks," and he simply could not imagine a different scenario. That contractor's experience was very real and heartfelt, and each owner in the room could relate to his concern. Unfortunately, that seven-minute exchange of real life angst was enough to neutralize 90 minutes of a well-presented case for changing the system.

The moral of this story: If we try to reason someone over the mind-shift bridge into a world of trust, it won't work. The only thing that *will* is showing them by moving across the bridge yourself.

But be prepared! If you can't set aside feelings like those noted above, don't venture into this new territory. Your effort will boomerang, and you and your management will conclude that "This trust-based stuff is a lot of wishful thinking, and we won't make that mistake again."

Here's what can happen if you go in naive and unprepared. One contractor told us this sad tale: "We made the 'trust pitch' to one of the clients with whom we had a great relationship, and it backfired on us! Some of the same suppliers had worked on several projects for this client, and we suggested that instead of bidding the next project, the owner instead allow us to develop the budget collectively. We put a lot of effort into it, and we did some really good work. But when we gave the final proposal to the client, she sat back and said, 'Wow, I wasn't expecting this. The price is a good bit higher than I planned. I'm going to have to bid this out.'

"Our team looked at one another and asked if we could take another look at our proposal and get back to her. Well, we turned this around quickly and showed her a price 10 percent lower. Now it was *our* turn to be surprised. She was actually visibly upset. In so many words, she expressed that we had taken advantage of the situation. She put it out for bid and got a price a good bit lower than ours. Our competitors were waiting and had been tracking our efforts. When they saw we had shot ourselves in the foot, they rubbed salt in our wounds with a particularly competitive price."

What went wrong? Although this team certainly had good intentions, they started from the wrong side of the mind shift. The team hoped to avoid the margin-punishing exercise of bidding by assembling a team of members the owner seemed to like and provide a fair price and earn a fair, higher margin. They did not use the opportunity to lower cost by removing waste and forgot to start with the client's goals and definition of value.

But it doesn't have to be this way.

A CASE FOR TRUST: THE BOLDT COMPANY, APPLETON, WISCONSIN

The Boldt Company is one of the pioneers of trust-based teams; it is perhaps not what you'd expect from a Midwestern firm whose expertise is building pulp and paper mills for firms like Kimberly-Clarke and Stora

Enso. This Appleton, Wisconsin-based construction company was founded in 1889. We asked its California Group President Dave Kievet how this 119-year-old firm from a midsized town in Wisconsin became an industry innovator.

"We looked to partnering as early as the 1970s, out of necessity," Kievet explained. "Paper companies often build additional plants during the bottom of a business cycle so they are ready when the market picks up. So, they want it in the ground today!

"Each building is a one-off, and a lot more sophisticated than an office building. There is complex equipment, and all of the mechanical systems need to be integrated. The need for speed also meant that we were typically building one and two days behind the drawings. We needed a different kind of approach with a deeper level of coordination and commitment.

"We had to sit down and work out all of the business details ahead of time, because there was no time to stop and dot some 'i' in the middle of the job. It raised the level of quality for the kind of partner with whom we needed to work. We developed a process that looks a lot like the IPD (Integrated Project Delivery) process used by the AIA."

"In January of 1999," Kievet continued, "our productivity expert, Paul Riser, met Glen Ballard at UC Berkeley and introduced our group to the whole concept of Lean. We joined the Lean Construction Institute (LCI) in October and started our first project with it in November. During the same time, Paul met Sutter Health's Dave Pixley at some of the LCI events. Eventually, Dave asked us to consider submitting for one of their projects in California. We told Dave that we would look at the market and interview several potential trade partners to see if our way of doing business is something they would be comfortable with.

TRUST-BASED TEAM SELECTION

Boldt is firm about selecting team members who meet their criteria. "There is so much waste in the current system," Kievet said. "Our focus is to bring value by reducing the waste, and that takes a different kind of thinking and a different kind of partner. We don't line up resumes and pick the lowest price! Our preselection process first determines which firms are capable and solid. We also drive out to visit potential firms and explain our approach. We may visit a dozen electrical contractors and find several that tell us, 'No, thanks; our strength is competitive lump sum bidding.'

"The success of our projects is completely dependent on our interview process. There is no formula, because each project has very different requirements. A $20 million project is larger than a lot of small businesses. When you consider the size of our projects and the number of people who will be working on it, we're essentially creating a company when we form a team.

"Right now," said Kievet, "we're getting ready to kick off a project for more than $1.5 billion. We're looking for partners, not vendors. So, once we complete our prescreening, we ask each firm to interview. It is like a job interview, tryout, and a bit of pre-marriage counseling rolled up in one. We don't want any PowerPoint or marketing material; we want to have a conversation. We care more about that company's point person, what they're like, and what they care about.

"We look for correct behavior and problem-solving capabilities," Kievet explained. "Do they think about their work, or just follow lines on a plan? How early are they willing to get involved? How much of the design process are they willing to participate in? A lot of this is how well they can play in the sandbox with others. We purposely talk to them as trade partners and not as subs, so we can create that level playing field.

"We also have a process and requirements for learning Lean and being able to fully function on a BIM platform, but at this point, we're looking more at honesty and perhaps a little humility because they have to be willing to learn a new way. They're not the experts in this model. At the same time, we don't use our experience as a lever to force them into this. You can't force people into a system that is all about philosophy and relationships. We're looking for people who want to take this path together—not wishy-washy, but excited about it. We can tell them that they won't have any more fun on a project than working in this kind of environment!"

DPR's Dean Reed, another Sutter team member with Boldt, explained that picking the primary players is fairly easy. Usually, this core group consists of the owner, the general contractor, the architect, and often a construction manager, whose role shifts to team formation and leadership. The traditional areas that the CM has historically overseen—procurement, schedule management, and field coordination—become collaborative team functions. Because of this shift, some projects call this position "alliance manager."

Dean claims that the role of leadership in this new model is to "articulate and facilitate the various networks of relationships required to carry out the project." The leaders bring continued coherence to teams handling the shifting requirements of a project.

Once the core team is in place, they take time to determine the secondary team members needed at the front-end of planning: MEP, structural engineer, electrical contractor, landscape, civil engineer and site development, construction tax specialist, and site planner. This is where 80 percent of the knowledge base and cost for the project reside. Once the positions are decided, players are selected based on their character and competency.

TRUST = CHARACTER + COMPETENCY

Steven Covey makes it clear there are two key components for establishing trust: character and competency. Boldt understands this concept. Their pre-selection process is based on competency, and their extensive personal interview process explores character.

It's tempting to let character slide when a potential partner is strong on the competency. Although they might excel on the job, they may cut corners, treat others with disrespect, or shade the truth to get the job done. But it's equally tempting to select someone with high integrity and great motives who is not fully capable, hoping that they will grow into the role, and only come to see your project founder as a result. Choosing someone with neither character nor competency (a likely possibility in a bid process) can sink a high-stakes project wherein trust is required to achieve speed, innovation, or high levels of coordination.

When it comes to competency, Boldt considers two factors: how well the business is run and the quality of work in the field. They also need partners who can function in a BIM environment, learn Lean delivery, and engage in cost estimates at a conceptual level—not just by doing conventional take-offs. Team members need to be able to make commitments on behalf of their company during collaborative planning. The crew leaders need both technical skills and relational team skills, and the team's success is based on how well everyone plays in the sandbox. Of course, not all good candidates have these capabilities in place, but a big factor for Boldt is a firm's willingness and ability to develop these capacities.

When it comes to character, the criteria must involve more than good intentions. Boldt will consider whether the company and its point person follow through on commitments. They also look at whether the company leader considers the impact of changed circumstances on other members, or if he just looks out for their own interests; how they have handled disputes in the past; whether there are any open disputes or claims; and how they have paid their partners. They want to know whether a candidate will present their own problems and mistakes to the team, or cover them up. They will look at a firm's values and philosophy and explore how consistent they are with performance. When there is a breakdown in practice, how is that repaired? What kind of voice do employees and suppliers have in a firm's behavior? Finally, does the firm have a consistent process of review and feedback and means of putting that feedback into practice?

COMPATIBLE TEAM FORMATION

To Covey's criteria, Boldt might also add "compatibility," in other words, the rapport and chemistry—as well as a good match of complementary talents and skills—that exists between team members.

Remember the tale of the 2008 U.S. Ryder Cup team from the beginning of the chapter? Azinger relied on matching and leveraging talent to make it easier for team members to gel, and to create a context in which players felt comfortable voicing their opinions or offering ideas. Azinger's life coach used the DISC[12] assessment as a tool to identify and explore each player's natural strengths and how they interplay with other members. These natural groups allowed strong bonds and safe forums for open communication.

According to Dave Kievet, Boldt follows a similar process once their trade partners are selected. The firm uses an assessment tool called the Integrated Performance Management system (IPM).[13] They favor this technique because it focuses on identifying and developing strengths. Boldt has also used Gallup's online *Strengthsfinder* assessment, which also follows a strengths-based philosophy.[14] One architectural firm we spoke to uses another team and project development tool called CoreClarity,[15] which builds on the five strengths provided from the *Strengthsfinder* assessment. One of this firm's teams produced some of the best work in the company, but never on time and usually over budget. However, when they used CoreClarity's team profiler, it became clear that they were lacking a team member who was naturally focused on things like schedules and budgets. They shifted a member from another team into the mix, and the results improved. They continued to produce great work, and now it was on time and within budget.

In addition to strategically recruiting the right kind of people for a team, identifying each person's unique areas of contribution and their role within the team is the next order of business. Contrast this to the old model, where the conversation between the successful bidders who met around the table for the first time went something like this: "Here's a checklist, here's how to submit questions, here's a review of the schedule—oh, and are there any questions?"

No contest.

THE LIFE OF THE TEAM

Both Kievet and Reed describe a similar process for bringing the team together. They begin with a summit to introduce not only the project, but also the new model. This initial meeting includes team-development exercises based on the individual assessment profiles, and introduces members to the Lean process, a review of the BIM platform, and the common technology for the project. Sutter Health uses a new relational contract that is structured to tie everyone's incentive and risk to the outcome of the project. The agreement is a dramatic departure from the standard scope-based, litigation-oriented contracts. An all-for-one-and-one-for-all philosophy is a great concept, but it takes time to explain and overcome old ways of thinking when it is actually written down as a form of contract. (We will review the nature of this and other agreements when we cover the different tools for enabling trust-based teams.)

The summit's facilitator needs to make sure the dialogue stays open. Some of these practices will be new to firms, and it is important for everyone's concerns to get on the table and be resolved before the project begins. One multinational owner, for example, quickly learned that trust does not automatically appear when you first change from the old paradigm to the new. Conceptually, all of their stakeholders liked the idea. The firms were competent and had good chemistry; they'd worked well together on previous projects. But when the owner presented an incentive structure that tied everyone's compensation to the outcome of the project, everything came to a screeching halt because they all knew that past projects had come in over budget and late. Although the process had been slightly changed to include more input earlier in the design from other players on this project, the owner's corporate real estate group had already set the budget. This left an obvious question: "What is so different about this project that would compel us to tie our compensation together?"

The suppliers reacted appropriately to this legitimate concern. In fact, this is just the kind of gut reaction that you aim to get out in the open at the team summit. In this case, the owner had an opportunity to respond to their concerns immediately. He could have asked, "What changes would have to be made right now for this team to believe that it will be more successful tied together in this way than if we went back to each person doing their own thing?" Instead, the questions raised took all of the positive momentum away.

One of the members said, "We had nothing to do with creating the budget. How do we know that the budget is sufficient?"

Another said, "This project includes significant interior renovation. We all know that one of the members on this team has very little experience in this area. How do we know they'll pull their weight?"

This is the kind of open dialogue, questioning, and push back that's necessary to build trust—not only in the stakeholders involved, but also in the strategy and process. Leaders in this new model will see these questions not as obstacles, but as road markers to creating a true team-based solution. The leader will also quickly discover if there are any members who just can't let go of the status quo and need to be replaced.

Unfortunately, after a genuine start toward open and honest dialogue, the owner and suppliers pulled back. They made a few small process changes, brought some of the other stakeholders into the design process earlier, and used a modified incentive arrangement. They stayed safely on the conventional side of the mind shift. Still, it was the beginning of a new way of doing business. It is easy to underestimate the significance of the reorientation needed to bring everyone to the same level of understanding and confidence in the new model.

Once the project is underway, the team leader's role continues to weave relationships and provide open conversation. Integrated architectural and engineering firm Ghafari Associates describes their use of relationship-building community events, like cookouts or sports outings, in building a sense of connection apart from the daily pressure of the project. They also encourage informal "meet-ups," where members go to a local pub and say what they might not feel comfortable saying during a coordination meeting. In essence, the new leadership role is more like a coach than the old top-down leadership model of trying to predict, plan, and control the process.

INSIDE THE NEW PARADIGM

Boldt's process shows us how trust-based teams work, and it answers the question we posed earlier in this chapter: "Why don't project teams engage?"

In the cases where they *do*, here's why:

- Members are recruited, not bid.
- They are trade partners, not subcontractors.
- They were selected because of common capabilities, values, and high character; they're not a just a random collection of firms who share nothing more than a low bid price.
- They can focus on developing measurable value and are not forced to play futile bid wars.
- They understand that they don't have to play games to make a fair profit; there is an incentive structure that allows them to care about the whole job.
- They will be asked to participate in the earliest phases of planning and will have an opportunity to make sure their knowledge is considered before it is too late.

Once you're operating inside the trust-based paradigm, one thing becomes obvious: When you have a team you trust, you don't need to bid. In fact, this approach is so different that bidding doesn't even make sense. A team-based partnership begins with the owner's business plan. The team's value is to see how much waste they can remove to finish faster and for less money than the owner's plan specified, or to add value to the project and improve the performance of the building.

Let's recall Azinger's lessons for this chapter one more time:

- If the model you've been using is losing, adopt a new one.
- Leadership is at its best when it is helping others perform at their best. People perform better when it's personal.
- And the best way to ensure success is in the selection and formation of your team.

Chapter 7 Key 2: Early Collaboration

"Conversation enables us to rapidly build shared contexts. If the world isn't changing very much, then the shared context you had a year ago can be brought up very easily. But to interpret rapidly changing phenomena or generate radical change, you have to be able to rapidly create new shared contexts."

—John Seely Brown[1]

Collaboration is a social technology tool. For much of the commercial real estate world, though, it's a rusty one that's hidden underneath the pile of instruments we use every day. We occasionally pull it out because it looks cool, but we can't really seem to remember how it works. The members of Mindshift have reached this conclusion based on the following evidence:

- The lousy results chronicled in the first half of the book;
- A startling lack of any training in collaboration either in schools or business;

- A current generation of senior leadership raised under different rules, when collaboration was not a general discipline needed for success; and
- Teams that really do want to collaborate, but stumble over the basics and give up too soon.

Collaboration without context is merely managed chaos. At best, every project is like assembling a mini-company with hundreds of sub-trades, varying levels of technology, complex building systems, sophisticated finance, and new demands for sustainability, local codes, safety, and timelines—all of which require seamless delivery. Trying to kick off a project with a table full of strangers—and attempting to achieve some level of shared understanding and coordination given the current structure of meetings, spreadsheet tools, and project delivery methods—defeats any hope of attaining coherence right from the start.

Trust-based teams provide a context for collaboration. That group effort creates alignment through a shared understanding and mindset—in purpose, process, and final product. These efforts are not effortless; though by comparison to conventional projects they may appear that way. The hard work is channeled to the beginning of the project, especially during the pre-design and design phase. It is, at times, stressful, contentious, mind numbing, and different in every respect to the phased participation and construction meeting format in conventional delivery. The stories of successful trust-based projects in this chapter will highlight factors common to these high-performing teams, old habits and tools that need to be identified and discarded, and new habits and tools to fully embrace.

But the tools and methods are not the secret. Some projects we'll discuss were low-tech in their approach, but successful because the trust-based teams started collaborating early and often. In fact, as we'll see, one of the keys to this new form of collaboration is to "build it before you build it"—the twenty-first century-version of "measure twice, cut once."

PSYCHO-TRACKING: KLINGSTUBBINS AND NOVARTIS

Early cooperation between all levels of the team provides the collective brain for a project. When that brain is fully engaged, it can and will take on challenges that the rest of the industry may consider crazy. Scott Simpson, a principal and senior director for the architecture and engineering firm KlingStubbins, is one of those collaborative project savants. He is well respected in the industry, loved by his clients, and embraced as an enigma within his own firm. Scott is the inventor of a project delivery model he calls "psycho-tracking."

"In late March 2003," explains Scott, "I was contacted by [pharmaceutical corporation] Novartis for a possible highly confidential project near MIT. Novartis was in the final stages of deciding whether or not to locate its global research headquarters of 500,000 square feet to Cambridge, Massachusetts. They set a very aggressive target of February of 2004 for project completion, including fully operational and commissioned." This involved process also tests all of the building systems to make sure they work as designed, and it was less than 11 months away.

Scott continued, "The selected site had a conventional office structure under construction that would not be complete for fit-up until Labor Day 2003. That left only six months to convert the eight-floor building into a world-class biotech lab, including two floors of animal care labs!" He shakes his head at the mere memory. "When it was first presented, it seemed like an impossible task. We immediately met with a partner of ours—construction management firm Walsh Brothers, Inc. We had a high level of trust with their players and worked through several approaches. Once we had a workable scenario, we finalized our discussions with Novartis and were given official approval to proceed in mid-April of 2003." (See Figures 7.1 and 7.2.)

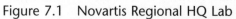

Figure 7.1   Novartis Regional HQ Lab

Courtesy of KlingStubbins.

"We then quickly assembled the rest of the team (trade partners and suppliers). With all of the right players on board, we were able to immediately order long lead time equipment like the lab casework, hoods, and MEP systems. We also started simulating and testing the construction logistics. We then contacted the labor unions to make sure that there would be no work stoppages, and of course, began coordinating with the Cambridge city officials to help streamline the approvals process.

"The building footprint was an unusually curved trapezoidal shape, because it was bounded by a railroad track (not an ideal adjacency for highly sensitive scientific equipment!). This presented a real challenge in designing an open and flexible research space, [since] labs are much better suited to rectangular layouts. It also required close coordination with the contractor, subcontractors, and suppliers. We broke out the work packages and mini-drawing sets to allow our trade partners to immediately begin modeling their work.

"As we were modeling the infrastructure, we also had intensive user-group meetings with teams of Novartis scientists to quickly develop design concepts. To add to the challenge, Novartis wanted a totally different kind of lab—neither a corporate-style nor an academic-style, but one that would encourage teamwork through openness and transparency of the key functions. A lot of sketching and modeling was done very quickly to test initial concepts. We called this 'changing the sociology of science.' "

This early collaboration and modeling gave Scott's team estimates to order material and equipment, even before the design was complete. They also simulated a construction logistics, staging prefabricated components in preparation for their access to the building the day after Labor Day. The work required three shifts, working 24 hours a day. "Our level of trust with one another allowed us to develop unusual contractual arrangements," Scott explains. "Our trade partners were willing to provide their fees based on the early models—not completed drawings. In turn, we agreed to pay them every two weeks. Drawing production flowed on a 'just in time' basis . . . one step ahead of the workers on site."

It took a month on site for the project to come into focus, and then it picked up steam. In a mere six months the sophisticated biotech labs were constructed and commissioned; the job finished exactly on time—to the day—and 7 percent under budget. The scientists were able to move in and start work immediately.

"Novartis was extremely pleased," says Scott. "There was a sizable bonus paid to the entire team."

How did they pull off this miracle? "Our strategic partners really give us that competitive edge," says Scott. "There is no manual for how to tackle a job like Novartis. You have to have trusted partners and take the time up front to invent a new way to digest a project. The benefits speak for themselves; the bonus [that we] made on the project nearly doubled our original net profit. When you consider, however, that we earned our fee in less than half the normal project time, you begin to see we've entered into a dimension of value—both to the owner and for our company—that was previously unattainable. The hands-on involvement of all of the key players gave us a high degree of control over the cost and quality, and we were able to work at an incredible speed. There were no delays, no cost overruns, and no construction claims!

"Attempting a project like this using a standard fast-track approach would be courting disaster. We have come to call the Novartis project and others similar as 'psycho-track'—they would be crazy to consider if it weren't for taking the completely unconventional approach we've developed."

Once a company leaves the gravitational pull of the old system, they find themselves in an entirely new universe. The rules are so different that the impossible becomes doable.

THE NEW NORMAL?

With results like these, you might think that that early collaboration is an easy sell for KlingStubbins. So why hasn't this style of working already become the new normal?

Projects like Novartis defy conventional wisdom—and that's the problem. "Every aspect of commercial real estate is inherently risky; so minimizing this risk is the primal instinct that runs through the entire industry." Plans and numbers on paper still convey a sense of certainty, regardless of how closely they match reality. Scott is the first to recognize that on the surface, the collaborative planning process looks more chaotic and less certain than a clean timeline and task list.

This may be the stickiest sticking point in making the mind shift. The new normal is appealing, but counterintuitive. The idea of trust-based teams working through early and ongoing collaboration sounds logical, but feels precarious. So we hold on tight to our tabulations, checklists, and bottom lines. The trick is to remember that this process is inherently open and flexible—you won't see intricate timelines mapping out the entire project, with every trade's start and end date posted to a wall 20 sheets wide and 10 sheets deep. But you know from experience that those neatly ruled lines hide a chaotic process that will just as likely take the project down as finish it. Collaboration and trust may seem chaotic, but the reality is that this is what creativity in action looks like. People who are truly invested in every aspect work toward a tight-knit organization that will get the job done—on time and on schedule.

If you can remember this going in, you stand a good chance of overriding the gravitational pull back to the old normal.

REDEFINING PROJECT MANAGEMENT

What makes collaboration different from traditional project planning is the level of trust and familiarity with one another that allows people to function outside their typical roles to leverage their strengths.[2] This allows a team to redefine project management around a specific job's unique requirements.

Let's compare this to the current definition of project management:

"Project management is the discipline of planning, organizing and managing resources to bring about the successful completion of specific project goals and objectives."[3] The leadership role within this paradigm predicts, plans, controls, and directs resources to accomplish the project goals and objectives. Alternatively, DPR Lean Construction Coordinator Dean Reed's take on collaborative project management, delivered at the 2008 Lean Summit, is as follows:

"A project is a network of commitments to fulfill a collective outcome." Leadership, then, brings coherence to these relationships by facilitating the kind of dialogue that uncovers the talents and skills to best aid one another toward fulfilling their collective promise.

Dean goes on to say, "The old assumption is that design can be successful separated from the construction. However, design is an iterative conversation, and each element is intimately linked to the others. For example, design affects the means and the methods of delivery. Those means and methods affect the design. The ends and means affect each other and have to be part of the same conversation."

If you are in the trust-based world, a project opportunity like Novartis generates a different kind of speculation. No longer do you waste time finding reasons not to take it on. Now you ask, "What would it take . . .?"

"WE REVERSE ENGINEER THE DESIGN FROM THE BUSINESS PLAN"

Scott Simpson's team cut the normal project time for Novartis in half. If they had followed the old approach, it would have taken up to three months just to conduct a thorough needs assessment (programming), develop concept drawings (schematics), make changes, receive the sign-off, and then develop a preliminary budget. The old normal follows a sequential process: programming, schematics, design, and then construction documents. Each sequence has a cycle that feeds into the next. In many cases, new information will require backtracking and the need to work through the sequences once again. Dean Reed calls this "negative looping."

Simpson's team was able to reduce errors and make better decisions faster because they practiced what Scott calls simultaneous design. Once they had a 3D model of the structure, each of the trades modeled their portion at the same time and then integrated their portion into the master model. All of the knowledge is brought to the table at the front end. There are no conventional cycles, delays, gaps of information, or surprises that pop up late in the process that require going back to the drawing board.

In the new model, the business plan drives design. In the old model, design drives the budget. That is why you will hear the phrase Target Costing instead of Budget or Guaranteed Maximum Price (GMP)[4] from some of these new practitioners. Ghafari's Bob Mauck explained, "We reverse engineer the design from the business plan."

ITERATIVE DESIGN

Moving quickly also requires a great deal of flexibility, and the kind of flexibility that this structure provides allows a team to plan, do, and modify in real time. This is called *iterative design*. Instead of designing to some predetermined level of detail, design stays far enough ahead of the construction to maintain a continuous flow of work, but not so far ahead that new problems require backtracking and redesign.

In today's process of change orders an overlooked detail holds up a trade. An RFI is then sent to the architect, who has up to 10 days, on average, to review the request for clarification on what to do, redesign it, account for the domino effect on other trades, re-estimate the cost, and then approve the work and the associated cost. Instead of being 10 miles off-course on a one-lane country road at night with a lousy map, you are a block away during the day on a major thoroughfare.

Dean Reed describes collaboration as "maximizing positive iterations while minimizing negative ones." Project managers can think of many situations where the plan noted a "critical dimension," a space for equipment that required six feet of clearance. Sure enough, when that equipment arrived, they found that the space had been built with only five feet, eleven and one-half inches of clearance. In a collaborative process, the builder of the space would have communicated with the provider of the equipment, and that small line on a quarter-inch-scale plan would have a completely different meaning for the builder of the wall.

The advanced use of BIM technology changes another important dynamic of construction: fabrication. A large portion of the Novartis

Figure 7.2   Novartis Interior Wall System

Courtesy of KlingStubbins.

project was pre-built and then brought to the site ready to assemble. The HVAC, for example, was fabricated working directly off of the 3D BIM models. The units were brought to the site and simply set in place and connected to its adjacent run. There were no cutters on site, no raw sheet metal—it was already built. The interior walls were pre-fabricated and included the glass, electrical, plumbing, doors, and hardware. Instead of having multiple trades working on top of each other with the pressure of a tight schedule, most of the work was completed in the controlled environment of a factory. Several components (HVAC, plumbing, interior wall, and millwork) were built simultaneously, alleviating the onsite bottleneck that sequential construction creates.

Novartis was built *before* it was built—allowing the project team to execute with almost flawless accuracy and speed.

LIVING IN 2D

One of the hurdles we have to overcome is our orientation toward paper-based planning, thinking, and control. The design, breakdowns, and constraints of spreadsheets and blueprints drive us to behave as separate, disconnected entities. Paging through a set of blueprints really brings this point home.

Each page provides the outline of the building or the interior space; however, each individual page also represents a layout for only one particular trade. There is one page to view the core and shell (outside walls, foundation, and floors); a page to look at the mechanical systems; a page for the plumbing; a page for the electrical; a page for the lighting grid; a page for the data lines; a page for interior construction; a page for the furniture; and so forth. A recent $40 million middle school project contained more than 300 drawings. The architect flips from page to page looking for key coordination points and potential interference between pages, which aren't always there.

When the sub-trades develop their layout, they have no reference of the surrounding work and trades. Contracts *do* stipulate that the sub-trades are responsible to review the drawing set (all of the layers) and catch collisions—errors or omissions on the plan and places that their portion of work might interfere with another. Their job is to check to make sure that what looks like clear straight lines on your paper do not interfere with the clear and straights on everyone else's paper.

Will a sub spend the $150 for a set of blueprints with less than a 5 percent chance of winning a project, or simply buy the sheet with their layer to work off of and build in a cushion for any oversights? Sutter Health's Dave Pixley blames this fragmented 2D approach and mindset for making projects commitment-free zones. There is always some missing piece that one can point to that causes the problem.

Arol Worlford,[5] with Reed Business Data, estimates that up to 10 percent of the cost of construction is consumed in all of this manual connecting the dots, which includes measuring, counting, and pricing. One would think that there must be a better way, right? There indeed is, it's called 3D collaboration.

THE DIFFERENCE BETWEEN 2D AND 3D

Vice President and Director of Design Practice for Jacobs Facilities Inc. (JFI) Thomas McDuffie offers an excellent comparison between 2D and 3D collaboration in an article that he wrote for an AIA publication:

> As we looked at our use of the traditional linear design process, two opportunities for improvement became evident. First is accelerated decision-making. Early decisions based on good data save time and money. Second is to create a more collaborative concurrent process. Removing the stops and starts inherent in the linear model results in improved coordination. Individual phase activities are pulled forward into the "big picture" context. This not only increases interaction between disciplines, but importantly provides added opportunities for front-end involvement by stakeholders. Increased stakeholder involvement, particularly during early project activities, significantly enhances the ability to fully identify and address owner objectives and expectations, benefiting quality and functionality.[6]

The 3D world connects the dots: the right and left brain, data to images, form to concept, and granular to big picture. It allows the people responsible for these different dots to see exactly how their dot relates to those adjacent to them.

As Michael Schrage describes in his book *No More Teams!*, the planning tools and methods used reflect our assumptions about how the world works.

- Linear or iterative
- Individual or collaborative
- Abstract or prototypical
- Analysis or play

Each method frames a range of thought, and has a built-in process that we follow. A linear approach works fine when the process and final outcome is predictable or fits within a set of defined solutions. But when success is determined by the quality of interaction, then a linear approach impedes free interaction. When there are tight constraints, high risks, uncertainty, or complexity, these conditions require a high quality of interaction and coordination. Again, a linear process interferes with the necessary dynamic of a tightly aligned but loosely structured team that has to grapple with challenging conditions.

In the 2D world, we end up with projects where the client says, "You built what we asked for—just not what we wanted."

Craig Janssen notes, "Well-designed modeling tools and processes help decision makers see the big picture, [and] understand the interrelated effects of their choices that make decisions stick. The presentation of information in clear, visual, and interactive form greatly enhances the effectiveness of the decision-making process. The business case—and the myriad variables which comprise it—is often presented in a very left-brained, data-centric fashion using columns of disconnected information. Our team has found that, in the absence of interactive and graphical—or right-brained presentation of the information—many clients simply jump to intuitive conclusions which largely ignore the data."

We now know that when designing collaboratively, we have to ask what kind of thought and behavior our context rewards or resists. Our current process leads to quick conclusions and quick action. But if those quick conclusions and actions are not delivering good results, what context might produce more effective results?

THINKING COLLABORATIVELY

Ray Lucchesi, principal at Lucchesi Galati, asks new clients to spend three days with them doing nothing but thinking collaboratively. The initial response from most clients is predictable: "Why do we want to spend three days together?"

"There is not much value placed in thinking," Ray explains. "There has to be a mind shift to even tolerate collaborative thinking and planning. In most projects," he continues, "the problem is framed as a time-money question along with some functionality. There is really no new value brought to this discussion. This analytical constriction is the first barrier to come down."

The second barrier to come down is the filter each stakeholder brings to the table. "If we are successful enough to get an engineer and an architect willing to sit next to each other for three days, our next goal is to open up the filters so that they can listen to each other—no small challenge. It's not until people can begin to step back and ask the kinds of questions that help them see through another's lens that these less visible but more rigid barriers begin to come down. That does not happen in a day, and often not until part way through the second day together.

"Once we can move beyond framing questions in terms of direct answers, the conversation shifts, and the real interest becomes the nature of the dialogue. It is at this point that priorities surface in the form of passionate concerns, hopes, or goals. At this level, we begin to see the real barriers getting in the way of our work together. It is [also] at this level that a group will see that the problem isn't really the contract, the schedule, or the process—it's a lack of trust. When we explore that more deeply the root may simply be, 'I really don't know you.' There can be any number of deep-seated barriers that will never be reached using old problem-solving approaches."

Ray's firm practices an important quality for gaining collective insight. That quality resists the tyranny of the urgent to "not just stand there but do something." Whether he knows it or not his method of collective dialogue and emergent thinking has a scientific foundation. Neuropsychologist and author Maryanne Wolf writes, "In music, in poetry, and in life, the rest, the pause, the slow movements are essential to comprehending the whole."[7]

THE LEARNING CURVE OF 3D COLLABORATION

In his book *No More Teams!*, Michael Schrage writes, "Organizations that attempt to substitute increased communication for increased collaboration learn the hard way that there is a tremendous difference."[8] Let's take a look at the various levels for teams who are working on the development of collaboration skills.

Streamlining

Streamlining involves working on coordination, rehearsing the process, and deepening trust so that conflicts can be handled relationally in real time, and not through a trail of paperwork and change orders. The purpose is that when you execute, it is flawless. The Novartis lab provides an excellent example of streamlining.

Better Value

Better value involves a significant reduction in the cost and schedule or a marked improvement quality. "We don't want the low bid on a higher-cost design, but the lowest true cost on the right design," says Eric Lamb, EVP for DPR. Some of this takes place when streamlining, but another level of collaboration occurs when the different trades work together to develop better overall solutions.

Remember the curtain wall problem for the East River Science Park in Chapter 5? The architect and fabricator worked together to model and design a less-expensive custom solution. The context is very different because the relationships and tools are different. The shift goes from "What options do we have?" to "What will it take to make this happen?"

Better Choices

When owners work with their teams early, during the business case phase, they make smarter decisions. Better choices involve exploring options to better understand trade-offs. Rapid prototyping is one of the tools that aid a deeper understanding of options. A prototype can be built around an attribute or advantage to see how it impacts other factors.

- How does more daylight reduce energy use or improve productivity?
- How does a particular curtain wall reduce heat absorption?
- How does one layout provide less distraction than another layout, and what is the trade-off of cross-communication?
- If we use a modular interior wall solution, what is the reduction in operational expense for the current churn rate?

The Novartis lab used old-fashioned prototyping (sketches) along with digital 3D modeling to aid researchers in developing their new lab space and considering the implications of one layout over another.

Innovation

Innovation involves gaining deeper understanding of the environment and the human interaction that takes place within that environment. Some describe this as a discovery process—deep observation with some structured reflection and search for deeper unifying patterns. Innovation goes outside our boxed set of options.

Renowned industrial design studio IDEO was asked to work with some hospitals to help improve patient care. Instead of using a traditional approach—bringing experts into a room and storyboarding the challenges—IDEO designed a "patient journey." This real-life, real-time experience took caregivers through the same experience a patient goes through: from the waiting room, to the exam room, to the patient room, on the gurney—the works. One of the gurney participants noted how boring the ceiling tiles were, and how they counted the holes in the tiles while waiting to go to the next stop. This immersion completely changed the paradigm and the dialogue and opened a whole new range of considerations. This is a perfect example of what we mean by gaining deeper understanding of the environment and the human interaction that takes place within that environment.

These insights led one hospital to dedicate one floor in their corporate headquarters to a life-size 3D model. They worked with IDEO and their architect to create five patient rooms with different configurations. The rooms were set far enough into the space to allow observers to walk through them, and windows were spaced along the outside so that the room could be viewed from different angles. This is one example of 3D collaboration and the way in which this particular hospital has changed many of its practices because of the patient journey experience.

If solutions require innovation, then that innovation has to come from a different mindset than the one with which we wake up every morning. Innovation naturally deconstructs our initial premise. It takes ideas and issues that look separate within the current context and creates a new context that reveals some deeper connection. An example of that deeper exploration can be as simple as employing Toyota's "five whys"[9] as a process to find root causality.

Another key to innovation is to find ways to take ideas out of the abstract and make them explicit—to make the intangible tangible. Michael Vance, former dean of Disney University, explains the process of "quinter-sensing" (using the five sensing). What does it feel, look, smell, sound, taste like? Prototyping—and more recently, rapid-prototyping—has become one of the essential tools to provoke deeper thinking around questions and problems.

IDEO employs a trust-based immersion strategy in its process called "Design Thinking." Tim Brown, CEO for IDEO, says, "Design thinking is a prototyping process. Once you spot a promising idea, you build it. The prototype is typically a drawing, model, or film that describes a product, system, or service. We build these models very quickly; they're rough, ready, and not at all elegant, but they work. The goal isn't to create a close approximation of the finished product or process; the goal is to elicit feedback that helps us work through the problem we're trying to solve. In a sense, we build to think."[10]

Context Is the Key

Context separates successful attempts at collaboration from those that fail. For example, top-down or owner–initiated collaborations and peer-to-peer collaborations can both work. But it's important to recognize that it will take longer for team members in the top-down approach to develop mutual trust, and peer-to-peer situations might give the owner some pause. The following provide other elements that create a context for collaboration.

Respect and Candor

The key to developing collaboration is to express the feeling that everyone brings value, can be trusted, and can freely speak their minds. Michael Vance says one of the key components to a creative culture is that "A is A." In other words, if I can't express what I really think but instead have to dance around it, then it kills candor. Once candor is gone, it is replaced by politics, and politics, in this context, merely fulfill one's agenda through indirect means. Respect and candor are not assumed behaviors; the team has to spell out and establish their own code of conduct, which includes how conflict will be handled.

Co-Location

Having the team together geographically for the duration of a project is a common feature. This ensures that the right information is immediately available, and that decisions can be made in real time without reverting to requests for information or holding numerous meetings. Since decisions are made during the flow of the project, everyone on the team is a decision maker within this context. There are no note takers, which reduces the latency of decisions, the time between the making of a decision and its effects. DPR calls this facility their "Big Room."

Highly Visual

A slide projector is the most commonly used tool during these kinds of gatherings. Teams will meet to project 3D models of planned areas and to work out clashes and constructability issues before they get on the job site. Wall space allows the team to map out a process and to improve coordination or remove steps that add no value. Visualization tools and props make work flow tangible and reveal links that allow the entire team to participate in the conversation. Software tools like Mind Map enable one to quickly capture ideas and easily arrange and rearrange them to offer different views or restructure how ideas relate to one another.

Good visualization tools allow the team to collect ideas, sequence them in different ways, create links, develop frameworks to organize these concepts into themes, allow group participation, and then develop different narratives or stories that give meaning and context behind these ideas. The tool can be as simple as note cards pinned to a wall. Working thoughts that remain visible allow members to see them as they take shape. These can become ongoing dialogues that do not require meetings to keep the flow of ideas moving. Michael Vance, who was in charge of Idea and People Development for Disney in the 1970s, adapted a form of visual thinking for business called "Displayed Thinking." HOK offers a similar visual architectural programming approach in their book, *Problem Seeking*, first published in 1974. No matter what method or tool is adopted, this is a vital element for any collaborative process.

Immersion

Ghafari's Bob Mauck says that when a team works together and is immersed in the evolving details of a project—its images, ongoing dialogue, and problems—then they develop a familiarity with the project that leads to fresh and novel solutions. They're able to anticipate issues or opportunities, and ensure a smoother, more predictable flow of work.

Front-loading Knowledge and Planning

Owners and teams will need to adjust their project rhythm to expect more people to be involved on the front end of a job longer. Patrick MacLeamy, CEO for HOK, has developed what has become called "the MacLeamy Curve." It contrasts the traditional knowledge curve for design with that of an integrated team.

The X axis (horizontal) lists the different phases of design: pre-design, schematic, design development, construction documents, bid and then construction management. The Y axis (vertical) shows the degree of impact for the effort invested (see Figure 7.3).

Figure 7.3   HOK Patrick MacLeamy Curve

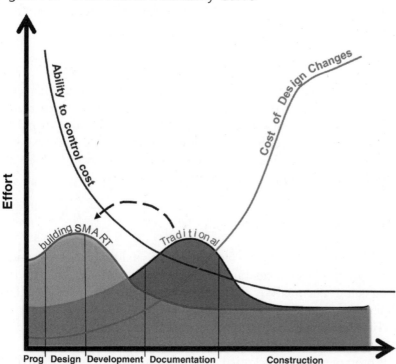

Four components are measured. The graph shows that the ability to impact cost and functional capabilities is greatest during pre-design, and decreases as the project works through the different phases. It also displays how the cost of changing the design is least during pre-design and increases dramatically through the different phases. Within a traditional design project, the greatest amount of design effort takes place during construction documentation, but within an integrated team scenario, the graph moves the peak of the curve up to the schematic or conceptual phase.

Set-Based Design

Set-based design refers to the process of developing a range of possible solutions at a conceptual detail level. Those solutions are carried through the evolution of the project until a clear winner is determined. We'll look at this in more detail in Chapter 11, Integrating Project Delivery.

Just-in-Time Drawings

Instead of batching drawings, integrated teams are able to develop ongoing drawings that reflect the latest conditions. In many cases, the sub-trades are modeling their own portions then integrating them into the master model for full team review. Chapter 10, Big BIM will explain how 3D modeling is not only moving design away from its 2D platform but changing the entire process of design.

Model, Prototype, and Simulate

Modeling, prototyping, and simulating are vital to 3D collaboration.

Modeling makes ideas tangible. It moves questions and inquiries from left brain analysis to a right brain synthesis. Models allow someone to examine an idea or problem from above, below, inside, and out. They do not have to be polished; in fact, a rough model often allows more open-ended thinking.

Prototyping uses conceptual props that are meant to test different ideas or scenarios. Lean construction training, for example, includes an exercise that uses Lego blocks to simulate the flow of work, building a simple airplane among a team of six assemblers. (We'll see this in action in Chapter 11.) This exercise allows participants to better predict performance, observe the effects of interaction, or rehearse an upcoming set of events.

Simulating lets you see your ideas in action and tweak them. Three-dimensional modeling software offers a wide range of simulation opportunities—from design to constructability and operational performance.

A Common Language and Tools

Communication is an ancient construction problem that plagues projects to this day. In addition to being a construction project—a tower—that never was completed, Babel has come to mean utter confusion. So it is worth taking note that one of the first challenges in team formation is to develop a common language among players from very different disciplines and cultures.

A common language helps to guide group conversations around problem solving, resolving conflict, planning, and team formation. This makes it easier for everyone to quickly get oriented and to anticipate where a discussion might lead. For these and other team interactions, there are host of tools available. We'll review just a few so that you have some ideas to further explore.

We've already discussed a tool that Boldt uses for a common reference point—the Integrated Performance Management system—as well as DISC and Gallup's Strengthsfinder.

Lean construction provides a universal language, values, and system for a team to create the flow of work and resolve clashes that arise from errors and miscommunication. When it comes to discussing the merits of new ideas, gathering creative input, or gaining a deeper understanding about an issue, some common structure and language will aid the process. Without that shared platform, discussions can easily get derailed or fall into common ruts.

One particular rut is the role team members begin to adopt in meetings. Often, one individual seems to routinely input new ideas, while another will consistently play the devil's advocate. But the goal is for people to listen deeply and develop the ability to hear and take on different perspectives.[11]

Every team will find its own tools to develop shared awareness and shorthand for working together. Michael Schrage points out that "Virtually all cultures have some proprietary vocabulary." Teams, families, colleagues, even groups of friends all function better when they have cultivated a universal way of communicating. Language is the external reflection of the shared mind. If the group speaks in different languages that have different meanings to different people, then we can expect to continue to have projects that turn out to be equally incoherent. The best time to start forming a common language is at the team formation phase, simply by putting language differences out in the open and asking about approaches that have worked for them in the past.

THE VALUE OF 3D COLLABORATION

Three-dimensional collaboration enabled Ghafari and GM's World Wide Facilities group to transform the design and construction of new factories. The initiative, called the "Virtual Factory," was implemented over five projects. The team was able to create a 3D composite with a level of detail that translated directly to field constructability. Vice President of Virtual Design and Construction for Ghafari Bob Mauck explains: "The highly collaborative, co-located approach eliminates waste along the supply chain by replacing 2D drawings with bi-directional digital exchange between the owner, A/E (architect/engineer), fabricators, and subcontractors." Having the entire team in the same place allowed full design integration, on-the-spot value engineering, automated collision detection, visualization of the construction process, and subcontractors' ability to fabricate straight from the models.[12] At Lansing's Delta Township site, the team of Barton Malow Company and Gharfari was commissioned to build a 442,000-square-foot manufacturing facility in 12 months. The project was completed in nine months with costs savings of 15 percent and a 90 percent reduction in change orders. In another facility, the team delivered the building in 40 weeks—compared to a typical 60-week schedule. A key to this success was the ability to accelerate the order of 4,500 tons of steel. The normal 12-week process to complete and issue a fabrication-ready drawing to the mill was reduced to three weeks (a 75 percent reduction in time).

"In 26 years, I have never seen a project run with more collaboration and be so simple," says Michael Neville, Ghafari vice president and project principal.

Todd Pugh, estimator for one of the trade partners commented, "We had the entire job detailed and coordinated before we stepped on the job site."

We close with a more recent story: Autodesk's new 60,000-square-foot headquarters. This project combines co-location, virtual design, and construction, Lean delivery, and a single shared risk/reward contract. The trust level on the team allowed a contract stipulating no lawsuits to resolve possible disputes, and every party worked through the project on a break-even cost basis. The project created a shared incentive pool.

The collaboration produced a significant portion of offsite pre-fabrication. The ceiling, for example, is a custom three-quarter-inch wooden boomerang-shaped design. The virtual models included all of the routing detail, and they were able to go straight to the milling machines for fabrication (see Figures 7.4 and 7.5). The millwork was similarly designed and fabricated. The sprinklers are typically built on site because of all of the complex bends to work around the other fixtures in the ceiling. In the old world, the first trade who arrives gets to build it the way they want, and then the other trades have to adapt by issuing change orders. In this case, the detail had a level of accuracy

Figure 7.4   Autodesk BIM for Custom Ceiling

Courtesy of KlingStubbins.

Figure 7.5   Autodesk Custom Ceiling Installed

Courtesy of KlingStubbins.

that allowed prefabrication of all of the bends. The sprinklers fit in place like a 3D jigsaw puzzle without any adjustments or interference. This LEED Platinum project kicked off in May 2008 and was completed in December less than seven months later.

Instead of relying on an "inspect and correct" form of quality control, quality can be built in from the start. The "build it before you build it" approach is the secret to breakthrough success. Trust-based teams and 3D collaboration changes the construction game completely. This approach will expand to impact and transform the entire commercial real estate world. Firms like KlingStubbins, Ghafari, DPR, Swinerton, Boldt, Lucchesi Galati, Strategic Dimension, Solidus, and other early adopters have successfully broken out of the tightly defined protocols within which the rest of the industry operates, and they have created a new market space without comparable competition. When you hear Dave Pixley with Sutter Health admit that "insurance companies and the legal system haven't caught up with what we're doing, but we can't wait for them," or Scott Simpson proudly express the same sentiments, it is both a victory cry and a warning to anyone who is attracted by these results, but who has not crossed the bridge to trust-based teams as the starting point for everything else.

Chapter 8 Key 3: Built-In Sustainability

"For the first time, the so-called 'Left' and the so-called 'Right' got together on the subject of Climate Change. This has unified some very high-level discussions. Within the next five years this will become a moral imperative."

—Craig Janssen

"Two facilities changed the course of our company," says The New York Times Corporation's David Thurm. This senior vice president of operations and veteran of journalism for almost three decades explained the corporation's transformation from a utilitarian-driven company—publisher of the *New York Times, International Herald Tribune, Boston Globe*, and 15 other newspapers—to a world-class green leader.

"We had built about a dozen print production facilities," he said, "and each one worked fine for us. We followed a cookie-cutter approach and that allowed us to build them quickly and within budget. It wasn't until the industry began to convert to color printing that we also had an unexpected 'Aha!' that would carry over to our headquarters."

He explained. "Two facilities changed the course of our company. We moved our printing operations from our Manhattan location to one in Edison, New Jersey, and the other to College Point in Queens, New York.

"Production facilities are measurable; and because of that we are always pushing the limits to find ways to improve our output. When we started the process, believing the conventional wisdom, we thought we only had two choices for printing color. We could either produce it efficiently or aim for high quality, but we couldn't achieve both. We worked directly with some of the manufacturers to push for a better solution. Our drive for innovation produced an epiphany. By pushing the limits, we found that in order to be really efficient we had to also produce high quality. Conversely, in order to produce high quality we had to be really efficient.

"That process," he continued, "showed us the importance of demanding innovation and the difference that design makes. We carried that through to the design of Edison and College Point. We wanted to push for an innovative facility for the people to work in and leverage the benefits that good design can deliver. Edison came first; and instead of our normal cookie cutter approach, we hired Polshek Partnership Architects and worked with Jim Polshek and Richard Olcott.

"Design, for us, meant a facility that was well thought through from the work flow, the environment for the people working in it. Edison was 1.3 million square feet and became an industry benchmark on many levels. When we began College Point, we took the same thinking and came in pushing the standards we achieved at Edison."

The upshot? "We improved the environment for the people working at College Point and built a facility for half the cost and half the size, but it produced the same output as Edison."

That was the beginning of a new attitude to designing buildings. "When we approached building our new headquarters in Manhattan, we carried these lessons with us (see Figure 8.1). We believed that innovation is essential and that design makes a difference. When we began investigating sustainability and LEED certification, we took a different approach in our green strategy. Instead of trying to follow a point system or a blueprint, our strategy was to provide a better environment for our people. The guiding lesson for us came from the wall we first ran into when we transitioned to color printing. Do we want quality or efficiency? When it came to a green strategy, we felt that building a great environment for our people would also produce a

Figure 8.1 NY Times HQ

Courtesy of Joe Schlabotnick/Flickr.

high-performing, sustainable building. It turns out our premise was correct." We'll look at what that meant in detail later in this chapter.

SUSTAINABILITY MEANS REDUCING ENERGY CONSUMPTION AND WASTE

Sustainability is a big buzzword these days. We all want to conserve local and global resources for the future in a way that will sustain the people and the planet. For the commercial real estate industry, the first item on the agenda for sustainability is straightforward: reducing energy consumption and waste.

Mindshift views built-in sustainability in the same light that Toyota views built-in quality: as a core principle. It should be intentional, integral to every project, and consistently achievable through trust-based, integrated teams and early collaboration. To our surprise and delight, we've found that building a green building costs no more than building a conventional building and delivers an immediate return on investment. The payback is now—not in three to five years.

So why aren't more people doing it? We think it's this simple: the knowledge gap. Broader adoption will mean challenging the conventional wisdom, overturning some widely believed myths, and showing how the foundation we've laid will achieve first cost effectiveness and an immediate ROI.

To do this, we need to get from the prevailing myth to the paradigm-blasting mind shift in four key areas that help people see: (1) sustainability is ready for Main Street; (2) sustainable building is cost-effective from the beginning; (3) buildings—not cars—are the biggest contributor to greenhouse gases; and (4) doing it will prove to you it's possible. Let's take a look.

MYTH TO MINDSHIFT #1: SUSTAINABILITY *IS* READY FOR MAIN STREET

Think the green movement is still on the fringes? Think again. An article is *Design Intelligence* says bluntly: "A Yale research survey reveals a significant shift in public attitudes toward the environment and global warming. In 2007, 83 percent of Americans said they believed global warming was a 'serious' problem . . . "[1]

An article, titled "Cost Benefits of Going Green," for the AIA stated this: "There has been a dramatic shift from the 'tree hugging hippy' greenie to the mainstream awareness of environmental issues which has permeated almost every home."[2]

It's clear that we no longer have to spend time making a general case for adopting sustainable practices: that battle is officially over. The question now is how to make the shift intelligently.

LEED Has Changed the Game

The primary vehicle for reducing energy costs and waste for new construction is a program through the U.S. Green Building Council (USGBC) called Leadership in Energy and Environmental Design (LEED).[3] The LEED rating scale provides a guide and benchmarks for owners and project teams based on choices that improve the environmental performance of a building. Those choices are validated through a commissioning process that tests actual performance against the targeted goals. LEED guidelines are heavily weighted toward reducing energy consumption (more than 50 percent of the points), in turn reducing the use of fossil fuels and greenhouse gases.

The EPA also has a program focused on energy efficiency (ENERGY STAR) and has been the primary tool for existing buildings interested in energy efficiency. Until recently, LEED only covered new construction; now it includes the conversion of existing buildings.

The New Buildings Institute's (NBI) Green Building Initiative provides a rating system called Green Globes. Its objectives and core values are similar to the LEED system. Green Globes provides an online evaluation and some feel it is more user friendly but less stringent than LEED. The American Society of Heating, Refrigerating, and Air-Conditioning Engineers (ASHRAE) is another key player providing improved energy codes and guides for advanced energy design. The field is rapidly improving and changing and at this time LEED is receiving the major focus.

LEED has given the industry an important set of guidelines that are accessible and easy to follow, even if challenging to achieve. It has developed specific criteria for different building types to account for the different demands of a school versus a hospital or a corporate office building. It has given developers and brokers their beloved apples-to-apples criteria with enough buildings to measure how they perform with lease rates and occupancy.

Rick Federizzi, CEO and president of the USGBC, offers some perspective on the future direction of LEED. He says productivity is "the smoking gun." It's becoming evident that a better building is a better place for people to work, and they are, therefore, more productive. This neatly accomplishes both the business and environmental objective.

Federizzi described the LEED program in a 2008 interview in the *Boston Globe*:

"I can explain LEED in the very simplest terms: if you had a box of crackers, on the side of the box it would tell you the nutritional content. And you would have the ability as a consumer to select that box or not, based on your health, based on your values, based on a number of different criteria. But in all the buildings that surround us, we've never had meaningful criteria to judge whether or not we should be in that building. Much like the nutrition label on the side of a box of crackers has been third-party-approved by the FDA, we do the same thing on buildings."[4]

LEED By-Products

Craig Janssen feels the LEED requirements bring back an element that has gotten lost in most conventionally designed projects.

"Part of the design process is finding out what an owner wants," he says. "That's called programming. In many cases, architects see their role as collecting what the owner wants and then try[ing] to fulfill that. We're trained as an industry to be pleasers. And because of the way the process is set up and how we are selected, there is not a good mechanism or tool to question the owner's assumptions or the value of what they 'think' they want. If you do—you are uncooperative and easily replaced.

"This 'basis of design' role that is built into the LEED guidelines," he explains, "provides us with a tool to ask why and set clearer performance criteria. The commissioning role adds another vehicle, or a person, whose sole job is to validate the purpose for specific design solutions and then test to make sure that the solution delivers the performance that was specified. This is more of a purpose-built process." Bill Black says that LEED shifts the dialogue to a more evidence-based design process.

LEED is not without its critics. One criticism is that LEED is biased toward energy reduction over other broader environmental concerns. Second, some feel Certified and Silver levels don't make a significant environmental improvement and yet allow companies an easy passport for green citizenship. Third, instead of sustainability being integral to good design, LEED can create an impression that sustainability is something separate and added to a building, with increased cost. On balance, however, LEED has changed the nation's building agenda in a positive way and has become the currency to measure a green building.

The recent growth curve for LEED-registered buildings makes it clear that the momentum has swept beyond early adopters: "A dramatic shift has been taking place in the green building movement in the last couple of years. As recently as [2002], the feasibility of designing and constructing projects under the U.S. Green Building Council's Leadership in Energy and Environmental Design (LEED) rating programs was in doubt." Three factors prevented market acceptance:

- Doubt whether the LEED process would produce significant results.
- A lack of readily available cost effective materials, methods, and expertise.
- A cost premium (or tax) to build a sustainable building.

"In recent years all three concerns have been largely put to rest."[5]

The LEED Flywheel

"Good-to-great transformations," says Jim Collins in the *Harvard Business Review*, "do not happen overnight or in one big leap. Rather, the process resembles relentlessly pushing a giant, heavy flywheel in one direction. At first, pushing it gets the flywheel to turn once. With consistent effort, it goes two turns, then five, then ten, building increasing momentum until—bang!—the wheel hits the breakthrough point, and the momentum kicks in its favor."[6]

The LEED program was initiated in 2000. Since that time, 2,021 buildings have been certified—that's it.[7] But the growth rate is the real story. By the end of 2009, we could easily see more than 12,000 registered projects in one year and by 2010 more than 18,000. According to McGraw-Hill's Green BuildingSmart Market Report 2006, new green construction could equal 10 percent.

Consider, too, that in 2006 there were 10,500 member organizations and 38,000 LEED-accredited professionals. By January 2009 that number had grown to 18,086 member organizations and 77,434 LEED-accredited professionals.[8]

Kyle Davy points out that this is a classic innovation growth curve. The USGBC (as a reflection of the broader green movement) is experiencing the kind of compounding that is still gathering momentum. When this compounded growth is projected out to 2020, barely a decade away, we will begin to see the full power and effect of this initiative.

MYTH TO MINDSHIFT #2: SUSTAINABLE BUILDINGS *ARE* COST EFFECTIVE FROM THE BEGINNING

In past years, many business leaders were resentfully biting the green bullet and asking, "How do we go green without committing balance sheet suicide?" Today, many are asking, "What do we need to do to take full advantage of this opportunity?" But in between are the majority of owners and developers, who erroneously hold to the idea that green design adds significantly to first costs.

It doesn't. Here's what we found:

- In 2000, when LEED was launched, some in the construction industry predicted LEED buildings would cost 20 percent to 25 percent more than conventional construction.

- In the 2003 *The Costs and Financial Benefits of Green Buildings* report Greg Kats and others compared a sample of 33 LEED buildings across the country and found the average premium was 1.84 percent.
- In 2004, a Davis Langdon report by Lisa Fay Matthiessen and Peter Morris evaluated 139 buildings and compared 45 LEED-certified buildings to 94 conventional buildings. They concluded that if a LEED building and a conventional building were designed for similar functionality their costs would be comparable.[9]
- In 2007, Davis Langdon issued their *Cost of Green Revisited* report comparing 221 buildings covering a wide range of function—schools, labs, libraries, community centers, and hospitals. Of these, 83 sought LEED certification and 138 did not. They concluded, "There is no significant difference in the average cost for green buildings as compared to *non-green buildings.*"

Nonetheless, some in the industry have a hard time accepting the facts. In a survey to the AEC community conducted by Reed Business in 2006, 75 percent felt there needed be more independently validated documentation for the value of sustainable buildings compared to conventional. The conventional wisdom says, "We don't believe that it costs less to build sustainably, and we don't believe there is a business payback, but we'd like to believe."

We did hear consensus on this: There is no cost premium until you reach a LEED Gold and Platinum level of certification. We also heard that the energy savings and the benefits of waste reduction don't have much of an impact until you reach a Gold or Platinum level. When we asked these experts how much more does it cost to reach Gold or Platinum, we heard a range of answers. Some were concrete: 2 percent to 7 percent. Some said there is no premium for the actual construction, but the consulting required to fill out the paperwork and do the commissioning (that is testing all the systems to ensure that they perform at the energy savings level specified) costs about 1 percent. And finally, some responses took a big-picture approach: "It doesn't cost any more at all, in fact there are enough tradeoffs due to lower energy requirements that it can cost less."

With such a wide range of answers from the experts, it's no wonder owners and developers are confused. The truth is, there simply aren't enough people who have sufficient experience developing high-performance buildings for there to be consistent feedback.

We decided to seek out those who have built LEED Gold or Platinum buildings for equal or less cost than conventional construction to find out what they had to say. Their message was clear:

- If you begin with the goal of building a sustainable building at the same cost as conventional construction, you can certainly do that with an experienced team.
- If you view sustainability as something you add on to the building, the project will cost more.
- The learning curve is important. It takes approximately three or four projects to develop a building for the same costs as conventional. This fact is all the more reason to select a trust-based team with experience instead of bidding it out and having perhaps one or two experienced members on your team.

LEED Gets Easier

Until now, achieving LEED Platinum has involved doing a dance around conventional wisdom, a lack of readymade products, a resistant developer community, expensive technology, outdated building codes, and an immature learning curve. Now, however, these projects achieving LEED Platinum certification cost equal or less than conventional construction:

Adobe: "To date, Adobe has completed 64 projects, spent nearly $1.4 million on energy conservation and related projects, received $389,000 in rebates from local and state agencies, and reduced annual operating costs by $1.2 million.[10] This 9-month payback gave a return on investment (ROI) of 121 percent."[11]

Johnson Controls: "Many green buildings cost no more to build—or may even cost less —than conventional alternatives because resource-efficient strategies and integrated design often allow downsizing of more costly mechanical, electrical, and structural systems. For instance, the cost of the Johnson Control's Brengel Technology Center in Milwaukee was on par with prevailing construction rates, despite numerous high-tech features . . ."[12]

"The 130,000-square-foot facility was built for a cost just under $17 million, which puts it in line with the market average construction cost of $125 per square foot."[13]

Banner Bank: "We created a beautiful, high-performance building that's good for the environment. And it didn't cost us any more to do it."[14]

"The building also had to compete in the speculative leasing market. At the very competitive cost of $128 per square foot, the Banner Bank Building, a 195,000-square-foot, 11-story Art Deco building in downtown Boise, proves that high-performance buildings are good for business.

"Raising the bar for performance has yielded impressive returns: reduced operating costs contribute to a $1.47 million increase in asset value and a 32.4 percent return on investment. The huge operational savings also enable (the developer) to charge rents comparable to those in buildings 20 to 30 years older and still make a healthy profit—which makes both tenants and owner happy."[15]

Signature Center: Ben Weeks, Aardex principal in charge at Signature Centre, says, "A vertical integration of the development interests— design, construction, and ownership—will result in significant savings to the project—as much as 15 percent or more of overall costs. This allows implementation of the most beneficial strategies and features at a delivery price at or below market rates for conventional facilities"[16]

Business Benefits of Green

DPR and Ray Anderson provide a good summary of the many business benefits for going green. Some of these benefits include:

- Discounted insurance rates
- Utility rebates
- Expedited permitting
- Reduced absenteeism
- Higher employee retention
- Higher rental rates
- Increased occupancy rates
- Marketing and public relations value
- Increased property/building value
- Tax rebates
- Lower capital costs for equipment
- Reduced operating costs
- Reduced risk
- Less dependency on external energy supplies
- Future proofing the company through greater adaptability

Ray Anderson says that taking this path has had a galvanizing effect on their employees. People are coming to work for Interface who would have never considered working for a carpet manufacturer: "They are not coming to make carpet—but to make history."

The Bottom Line

Some, of course, will still be skeptical. They ask, "What if we *can't* build it for the same cost? How do I recover that back?"

The current building classification structure only offers three levels: Class A, B, and C. Once you have a Class A building, pumping more cost into it doesn't turn it into a Class A+ building. It is common to hear developers or brokers use this rationale to downplay or ignore the value of a LEED or Energy-Star building.

But CoStar, the leading provider of market data to the commercial real estate industry, published a new study in March 2008 that even surprised them. The study compared 1,300 LEED and Energy Star properties to its database of 44 billion square feet. The comparison matched up similar criteria for location, size, class, year commissioned, and amenities.

A new study by CoStar Group has found that sustainable "green" buildings outperform their non-green peer assets in key areas such as occupancy, sale price and rental rates, sometimes by wide margins. According to the CoStar study, LEED buildings command rent premiums of $11.33 per square foot over their non-LEED peers and have a 4.1 percent higher occupancy. Rental rates in Energy Star buildings represent a $2.40 per square foot premium over comparable non-Energy Star buildings and have a 3.6 percent higher occupancy.

Energy Star buildings sell for $61 per square foot more than non-Energy Star-rated buildings, and LEED buildings receive a $171 per square foot premium over non-LEED buildings.[17]

These surprising findings go against the conventional belief that high-rated LEED buildings will require an investment that will take three to five years to recover.

"The information we've discovered is very compelling. Like all good science, we discovered it by accident," [Andrew] Florence said. "Green buildings are clearly achieving higher rents and higher occupancy, they have lower operating costs, and they're achieving higher sale prices."[18]

This is a significant change and a tribute to the USGBC's LEED program establishing a brand proposition. If a company wants a green building, then they will be looking for one with a LEED certification.

A second factor for the premium is the higher demand than supply. There are just over 2,000 buildings certified and 16,000 more buildings registered. The bottleneck to certify a building has to improve dramatically. McGraw-Hill estimates that by 2010, up to 10 percent of commercial construction starts are expected to be green. Some have recommended some form of self-certification that is followed by third-party auditing; the current structure of the USGBC may otherwise be unable to keep up with demand.

MYTH TO MINDSHIFT #3: A BROWN COMPANY *CAN* PRODUCE A GREEN PRODUCT

Ray Anderson states the myth this way: "A brown company cannot produce a green product." Yet Mindshift is primarily a collection of leaders of brown companies who also realize another equally powerful truth: Action changes attitude.

It's not an overnight success story; Anderson's Interface has been on their journey toward green building since 1990. They feel like they've climbed about halfway to their 2030 goal of zero carbon emissions.

The AIA began efforts in 1990 with the Committee on the Environment, which later linked up with the founding of the USGBC in 1994. LEED was initiated in 2000 and is just entering its power growth curve.

The good news is that these two initiatives affirm the magic of compounded growth, a lesson many of us heard (and some even learned!) when we began saving money as kids. We see Ray's comments as a hopeful stake in the ground. We are not disagreeing with the underlying truth of his comment. In the same interview, Ray pointed out that there are varying degrees of green and Interface has not attained its ultimate goal. They are true believers, however, and their green awareness informs every decision they make.

Innovators like the New York Times Corporation show us that aiming to design a wonderful place for their people led straight to sustainability. Trust-based project teams who work well together somehow find that they are designing sustainable buildings—whether they intended to or not—because that's what makes sense and saves money. Firms using 3D modeling tools to their fullest can see the life cycle of a building better, and that flows directly into green design.

MYTH TO MINDSHIFT #4: GREENHOUSE GASES? IT'S NOT THE CARS, IT'S THE BUILDINGS

Here's a simple question: What is the biggest source of green house gases (CO_2 emissions)?

Cars, right?

Ed Mazria, an architect who has a longstanding record for sustainable design, disagrees, and he's got proof.

"All the cars and trucks on the road account for about 6.5 percent of energy consumption in this country," he explains. "If you figure SUVs as half of that, that's 3 percent, maybe 3.5 percent. So even if you doubled the gas mileage of every SUV on the road, you're talking about a marginal effect in a marginal area, all things considered. That kind of misguided focus keeps us from addressing the real issue." In other words, we're worrying about cars when we should be worrying about buildings.[19] Here is what he discovered once he reassembled the pie chart:

Here is Mazria's breakdown.

- Buildings 48 percent (commercial and industrial accounts for approximately 25 percent)[20] (See Figures 8.2 and 8.3.)

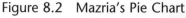

Figure 8.2   Mazria's Pie Chart

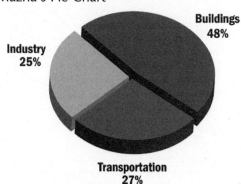

US ENERGY CONSUMPTION

Data Source: US Energy Information Administration

- All transportation 27 percent (cars and trucks are 6.5 percent)
- Industry 25 percent
- Buildings also consume 75 percent of electricity production.

Mazria estimates that architects (including in-house corporate design groups) control over 80 percent of the potential decisions for buildings. If you approach this challenge with trust-based teams using early collaboration, future buildings can reduce energy consumption by 35 percent to 50 percent immediately, for the same or a lower cost than conventional construction.

The Implications

A 2007 University of Michigan study reported that in 2003 there was 72 billion square feet of commercial building space, an amount projected to increase to 108 billion square feet by 2030.[21] More than 20 billion square feet will replace existing buildings—that is, more than 50 billion square feet of new construction.[22]

In 2004, commercial and industrial buildings consumed $234 billion in energy.[23] At the same time, commercial and industrial

Figure 8.3   Building CO2 Comparison

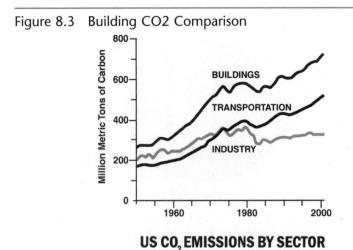

US CO$_2$ EMISSIONS BY SECTOR

Data Source: US Energy Information Administration

© 2009 2030, Inc./Architecture 2030.

buildings accounted for up to 7 percent of the world's CO_2 emissions. A 35 percent reduction in energy (a current conservative goal) saves $82 billion a year in 2008 dollars. That also translates to a reduction of 675 million tons of CO_2 emissions.

Here's the global scorecard for emissions:

- World emissions are 27 billion tons
- U.S. emissions are 6 billion tons
- U.S. buildings are approximately 3 billion tons
- U.S. commercial and industrial buildings are 1.53 billion tons

If the United States were to comply with the goals set by the Kyoto protocol, we would need to reach a level of 7 percent below our 1990 levels (5 billion tons) to a level of 4.65 billion tons.

Reducing all commercial and industrial building emissions by just 35 percent achieves half of that goal. If the flywheel reaches its full momentum in 2020, it is conceivable that by 2030 we will reach something close to zero carbon emissions.

How does that compare with cars? Toyota claims that its hybrid Prius reduces car emissions by 45 percent.[24] If every car in the United States were replaced by a Prius that would reduce emissions to 175 million tons—one quarter of the reduction that improving buildings would have with today's capabilities.

Mazria's insight that buildings offer the motherload of opportunity has dramatic implications. Currently, the Obama administration is considering plans to run a pilot program to retrofit several Veterans Administration hospitals using the latest 3D virtual design and construction capabilities to simulate improving the conditions and operations of these buildings with an eye toward reducing the carbon footprint. The federal government is the largest landlord on the planet. Once their flywheel begins to move toward zero carbon sustainability the whole market will shift more rapidly.

LIGHT, AIR, AND POWER

Remember the building design lessons David Thurm recounted at the beginning of this chapter? He put them to work big time in creating The New York Times Building on the east side of Eighth Avenue between 40th and 41st streets. Completed in 2007, the building stands 52 stories. Its clear glass exterior reflects the pace and energy of New York City. From inside looking out, the story is even better.

Above street level, a unique ceramic rod curtain wall acts as a visual and light shield that allows a level of transparency rarely seen in a high-rise building. With no tint or filter, one can stand inside looking out and actually tell what time of day it is and see what the weather's like. The offset curtain wall provides a sense of separation, and it also keeps the direct sun from becoming uncomfortable inside the building. Architect Renzo Piano translated the company's vision into structure. In Piano's words, "The story of this building is one of lightness and transparency." But that is not the whole story.

Although the New York Times chose not to register for LEED certification, the building's performance would probably surpass many higher-rated LEED buildings. Considering this building was originally conceived a year after the LEED rating system was put in place, the advances it incorporates are still forward thinking.

Thurm says, "We checked into the LEED process and I think it is a great blue print. However, at the time we looked at it, the criteria was more for suburban office campuses and had not fully developed for urban application.

"Our guiding principle," he explains, "was to create a better facility for our people. That led us to ask what makes an environment healthier and more productive. That led to exploring light and air quality and put more thought into the design of the interior work flow and people interaction. We think that these converge; good design is sustainable design and true sustainable design is good design. Again, our long-term view took us down the path to examine the performance of our space in greater detail than owners that consider themselves as simply tenants."

An innovative lighting system reduced the original requirement for electricity by 70 percent. Forty percent of the power is co-generated using clean natural gas. This is far more efficient than energy generated from the power plant, where the heat is lost up the smokestack. The Times building recaptures the heat from their co-gen facility and turns it into air-conditioning for its data center using absorption chillers.[25]

The building also handles air flow differently. Instead of sending air through the ceiling and pushing it down into the space, the project team used a raised floor solution to run all the air under the floor (as well as the power and data cabling).

"We had to push against conventional wisdom," says Thurm. "When the CEO for a large company came by to look at our mockup for lighting, he also noticed our raised floor and asked about it. He liked the idea, turned to his consultant, and asked, 'Did we look at raised floor for our project?' The consultant said, 'Yeah, but it's $9 per square foot.' End of discussion. That should have been the start of a discussion, not the end. But that's the problem with consultants. They will give you the easy answer or not really answer the question you are asking. That answer doesn't tell the real story. The consultant just presented the line item cost for underfloor air but did not tell his client the tradeoff savings.

"For example, the concrete slabs do not need to be power troweled to smooth out the dips. The raised floor sits on top of the slab. The ductwork in the ceiling is almost eliminated because the floor becomes the plenum. The underfloor air distribution requires less pressure and so the fans, chillers, and base equipment can be downsized. The air that diffuses up through the floor doesn't have to be cooled to 55 degrees. It can go in at 68 degrees and then rise naturally to the ceiling. You are also getting cleaner air because it is not being mixed with the return air. With all the electrical and data under the floor, it makes changing our space less expensive. The cabling doesn't run through the furniture, so I don't have to hire an electrician and a carpenter to move things around. The ceiling goes in faster, the cabling installs faster, the carpet is laid in faster—none of these tradeoffs were mentioned. So when you add these up, if there is a premium it is small, and when compared to the benefits—a non-issue."

"You can see we did our homework and chose Haworth's raised floor, convinced this was the logical way to go."

So, how did they select the right crew to install it? "Our process was a bit unusual. We invited nine bidders and gave them a series of essay questions. 'Do you build the floor first or the ceiling? Do you level the slab or leave it? Do you cut your cable in the shop and bring it to site or do all of your cutting on site?' And several others. One firm amusingly said they would begin with the ceiling on one end and the floor on the other and then somehow trade positions when they met in the middle. I'm not sure what their logic was.

"We weren't done with our research," he continued. "The winners were sent to view the most recent projects we could find. That process was invaluable. Before we tried this for the headquarters, we used it on a project in Sarasota. Both teams met together, however, to debate the best approach. Our strategy was to get all the smart people in one room together and then walk away with a plan of action.

"Since we were planning to live in this building," Thurm said, "we did not view it as a tenant but as our home. That influenced our approach. We looked at solutions for actual performance rather than taking the consultants' first answer."

Thurm sums it up: "In the future, we will definitely use BIM because we see that adds to integrating the process and provides a better structure for engaging the different trades in conversation. We will also seek LEED certification, but not because we think there is something inherently valuable with LEED. We see our values as consistent with sustainable design, and so it would be natural for us to connect that to USGBC initiative."

The story of the New York Times building teaches two important lessons. First, their mission was not to go the cheapest way possible but to create a better place for their people to work in. This is the best way to build a highly sustainable building. Cost and good design are not in conflict. The two are connected.

Second, a great mission requires engaged leadership. The owner has to be the master of his own house. David Thurm wrote an article to this effect published in the October 2005 edition of the *Harvard Business Review*.[26] He backed up the mission of creating a better place to work with extensive research, experimentation, and a willingness to pull in the experts and engage them with their people.

SEEING THE CONNECTIONS

By now you should be seeing some important common connections:

- The quality of the work we do is directly related to the quality of relationships we hold (trust-based teams).
- The reasons behind what we do determines the quality of what we do (intent of design).

- Building a better place for people to work produces good and sustainable buildings.
- Buildings are really about the people who work in them, not pro formas. But, if you build a great place for people, you will improve your pro forma.
- If we reduce the harm to the environment, we might also begin to see a corresponding improvement in the health of our company cultures (Gallup).[27]

Buildings are expensive—the largest capital expense for any company. But a building and all of its operational costs are only one-eighth of the cost of its employees. We think the lessons learned from reestablishing trust, developing collaborative partners, and discovering the laws of sustainable practices will unlock our understanding of employee performance and engagement.

Where can a company go with all of this? Interface certainly offers one benchmark worth noting. In a 2008 interview with the website Treehugger.com, Ray Anderson made the following assessment of their progress: "We took (Paul) Hawken's challenge . . . to become the world's first truly sustainable industrial enterprise. . . . Doing no harm to the biosphere. For a petro intensive company, that's a tall order. But we're well on our way to the top of the mountain, Mount Sustainability. The point at the top signifies zero footprint that we aspire to."

Here are some of those milestones attained:

- 82 percent reduction in emissions
- 66 percent reduction in landfill
- 75 percent reduction in water use
- 88 percent of the electricity is from renewable sources
- 25 percent of the materials used are from recycled products
- 133 million pounds of materials are from recaptured product
- The company has grown 66 percent
- The savings represent $372 million

Interface is finding ways to profitably connect commerce and conservation.

For more than 45 years there has been an open war between the interests of business and the environment.[28] Today, that war is not only over, but the future well-being of both are now tied together. We began this chapter with the proposition that we would focus on affordably designing buildings with reduced energy consumption and waste. We close by recognizing how rapidly and recently the green movement has worked its way into the boardroom. That momentum has a trajectory that will soon require more than plucking low-hanging fruit. The lessons are just beginning.[29]

Chapter 9 Key 4: Transformational Leadership

"You are here because you know something. What you know you can't explain but you feel it. You felt it your entire life. There is something wrong with the world but you don't know what it is. But it's there like a splinter in your mind."

—Morpheus to Neo in *The Matrix*

Fifteen years ago, a prominent flooring manufacturer began receiving requests from some of their clients asking what they were doing about the environment. Charles, the CEO, was a second-generation factory guy. When new VP of Sales Jane approached him with the question, he gave her a funny look.

"What environment? We make the best floor products in the industry. Our factory is one of the safest and cleanest anywhere. I'm not going to sacrifice the quality of our products to satisfy a few people who feel like the sky is falling. Just tell them that we follow all of the EPA standards, and we'd be happy to show them our track record."

Jane responded by explaining, "Charles, I don't think that's what they're really talking about. I've met with manufacturing and engineering, and they say we're not even looking at how we can make safer products for the environment."

However, Charles would not be easily moved. "Jane, I appreciate that your job is to make customers happy. But we can't please everyone. We can't afford to change our products to satisfy every group with a cause. Just tell them our 50-year story and the quality of our products. They'll understand. We'll be fine."

Over the next two years, Jane continued to field more questions about the environmental policy of the company from clients and prospects. Frustrated, she finally stopped asking Charles about the various queries and drafted a statement that basically said, "We comply with all of the government's standards for safety." Charles approved the document, and it became the company's official stance.

Not long after, one of their oldest clients in California removed them from contract renewal talks. When Jane gave Charles this disappointing news, he went ballistic: "What are you talking about? They've been a close client of ours for 15 years. Heck, I closed the deal while my dad was grooming me to take over the company. Sarah Cummings was the head of purchasing back then, now she's CFO. I'll call her. Whoever they put in purchasing has stepped way out of bounds on this!"

Charles called Sarah, but before he could move past hello, she broached the very issue he wanted to address. "Charles, I probably know why you're calling. I'm the one who removed your company from our suppliers list. I should have called you directly, but we've been requesting for two years that your company help us create a healthier work environment. We're selecting suppliers who have this on their agenda and who feel that it's part of their mission to improve the world we live in. I know you make a great product, but we want more for our employees and our community. I'm sorry."

Charles was stunned. "Sarah, could you give me some time and let me see what we can do? Your account is not only important to our company, but to me personally. I promise, we'll do whatever it is we need to do to keep your business."

Sarah reluctantly replied, "Charles, I appreciate that, I really do. But this is not something you'll be able to fix in 90 days, or even a year. Before you would make a commitment like that, I'd have to be sure you really know what you're prepared to take your company through. It's too late for this round, but you know we review our contracts every three years. Think about it. If you're still interested, I'll be happy to share what we've done and what our suppliers are doing."

Charles didn't know what to say, but Sarah continued. "Charles, this is something I really think you'll want to investigate further. I know you have a lot of accounts in California, and we're concerned with the environment out here. You know that what starts in California eventually spreads across the country, right?" Charles nodded, but was still speechless.

"Well," Sarah said, "I meet with a group of corporate leaders every few months to better understand where this mission might lead. We are also using our leverage to influence other companies and the state. That means that in a year or so, it won't just be *our* account that takes you off its list."

"I'll do anything I need to, Sarah," said Charles.

But when he hung up the phone, Charles slumped in his chair. He had no reference points for what had just happened. He had only told Sarah that he would do anything out of sheer desperation. He truly had no idea what he would do. California was a major market for the company, and he really didn't know whether to take this environmental stuff seriously or not. A few weeks ago, he and some of his golf buddies were laughing about a colleague in the flooring business who had some "personal epiphany" and became a tree hugger. He was going to make his company the "first sustainable industrial enterprise. . . . Doing no harm to the biosphere." Charles recalled that he joked, "Now what in the heck is a biosphere?" They'd all laughed.

Charles was no longer laughing. In fact, he felt sick. Sarah said they had chosen to partner with the company he was ridiculing a mere few weeks earlier—the tree huggers.

He became regretful as he pondered his current situation. "My dad and I built a great company, but somewhere we must have missed a turn. If this is where the industry is headed, I'm not sure I can get there." What hit Charles was not just the loss of an account, but deeper doubt about the future of his business and even the values that he had been proud to represent for more than 30 years. For several weeks he felt angry, sad, confused, and exhausted. He wasn't dealing with it well, and it unsettled his direct reports—including Jane.

A few months later, Jane told Charles about a local luncheon on the topic of "Building a Sustainable Business."

What the heck, he thought. *Let me go and see what all of this frenzy is about.*

When he arrived, Charles saw a few of the other local business leaders and some longtime friends at a table near the front. He went over to sit at that table and greeted several more friends and town acquaintances along the way. After several hearty handshakes and some small talk, the luncheon was called to order. Charles picked up the program and saw that the president of the company to which he had lost his long-time account would be the guest speaker. The tree hugger! That was almost too much to take. He quickly lost his appetite, but he couldn't leave now. People would notice, and that wouldn't go over very well.

So Charles pretended to eat his lunch as he listened to the man's story. But instead of feeling angry or awkward, he found that he actually connected with the topics that the speaker was covering. In many ways, he was like Charles—a factory man at heart. Charles had just never considered how much waste and harm a factory produces; even if he had, he never really thought that there was anything he could do about it. But the speaker's story made sense. Hearing about where that company had started in their new effort—from scratch, basically—made Charles feel like it was something that he just might be able to do, and just might *want* to do, at least for business reasons. The weight of having to solve the problem overnight lifted when he heard the path the speaker was charting for his company.

He left the luncheon thinking to himself, "It's going to be okay. If this is where the game is going, I may as well get back into it."

Charles' story is actually a composite of stories we heard from several leaders who each arrived at their personal crossroads. Like Charles, as long as these leaders did not have to face the facts directly, they were able to continue and even reinforce their old way of looking at their business. When it became personal, however—when it looked like business might suffer or go elsewhere—that line of thinking no longer worked. These old school corporate giants were forced to see what was really going on: They were needlessly wasting money and materials, and yes, they were probably doing some environmental harm they didn't have to do. They could no longer write it off, blame others, or buy time. Like Charles, they reached a moment of truth—one from which they could only move forward.

CLARITY BEGINS TRANSFORMATION

Ronald Heifetz, director of the Leadership Education Project at Harvard University and one of the world's authorities on transformational leadership, contrasts our current notion of visionary leadership and compares it to Charles' experience. He says that an earlier, more fundamental meaning for vision is the capacity to see and to see clearly. In other words, a visionary leader is not fundamentally someone who sees into the future. We're talking about a regular guy like Charles who begins to accurately see what is going on *right now*.

For Charles, the light went on *not* when he heard that this other company had started a green initiative and was attracting attention and some clients because of it. He was able to ignore that fact, because he figured it was costing his competitor more. He assumed that the other guy had gone off the deep end and was providing a premium product for a niche clientele. But when he realized that the green initiative was also standard business—and that it cost no more than the way that he himself was doing things—well, that changed the rules. Business books are full of stories of leaders who ignored early signs of a shift, and, by the time they realized how behind the times they were, their ship was sinking. That had almost happened to Charles, and he wasn't about to let it happen again.

LEARN FROM THOSE WHO'VE BEEN THERE

You won't learn the how-tos of transformational leadership at a seminar or in a book (even this book). You have to go and see for yourself. Plan on talking to a lot of people, following several dead ends, and eventually finding one or two similarly inclined leaders who unlock a new door for you. Get out of your current context and see what others are doing in their worlds.

KlingStubbins Principal Scott Simpson's aha moment became the liberating power of constraints. And that has become an organizing principal in every project he tackles. For David Thurm, SVP of operations for The New York Times, the process of building a dozen printing plants led him and his team to the aha that the Times was an owner, not just an occupier, of buildings and that the company had to become more assertive as an owner. They became the master of their own house and that changed everything. For Ray Lucchesi, it was realizing the connection between living systems, organizations, and design. For Mindshift, our aha comes down to connecting the dots in the emerging trust-based revolution.

In the movie *The Matrix*, protagonist Tom Anderson (also known as Neo) works as a computer programmer for a software company called

MegaCortex. He is a hacker at night, and begins receiving cryptic notes, like "The Matrix Has You." He is driven to find out what the Matrix is because he subconsciously knows there is something not right with the way things are. He just can't put a finger on what that might be. Tom's discontent and curiosity lead him to uncover insights about himself and the world to which he had been blind, and eventually, he crosses a threshold into the real world. A man who barely existed becomes a hero and a leader.

An awakening like this can happen to anyone—to the people profiled in this book, to Charles, and to you. Once that aha! moment strikes, there's no turning back. Ray Anderson, CEO of Interface, describes his journey of transformation as "epic." A lot of leaders, both men and women, described similar themes: Unlikely and seemingly innocent events propel the protagonist forward into a journey that changes their destiny. Some launched new careers; others reinvented their companies; and a few changed entire industries and even national priorities. If you believe at all that you are on this planet and at your company for a reason and that an individual can make a difference, then what we are sharing will not sound so far-fetched. If you don't, come along for the ride anyway. At the very least, you'll be entertained.

Dean Reed, DPR

We asked DPR's Dean Reed, "How did a construction guy like you end up in the architectural world of BIM? At that time, you must have felt like you were trespassing."

Dean explained by sharing the following story. "In 1996, I was working for another company [that was] building a pharmaceutical plant in Mountain View, California. Melody Spradlin [was a colleague of mine at the time]. She was really forward thinking and had just finished her master's in construction management at Stanford. This was a few years before Stanford's Center for Integrated Facility Engineering (CIFE) launched. While Melody was talking about 4D design, I was barely familiar with 3D.

"We struggled with the design of the project; it was the first time I saw detailed modeling and coordination of MEP systems. I left to go to work for DPR, but I carried that impression with me. I knew it would eventually be the future for how every building would be built, and I wanted to be part of that. Melody introduced me to Sheryl Staub and Martin Fischer, who had just started CIFE, which became the center for virtual design and construction in our area. Martin began connecting others who were interested, and soon this evolved into the Virtual Building Round Table."

Dave Pixley, Sutter Health

For Dave Pixley at Sutter Health, an unlikely future-shifting event came during a vendor presentation where the salesperson demonstrated a product within a 3D-modeled project. The product became secondary to the architectural software that the salesperson used to show his product. Dave realized that he needed to find out more about this software, which was "disappointing to the salesperson, but fortunate for me." Dave saw the potential to eliminate a lot of waste and errors by virtually building a project before it was physically built. After about six months of research, Dave laid down his now-famous challenge to Sutter's architects and engineers to drive down cost and improve safety. Sutter now leads a revolution that is changing an industry.

Mark Charrete, Solidus

Solidus started as a furniture dealership near Hartford, Connecticut. They represented one of the top five furniture lines as well as one of the largest wood furniture manufacturers. One day, their largest supplier came and told Solidus' president Mark Charrete and his brother John, to choose between the two furniture lines. Rather than bending to this larger supplier's demands, they parted ways and become more independent—a bold move that would set the stage for a final showdown.

Another top five furniture manufacturer approached Solidus, and Mark made the conditions clear: the manufacturer would have to accept Solidus' longstanding relationship to their wood manufacturer. The manufacturer agreed.

Solidus experienced success and growth, and sales for this new supplier surpassed the previous one. A few years into the partnership, a new edict came down. Once again, the manufacturer asked the company to choose one or the other. While this was another gut-wrenching decision, it was one to which they already knew the answer. They said goodbye to the other top five suppliers and promised never to make their company's success or failure tied to one particular manufacturer.

That's when Mark opted to rethink his entire business. He developed Solidus's current model around turnkey delivery of design, construction, and furniture. Construction services now lead their sales effort, and furniture is more often than not wrapped into the overall package. It has made Solidus one of the most profitable firms of its kind in the industry.

Larry Fees, Compuware

Compuware, a 7,000-person global IT software and services company based in Michigan, made the rare decision to move from the suburbs to downtown Detroit in 2003. Attracting and retaining top talent is the lifeblood of the company. Larry Fees, former vice president of real estate and facilities,[1] was an unlikely candidate to head their new headquarters' project and consolidation of five locations. As he describes it, "I'm an IT guy who knew nothing about buildings. But as a software engineer my experience defining requirements, developing specifications, and mapping out the process fit the assignment. In some ways it was actually easier than writing software because it is physical. You can see it.

"The keys to our success are familiar—assemble a great team, provide strong leadership, and be willing to take responsibility and make decisions quickly."

We asked Larry what it was like to get his hands around a project of that size. "It was exciting and intimidating. I had much to learn. Although we had professionals and experts in every area, I needed to learn about real estate law, negotiating with municipalities, accounting rules, excavation and construction techniques, tax abatements, design and architecture—almost every aspect you can think of. It was fun learning, and that was a real motivator. My interest and desire to learn was actually a strong team builder, spurring everyone to communication more and work together. Our project is very unique and something our people take great pride in."

David Thurm, The New York Times

David Thurm, senior vice president of operations for The New York Times, came out of production, the department that prints the paper.

In fact his whole real estate development team came out of production, and the Times' most recent large construction projects had been two highly automated facilities in New Jersey and New York. This background ended up being an important factor when it came to building the Times' 52-story corporate headquarters building. The Times' need for high quality and efficiency at their plants pushed the company to use technologies that had never been used before in newspapers. And this need to use new technology forced the Times and the team to learn how to deal with the uncertainties of managing innovation. Indeed, the team came to the headquarters project with a mindset that was open to trying new things or expecting to explore what was available and push for what was needed.

There were other drivers for the Times' approach. First, they owned their part of the skyscraper, and as such approached the building as a long-term home and not a short-term rental. Second, they early on defined goals for the project, and those goals helped guide the way. The Real Estate Development Team at the Times publicly asserted that just coming in on time and on budget wasn't good enough. An investment of this magnitude must further the overall goals of the business. The building must:

- Reflect the Times' values as a company and its role in the community
- Serve its long-term operational needs as an owner/user
- Enhance the way the way employees work

Being self-taught in construction, they didn't understand that most builders opt for the tried-and-true, and most owners take a more supervisory than participatory role.

"As autodidacts, we didn't know what could or couldn't be done. We just assumed if it made sense and improved the facility for our employees then we should pursue it. The lighting we selected is a breakthrough and a good example of our approach through the whole project.

"We worked hard to get a lot of natural light in the space including installing floor-to-ceiling glass and locating private offices against the core, not the windows. While energy savings are important, our focus was on improving the work environment for our employees. In the pursuit of this goal, we wanted to explore a shade and lighting system that would dynamically change to take advantage of sunlight and that could be tuned to match the particular needs of each group. We asked the design professionals, but they could provide little guidance.

"We refused to let the inquiry end so easily, so we started doing our own research. In the course of following leads, we got a call from a Swedish professor who happened to be in the United States for a conference on lighting. When he told me that, I said, 'Really—does the conference have a website?' On the website there happened to be a book on daylighting. I downloaded the 250-page book, read it over the weekend, and assigned it to the architects and engineers on Monday as mandatory reading."

The book seemed to be a breakthrough, and we asked where that led. "The book was edited by the Lawrence Berkeley Labs at the University of California. So I called up the professor who edited the book and said, 'You don't know me, but we have this project.' I described what we were doing, and that led to an all-day meeting in Berkeley's labs attended by our entire team, our lighting designer, and our architects. This meeting led to a research collaboration to test the feasibility of advanced lighting in an office setting. Indeed, as part of the project, we built an exact replica of a corner of our building in the parking lot of our production plant in Queens. The mockup served multiple purposes since it was a test of the furniture and fixtures. Most importantly, it was a laboratory for testing different concepts for controlling shades and lighting through sensors and computer controls. There was real science behind the work. Berkeley installed 107 sensors in the space, and automatically scraped information from these sensors every minute for a six-month—solstice to solstice—evaluation of competing lighting and shade systems. The testing proved out the concept.

"In particular, we focused on a new technology that puts a computer chip in the ballast that controls the light: Digital Addressable Lighting Interface (DALI).[2] DALI would allow us to automatically adjust lights throughout the space through programmable computer controls linked to sensors."

We asked David how his research was received by the experts he hired. "In the first instance, our lighting designer came back with a beautifully detailed 100-page report that "proved conclusively" that the DALI system was absolutely unaffordable. Instead of taking this at face value, we questioned his assumptions. The report was a topic of conversation at our meeting in Berkeley, and it turned out that the designer had used an inexact computer model. Incidentally, the designer immediately jumped on board. He was instrumental in developing solutions, and he is now a recognized leader in the field.

"We also challenged the pricing assumptions. The numbers came directly from the lighting manufacturers, but they were ridiculously high. We refused to accept this answer, and challenged ourselves and the extended team: How do we make this affordable?

"As a first step, we 'crashed' the annual trade show for the lighting industry. Again because we didn't know the rules, we came with our own sales brochure to interest firms in participating in our mockup experiment. We also sought out the ballast manufacturers to solve the mystery as to why the DALI ballasts were priced 10 times as expensive as conventional ballasts. It was sort of fun, since ballast vendors don't typically meet owners. They sell to the fixture person, the fixture person sells to the wholesaler, the wholesaler sells to the contractor, and then the contractor delivers it to the site. With only a few questions it was readily evident that the ballast folks expected the first purchaser to pay for all of their R&D. This approach imposes a near impossible barrier to entry, at least for us. Through the excitement and education (mutual education) of the mockup, we needed to find the vendors who believed in future sales and thus were willing to create a system that was competitively priced. We found those vendors in Lutron and Mechoshade.

The team's leadership and the innovation they drove created an impressive response from their suppliers, but we were curious about how the system actually worked. "So here is what that system does for us. Today is a rainy day. The radiometer on the roof signals the system that controls the shades to tell it that it's overcast and you don't have to use any shades today. So all the shades are up, and the lights are on. Yesterday, it was a beautiful day. The shades automatically lowered to block the glare when the sun was on that side of the building, and the lights dynamically adjusted to take advantage of the outdoor light. The shades and lighting dynamically change throughout the day. It makes the space feel quite organic.

"We knew that the natural light would be wonderful. The unexpected dividend is how the dynamic lighting creates such a connection to the outside world that is so intimate and immediate. When I worked in our old building, there was a sameness to the quality of the light. Sitting at your desk, you couldn't tell if it was raining outside or what season it was. In the new building, there is a palpable difference in the quality of the light in the morning and the afternoon, in summer and in winter. It is really very special and creates a much improved workspace for our employees"

CREATE A TRANSFORMATIONAL NETWORK

Transformation requires an incubation period, a time to unplug from the old rules of operation, a time to prepare and test new ideas in a safe place. This is also a time to meet other like-minded people and develop a small community and support network. Some leaders find these relationships within their immediate work, forming some version of the Pancake Round Table depicted in Chapter 1. Others have formed networks through different trade organizations.

The United States Green Building Council traces its roots to a few friends in the business who began meeting informally. David Gottfried was an environmental litigator in the same market as developer Michael Italiano. At the same time, architect Bob Berkebile founded a committee for the AIA called the Committee on the Environment (COTE) in 1990. They would intersect in 1993; together, they formed "a small group of like-minded people who were interested in genuinely addressing the total impact of buildings on the environment, human health and well-being, and communities."[3]

Many leaders look to found or join committees within their trade group or create networks with peers in their industry. The USGBC initially began as a subcommittee within AIA, and it then expanded outside of architecture. The 3xPT initiative is a collaborative effort between CURT, the AIA, and AGC to drive industry transformation. Mindshift did not begin with any agenda, but rather with individuals engaging with other individuals and talking about what the future might or could look like. That process took two years.

The evolution of Discovery AE[4] is another interesting case in point. The group's roots go back to the early 1990s, when architect Kyle Davy and Susan Harris, a PhD in education and a long-time change consultant, worked on the faculty of the Advanced Management Institute, which focused on developing the leadership in architectural practices. As Kyle tells the story, "In 1999, everything seemed rosey for the architectural world. It was the height of the telecom boom, [and] the economy in general was strong, but at the same time, principals were expressing a deep level of frustration. They were making higher fees because of the volume of work, but lower margins. Clients seemed to think architects were commodities. Something fundamental was wrong."

Kyle and Susan reached out to see how many others who felt the same way would be interested in their own collaborative discovery process. About a dozen firms met over four retreats. They explored cycles of industry change from experts like Clayton Christensen[5] and new leadership models from experts like Ronald Heifetz.[6] At the end of 18 months, the group came to more or less the same conclusion about their industry that Mindshift had about commercial real estate and construction: that the industry was fundamentally broken. Their findings, along with their suggested solutions, were recorded in a groundbreaking book for the architectural and engineering (AE) industry called *Value Redesigned.*

The group valued the relationships they had established during this process and continued to meet every six to nine months. In late September 2005, the group met again in what would be a redefining moment. The gathering was less than a month after Hurricane Katrina. The members had developed a strong sense of connection to one another and a high degree of candor. The discussion morphed into an examination of how the architectural and engineering industry had responded both before and after Katrina. The poor advice on the front end and the lack of action within the AE community despite repeated warnings were symptomatic of deeper problems. The industry lacked leadership.

They decided to concentrate on building that capacity. Over the next two meetings, the group also began to focus on sustainability. They found their unique identity in becoming a place for change agents championing sustainability to meet, learn, and encourage one another in their efforts.

TRANSFORMATIONAL LEADERSHIP BEGINS AT HOME

You can't just claim that "I've seen the light!" and say "Charge!"and expect your company to follow blindly. Your employees need to see reality with a similar clarity themselves and then reach their own defining moments. When each person feels that he or she owns the problem, they are motivated to wrestle with solutions. But if leadership simply hands them the solution after returning from their "transformation" retreat, it takes away the necessity for them to change. As

Heifetz explains, the critical role of a transformational leader is *"to help colleagues and employees see clearly, and allow the solution to emerge."*

This takes us back to the story of Charles, who came back from the luncheon a different person. Jane noticed it right away and asked, "What's up?"

"Nothing," he said. "I've got something I'm working on."

She didn't know whether that was a good thing or a bad thing considering the way he had been acting lately.

But Charles really *was* working on something: getting educated. He ordered some of the books the speaker referenced and checked out the organizations. He was coming to work earlier and leaving later, but he wasn't coming out of his office except to go to lunch, by himself. It wasn't just his direct reports having side discussion on "the state of Charles" anymore. Everyone noticed.

Then, seemingly out of the blue, Charles announced that the company would have a series of town-hall meetings. Jane thought, *He's never done that before. I wonder if he's found a buyer for the company?*

The first meeting that Charles held was with his direct reports. Everyone showed up to the executive conference room early and speculated about what was about to happen. Charles walked briskly into the room and asked everyone to take a seat. He was smiling. *Maybe that's good sign,* Jane hoped.

"As you all know, we lost one of our best clients last quarter, and it forced me to do some soul searching. We've lost clients before, but never for this reason. Most of you don't know the whole story, but in a nutshell we were canned because we don't have an environmental strategy."

Those who had been with Charles for a long time looked to the ceiling with disgust. They thought the same way Charles had a few months ago: "Tree huggers should plant trees and leave business alone!" But Charles didn't cut off the talk. Instead, he showed several images. The first was a river with a black outline a foot up the bank. The second was smoke billowing to the sky from several smoke-stacks. Over it was the number of megatons of carbon hitting the atmosphere. A third slide was a picture of around 50 train boxcars lined up on the tracks.

The room had gotten quiet and curious. "The first picture I showed is the river that we dump our processed water into. Do you recognize it? The second is the smoke pouring out of Factory Two; I asked our engineers to calculate what we send up into the atmosphere every year. Surprising, isn't it? The boxcars in the last picture are my way of trying to show how much solid waste we generate every year."

The room was silent. Charles took three jars out of a bag he'd carried in and put them in the center of the table.

"Take a close look at these three jars," he said. "These are the three chemicals we use the most to make our flooring products. In front of each of you is a list of the problems these chemicals can cause if you touch or breathe them."

Bill, the company's CFO for the last 20 years, leaned over to Jane and whispered, "The old man is serious about this stuff. What do you think he's going to do?"

That question did not take long to answer. "I want to thank Bob's engineering group for helping me pull this together and tutoring me on all of the environmental stuff," Charles chuckled. That also lightened up the tension in the room.

"I know I've hit everyone broadside, but that's what happened to me. If Sarah Cummings hadn't canceled her contract with us and talked to me straight, I probably would have gone along with business as usual. I think everyone knows that I lost my bearings for a few months. You may too, because I really don't have a plan. It's going to feel awkward around here until we can regain our direction and figure out how to move forward."

The noise level in the room grew substantially as everyone started commenting on what they'd heard and seen.

"Let me ask you something," said Charles. "Is anyone here okay with those pictures I showed? Or comfortable with the fact that our products could cause all of those symptoms in people if they are sensitive to those chemicals or exposed to them for too long?"

Charles opened the floor for discussion. At first, it was a bit of a free for all; tension had been bottled up all morning and then there were several months of wondering how Charles was doing. The first question was direct: "Are you getting ready to sell the company?"

Charles laughed, and said, "Hell no! Is that what some of you think this is about?"

Once that was settled, they got down to business and talked for three hours. Lunch was brought in, and Charles's team talked in a way they never had before. He saw his employees rise to the occasion. At the end of the meeting they were not only supportive but passionate about the opportunity to make some changes.

Charles ended the time with these words: "I was serious when I said I have no clue what to do. If we're going to tackle this challenge, it's going to have to come from you and your people. I can get us started and point toward some resources I've found, but don't count on me to decide how all of this is going to work out. I am forming an outside advisory team to help us with this, and I will look for a few of you to join that team. These are people who have done this kind of thing before. Sarah Cummings has volunteered to lead that effort."

Charles looked around the room and saw some encouraging smiles.

"I think we're going to have a much better understanding of how we make our products," he said. "We're going to have to take time to listen to our people, and hear what they say and how they feel about all of this. We're going to have to bring our clients in and discern what they think as well. We've got a lot to learn! From what I can tell, it will take us a few years until we feel like we know what we're doing. But I've seen that there is a lot of progress we can still make too. I am personally excited about this opportunity—and yes, I think an old dog can learn a new trick or two. In fact, it takes an old dog to really appreciate a new trick."

"For my part," he continued, "I promise to make any investment necessary to make the changes needed. Are you okay with that, Bill?" Bill cocked his head and nodded with a half smile.

"There are times in life that force you to choose between two roads. I think if we choose to transform our company we'll not only make a better company, but we'll also leave a lasting legacy our families and community will be proud of."

THE MINDSHIFT TOOLKIT

This chapter completes the four principles that frame the commercial real estate revolution: trust-based teams, early collaboration, built-in sustainability, and transformational leadership. The new paradigm that these principles describe is made possible and empowered by several tools. We have chosen four: Building Information Modeling, Integrating Project Delivery, Relational Contracting and Shared Risk and Reward Partnering, and Offsite Fabrication. Each of these tools improves project performance with our without making the paradigm shift. However, when you see organizations like Ghafari, DPR, and other industry giants excel on their projects using the techniques we cover—don't be tricked by what appears to be "magic" in the tools. The sleight of hand is really the cultural transformation—and that is something you don't see. One of the presenters we listened offered this formula: OO + NT = EOO. An old organization (OO) plus new technology (NT) equals an expensive, old organization (EOO).

Chapter 10 Key 5: "BIG" BIM[1]

"There are different rhythms of change. Technology is faster than business. Business is faster than infrastructure or law. We're just beginning to adjust to the technology of BIM. You can't move to BIM without the social change. That change is one person at a time."

—Ray Lucchesi, principal, Lucchesi Galati

If you were flying in June 1997, you may have accidentally booked a history-making United Airlines flight and been pleasantly surprised by what you found.

The overheads were easy to reach and closed smoothly and precisely. The seat was wide and plush, and a TV screen was set into the back of the seat in front of you. You even had a choice of channels to watch. The flight attendant provided you with your own set of headphones and a certificate pronouncing you a passenger on the first flight of the Boeing 777, the first plane to go straight from the computer into production and into the air without a real-world test flight.

Eight airlines collaborated with Boeing on the groundbreaking design. This collaborative endeavor—the "Working Together" group—first met in January 1990. To kick off the effort, each airline was asked to fill out a lengthy questionnaire listing all the things they would like to see in the new plane. Boeing started with the best of intentions, recognizing that "we know how to make planes, but we're not the ones flying them."

Reviewing the requests caused Boeing to reconsider some of the original assumptions about the plane. The initial meetings were challenging for the Boeing engineers. "In the past, the relationship between the manufacturers and its customers had often been confrontational. Now both sides were forced to overcome natural prejudices." Boeing added 300 design features that they would not have considered using the traditional process—something that passengers noticed.

The tool that made the process possible was a 3D modeling software called CATIA (Three Dimensional Interactive Applications) from French company Dassault. IBM provided the software behind the manufacturing interface. The 3D objects could detect if it was a proper fit or if there were interferences with any of the mechanical systems. The CATIA software not only tested for fit and interference, but also for ergonomics. Finally, CATIA could provide full simulation of all systems within the plane, including full flight performance. This allowed the engineers to bypass the prototype phase and send the models straight to production. Modeling allowed the team members to assemble a virtual 777 in simulation, to check for interferences, and to verify proper fit of the many thousands of parts, thus reducing costly rework. They could investigate assembly interfaces and maintainability using spatial visualizations of the aircraft components to develop integrated parts lists and detailed manufacturing processes and layouts to support final assembly.

The consequences were dramatic. In comparing with extrapolations from earlier aircraft designs, such as those for the 757 and 767, Boeing achieved:

- Elimination of more than 3,000 assembly interfaces, without any physical prototyping
- 90 percent reduction in engineering change requests (6,000 to 600)
- 50 percent reduction in cycle time for engineering change request
- 90 percent reduction in material rework
- 50 times improvement in assembly tolerances for fuselage[2]

Boeing's was the first paperless airplane. But what does this have to do with the commercial real estate industry? Actually, it was the adoption of CATIA that had an even broader and deeper effect. It changed their whole manufacturing process, their relationships with their clients and suppliers, and the industry at large. CATIA was a form of BIM—Building Information Modeling, something that is changing the commercial real estate industry in the same way.

BIM DEFINED

Some call it BIM, some call it Virtual Building™, some call it Virtual Design and Construction (VD&C), some call it Revit. But BIM is not a particular software package—it's a concept: Building information modeling.[3]

The *building* is the project.

The *information* portion can include almost anything. The most obvious is the building's geometric information, including size, shape, and properties. It can also include the manufacturer's specifications, warranty information, the hours estimated to build the object, location in the building, tax classification, maintenance schedule, energy use, rules for how it behaves in space, what it can or cannot attach to, and so on.

The *modeling*—along with the ability to manipulate the objects and simulate their behavior or performance—is the visual component. The information and the model are linked in such a way that changing the data will change the object and vice versa. We will talk more about what these features allow one to do later in the chapter.

BIM includes general architectural software, specialty trade software (i.e. for steel or concrete), spreadsheets, and PDF files—any digital tool that can in some way be extracted or linked to the data that defines an object. BIM provides a way to link and exchange the information back and forth, as well as a structure that allows the information to interact. Finally, BIM sets up rules or parameters (as commands) that determine how this information is to respond to other pieces of information based on the rules that guide it. For example, if the ductwork on a project were mistakenly placed so that it collided with a joist, the rules will communicate back to the designer, "You can't do that."

That's BIM in a nutshell. Now let's see why this seemingly simple idea is truly so revolutionary.

THE REVOLUTION TAKING ROOT

Here's the revolution: BIM allows us to perceive the whole in real time instead of looking at layers and layers separated by phase and discipline. This make everything that supported those layers, phases, and disciplines obsolete and maybe irrelevant.

The use and implications of BIM have far outstripped industry guidelines, practices, contracts, and standards. A variety of organizations are working hard to coordinate this growth.[4] But early adopters and power users can only go as fast and as far as the weakest link in the chain. If a contractor is capable of providing full project simulation but is only brought in at the end of the traditional design development phase, most of the decisions have been made. Here again, early team-based collaboration is critical to optimal use of BIM.

Because BIM is so early in its adoption curve, there are no established best practices. Firms use BIM for different purposes and in varying degrees of sophistication. The 2006 AIA survey of use among its members found only 16 percent had BIM software. In 2008, at a BIM roundtable for large architectural firms, every company was using BIM. A 2008 McGraw-Hill study of BIM users found that 62 percent of construction firms surveyed planned to use BIM on at least 30 percent of their projects in 2009. That shows incredible growth in use and a rapidly changing landscape.

On the other hand, Reed Construction Data's Arol Worlford, a former board member for Revit, estimates that up to 80 percent of BIM users only access its visualization capabilities and clash detection. When we spoke to the national companies in both construction and architecture, we found that only a few of their offices provide BIM expertise for their firms.

The question "Are you using BIM?" is a loaded one whose answers need to be pulled apart. Is it one office or just a few people? And to what degree are you using it?

OUTSIDE THE BIM BOX

Architect Frank Gehry is an unlikely champion for technology. He does not use a computer, and his design process is highly intuitive. Gehry works out his ideas on a sketchpad and builds a quick model out of cardboard and foam board. He plays with the models to test ideas. He says he likes to see how the model is going to irritate and make him react to the form. Yet his firm Gehry Technologies is perhaps the most advanced architectural BIM firm in the world.

Figure 10.1   Frank Gehry's Bilbao

The turning point came during 1987 to 1989, while the company was designing the German furniture manufacturer Vitra's main facility and design museum. When the snake-shaped exterior staircase was engineered and built, it lost some of the fluid form provided in the drawings. Gehry sought a design solution, which lead his team to CATIA.

The software let Gehry translate complex curves accurately, allowing him to go straight from the model into fabrication. The team created a digital wand that allowed him to capture a three-dimensional image of the model by touching the wand to points along its surface. In the true spirit of an innovator, he was able to combine the freedom of expression that his handmade models provided into digital precision and physical fabrication.

Gehry and Gehry Technologies, the firm he created to solve the problem of translate fluid design to structure, have reinvented construction to include sculpture and fabrication. The unusual angles of his Guggenheim museum in Bilbao, Spain, and the Walt Disney Concert Hall in Los Angeles, California, illustrate the power of BIM (see Figure 10.1).

THE BIM MIND SHIFT

The BIM mind shift can be hard for some people. Simply saying that BIM is revolutionary doesn't necessarily convey just how powerful those changes are. So let's break it down.

BIM is not just a faster, better machine for doing what we did before. A good parallel to BIM is the Internet. The first websites simply replicated company print brochures, and you had to be a geek to make one. Today—in a relatively few years—we have leaped to Web 2.0. Home pages are now interactive, animated, and collaborative. With the right software, we can (almost!) all do it.

The first awkward transition to a new technology is always challenging. When an industry is disrupted through innovation, survival depends on how we define what business we are in. It also requires a new appreciation for the implications of change locked inside the nature of the new technology or innovation. In other words, do we think we are in the buggy whip business or in the business of making transportation more efficient and predictable? One leads to extinction the other to transformation.

DPR's Dean Reed commented earlier, "The old assumption is that design can be successful [if] separated from the construction. However, design is (now) an iterative conversation, and each element is intimately linked to the others. For example, design affects the means and the methods of delivery. Those means and methods affect the design. The ends and means affect each other and have to be part of the same conversation."

Scott Simpson sits with a curtain wall fabricator, designing and creating a solution that goes straight from design to the fabricator. The line between design intent and manufacturing has blurred.

David Thurm, with the New York Times Corporation, crossed the line from owner into product development and collaborated with lighting manufacturers and engineers to develop a new lighting solution and product.

BIM is also changing the process of design and construction and reunifying the effort in the spirit of the Master Builder approach to construction. One architectural firm we talked to has hired a construction estimator to act as a translator between their modeling efforts and the different contractors they work with using BIM tools. To tap into BIM's potential, firms are beginning to realize that roles, processes, and relationships between the different stakeholders are up for grabs and undergoing significant redefinition.

The real questions we need to be asking right now are basic. What is the new business of:

- Architecture?
- Contractor?
- Specialty trades?

- Manufacturer?
- Facility Manager/Owner?
- Broker?
- Developer?
- Investor?

As BIM becomes better at providing accurate material counts, costs, and labor estimates, what becomes of the traditional estimator roles; as more of the actual design of work shifts to those doing the work like fabricators—and the model platform manages more of the coordination—what will the role of production architects be?

Ray Lucchesi explains, "BIM is a supporting technology for a change in perception that also changes the process for our delivery of drawings. BIM allows architects to uncover deeper definitions of the problem through a tool that is not about better ideas but about better interactions. We get to that deeper level by being able to surface our underlying assumption, holding those off to the side, and taking time to layer away the assumptions of others to retool the belief structure that is really running the ship. The underlying belief structure will always steer a course back to its basic behavior despite adding new layers of technology and process.

"For now," Lucchesi concludes, "most people are modeling to improve construction documents or drawings. They still see a building as a machine, a thing. If they design for high-performance sustainability, what they are thinking is a high-performing building. But it is not really about sustainability that is about performance. For many the low-hanging fruit of sustainability is making the building a better machine. Sustainability, however, is about how the building fits and interacts within the context of interlocked stakeholders, [and] the environment is one of those linked partners."

OUT WITH THE OLD AND IN WITH THE NEW

All technology brings change, but not all technology obliterates the previous reference points. BIM does just that: for architecture, construction, a building's operations, the financial model, and the future of urban planning. The implications will ripple through all the infrastructure of codes, equipment manufacturing, materials, insurance, laws, trades, disciplines, and the schools preparing the next generation. And that will take time.

EDS Fellow[4] and futurist Jeff Wacker presented an analysis in 2007 for technology adoption over the last 60 years and projected it out to 2024. He showed a common cycle of between 18 and 20 years for a breakthrough technology to reach its peak. The first half of the period reflects innovation and growth. The second half is refinement and optimization. That same timeline may not follow with BIM adoption, because compared to IT investment the AEC market is fractional. However, we can clearly see a similar adoption trend. Revit, at 80 percent market share in the United States, was introduced in 1997. Autodesk bought it in 2002, with annual revenues of less than $1.5 million.[5] In 2006, BIM had only reached a 16 percent adoption level among architects. That 16 percent, however, is a significant number.

In his 1962 book *Diffusion of Innovations*, Everett Rogers said that technology diffuses through stages of distinct kinds of users. The first to latch on to a new technology are "innovators." The next stages are the "early adopters." *Those two groups in his model represent 16 percent of the total pool of users.* The early adopters are those who prove out the idea and experience the first big breakthroughs. When enough of these stories diffuse through the market, the next group— the "early majority"—make the innovation common practice. They create the new conventional wisdom while the early adopters continue to push the innovation to peak performance. The fourth stage of adoption is by the "late majority"; these are the companies and leaders who will change when their existence is tangibly threatened if they don't change. Finally, there will be the "laggards"; they curl up like armadillos in a tight ball and disappear.

BIM VERSUS TRADITIONAL DESIGN

For owners, architects, contractors, and subs, the race is on. Your firm is late to the game if it is not converting 100 percent to a 3D world. The early adopters have proven the breakthrough with stunning results that are still just scratching the surface. Some of these firms have gone through the cultural transition, and some are making hay by capitalizing on streamlining and collision detection. If those firms making hay get stuck optimizing BIM as an efficiency tool and not investing in the cultural shift, they will be easily leaped. The big firms have committed to using BIM and may have an office or two that is proficient, but BIM has not made a big dent in most of their day-to-day operations.

The kinds of questions that a firm asks and the issues upon which they focus provide an indication of whether they get it. Firms that use surveys or competitors as their benchmark of whether they are behind or ahead of the game display late majority traits. We spoke with the leaders of the BIM transition team for one of the largest AE firms in the world, and it is clear to see their challenge when they try to analyze the handful of BIM projects they have implemented compared to the thousands they handle traditionally. The ratio of a few advocates and believers within an ocean of implementation experts is difficult and takes time.

We interviewed and met with smaller firms and early adopter offices within the larger firms to get a better sense for the social shift that uses BIM in a way that it was created to be used.

PAPER TRAIL VERSUS PAPERLESS

Conventional design is built around paper; even 2D CAD lives in that worldview. Each discipline creates a separate document, and then each phase requires a new document with different levels of detail.

Gary Skog, FAIA, LEED AP, describes the difference in a fall 2008 article that he wrote for NEXT entitled, "Bada BIM! Everything You Wanted to Know About Your Facility Will Soon Be in the Palm of Your Hand": "Industry studies show an actual decline in design and construction productivity over the last twenty years. This isn't difficult to understand when you think about the fragmentation of the traditional construction process with its layers of disconnected, discipline-specific construction documents, specifications, shop drawings, coordination drawings, as-built drawings, and record documents. Not to mention all the related building code and manufacturing information."

Design for the Boeing 777 was paperless. There were no layers, no shop drawings, no separate specification sheets or product manuals. The difference is this simple. Paper is a physical artifact. In the digital world, everything is created out of the same bits and bytes in a multimedia environment with no restrictions on combining elements. The physical world's space and time-sequential barriers don't exist.

2D OBJECTS VERSUS 3D OBJECTS THAT WORK

CAD accelerated the ability to make lines, arcs, and circles that can be configured to represent three-dimensional images. BIM provides

Figure 10.2   Time Savings Using BIM to Go from the Model
to Fabrication

SUPPLY CHAIN WORKFLOW

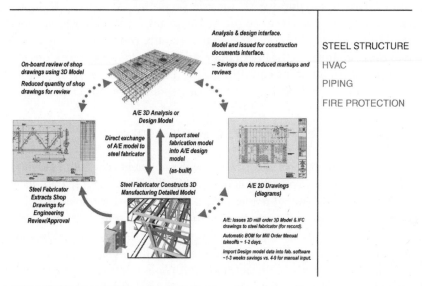

© GHAFARI Associates, LLC.

three-dimensional objects that have the same properties and behavior as their physical counterparts. Arol Wolford describes the transition like this: "Moving from paper to CAD is like shifting from handwriting to an electric typewriter. It's just a faster way to put lines, arcs, and circles on a plan. Moving to BIM is more like moving from typing to desktop publishing."

In the paper/CAD world, the architect draws the line designations for a wall, which the contractor then has to assemble trade by trade to price the wall: the metal stud supplier, drywall board distributor, the survey-layout for placement, metal stud framing, sheetrock hanging and installation, rough carpentry, insulation, caulking, taping, painting, electrical, glazing, door supplier, and hardware supplier. In a 3D world, a wall is a wall, called an object or an element. The BIM model will provide a price for the materials and labor for the object and break it down into the various trades.

DOMINO EFFECT VERSUS SEAMLESS CHANGES

When a designer changes something in the paper or CAD world, she creates a domino effect that someone has to recognize and account for.

In a 3D BIM world, however, objects behave according to predefined rules. Changes ripple through the drawing, either updating the information automatically or identifying conflicts that need to be worked out. There is no guesswork or interpretation. When the designer changes a sheetrock wall to glass, for example, the change is more than lines and symbols on a screen that require someone to reinterpret and make changes to the bill of materials, labor, and then work out the interface with adjacent conditions. The BIM objects carry all of that information as well as the implications to adjacent objects.

CHANGE ORDERS VERSUS NO CHANGE ORDERS

Architects currently provide drawings of design intent. The contractor and sub-trades must interpret the intent based on 2D lines and a separate sheet with the desired material requirements. If the contractor thinks there is a better solution, then that recommendation loops back to the architect for review, consideration for any adjacent implications, revision of the drawings re-review by the contractor, and finally, a change order.

In a 3D world, the contractor or sub-trade will pull up the model with the architect and test the recommendation, and if both agree with

Figure 10.3   Eliminating 3,000–4,000 Field Interferences

VD&C MANAGEMENT STRATEGY

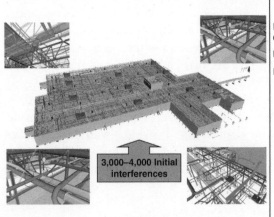

MULTI-DISCIPLINE
COORDINATION SESSIONS

BUILD TO THE MODEL MINDSET

RESULTS

3,000–4,000 Initial
interferences

the suggestion, there is nothing more to do. The model updates all the needed information.

RULES OF THUMB VERSUS ACTUAL MEASURE

In the 2D world, everyone develops shorthand to overcome the cycle time limitations of a paper and sequential process. This leads to a rule-of-thumb approach that is then manually stitched together. In the BIM world, virtual objects reflect their physical counterparts. The parametric properties provide the stitching in real time to provide an actual measure, with actual dimensions and actual performance in the real world.

WORK PHASING VERSUS INTEGRATED PROJECT DELIVERY

Traditional phasing of work no longer makes sense. That shift is reflected in some of the new AIA documents for Integrated Project Delivery. Currently, the AIA process makes its way through distinct phases: pre-construction, schematics, design development, construction documentation, and construction administration. The new AIA documents replicate the same number of phases, but with different terminology that more accurately reflects its function. The new approach, however, can be further simplified to include a conceptual, design, and implementation phase.

The reality beneath the 3D world blurs the lines even further, with concepts like iterative design, parallel work, offsite fabrication, and simultaneous design and then build. The new AIA phases were developed in part to realign the billing of work to more closely match the effort. BIM capabilities are still in front of process definition and contracts.

TRADITIONAL ROLES VERSUS REDEFINED ROLES

Roles change. The principal for a national architectural firm described a meeting they were in that included the architect, the MEP engineer, and the general contractor. During the discussion, the architect realized that the contractor's team knew a lot more about this problem than his consultants, and claimed that he wished he could have simply handed-off the design to the contractor.

Kurt Young, principal at Walter P Moore, describes a more common scenario on projects for which his team uses BIM. "The design team and construction team can work collaboratively and develop a structural steel BIM model that can be created to directly handoff to the fabricator. The fabricator can assume control of the model and assign a detailer to add the connection designs and detail work for each of the pieces. This joint model can now go straight to the structural steel fabrication machinery at the plant. With both the design and build entities involved in the process, they can approve the model at the end of the design phase, no shop drawings or submittals are required." (See Figures 10.2 and 10.3.)

COMPENSATION FOR TIME VERSUS COMPENSATION FOR VALUE

Compensation for value—instead of time—will need to shift as well. An owner may not see why they should pay 50 percent more for design time unless there is a way to link that directly to reduced change orders or reduced time.

Kurt Young explains this in the following way: "Owners are traditionally not comfortable with quantifying these savings. They feel they are at an 'information disadvantage.' If the owner typically carries a 5 percent contingency for design and 7 percent for construction, they have some expectation for how much of that will be left when the job is completed. They can then compare that to a BIM project and allocate part of that differential for compensation."

PLUG-AND-PLAY SUPPLIERS VERSUS STRATEGIC PARTNERS

Viewing suppliers as plug-and-play components in a project is easier in a sequential model. In a 3D world, however, the linkages will push toward greater integration and eventually lead to selecting strategic partners at predesign.

Milestones on the BIM Path

BIM is a technology shift, a process shift, a cultural shift, and a worldview shift. As with understanding sustainability, there is a mountain to climb and milestones along the way. Everyone sees these milestones differently. For example:

- 3D relates BIM visualization capabilities.
- 4D adds the time elements of sequencing and schedule.
- 5D adds quantity takeoffs and cost capabilities.
- Fabrication is still another level of use.

Others prefer to use the Maturity Model:

- Level 1 includes 3D visualization, the reference model, and contract documents.
- Level 2 adds 3D coordination, secondary structures, and the coordination of trades.
- Level 3 adds clash detection and tertiary components.
- Level 4 adds material properties and attributes and schedules.

We have broken this down differently again, describing depth of use based more on purpose than levels:

- Static 3D visualization
- Dynamic 3D visualization (Animation)
- Object intelligence: objects know what they are
- Relational intelligence: objects know where they are
- Analytics: clash detection, quantity and cost analysis, object property comparison
- Simulation: performance of materials, operations, logistics, what-if analysis
- Prediction: sequencing, scheduling, cost, and performance
- Fabrication: converting onsite construction to offsite manufacturing of subassemblies
- Operations: controlling the building operations and maintenance
- Virtual worlds: alternative environments for people to organize within to get things done. Kimon Onuma, FAIA, architectural principal, calls this initiative "low-carbon collaboration."

WHERE IS THE INDUSTRY?

BIM, like sustainability, has hit its rapid growth curve and is moving fast. Arol Wolford notes that a CURT study in 2006 estimated that

80 percent of BIM application focused on visualization. "Today," he says, "at least 50 percent of the users are performing some form of analytics, using clash detection. We still have a big 'M' on the modeling but a very little 'i' on the information and analytics. That is where the power is going to come from. The bottleneck right now for analytics is the number of objects available to use in design. Without the objects you are back to developing quantities and costs outside of BIM."

Arol sees a big shift for owners coming when BIM evolves to the point of easy life-cycle simulation: "Owners typically decide based on first cost, because they don't have the tools to look beyond." With Reed Business, Arol has launched three companies focused on developing and managing the "I" in BIM. SmartObjects provides a service to convert manufacturer catalogs into architectural BIM objects. SmartLibrary Manager functions like an iTunes platform, allowing each firm with its own library of objects to easily access objects from other libraries when working on projects together. The third component is directly related to Arol's mission to provide automated quantity takeoffs with material cost and labor estimates: MeansSmart Objects draws from the labor database for 165 markets across the country.

Steve Jones, thought leader for BIM at McGraw-Hill, sees the rapid growth in several areas. "We saw 2008 as the tipping point for the industry. An AIA survey showed that the numbers of their members using BIM in their billable work grew by 55 percent from 2007 to 2008 and 69 percent among larger firms. We project 2009 will be the year of the contractor transitioning to BIM. Architects are still the dominant user, but contractors are growing more rapidly, and when they get in they go deeper faster."

BIMSTORM

BIMStorm is a unique design collaboration platform created by Kimon Onuma. It is 50 percent technology and 50 percent redefining virtual collaboration. The technology is known as the Onuma Planning System, a web platform that enables all the numerous software platforms to "shake hands" or integrate: Excel, Google's SketchUp, Google Earth, Archicad, Revit, Tekla, and Vectorworks, as well as many others. This allows virtual teams to work together in real time on budgets, modeling, and analysis to quickly design, virtually construct, and test the work (see Figure 10.4). Contract

Figure 10.4   BIMStorm Kickoff

Source: Penn State iCON Lab.

teams can watch in real time as buildings evolve, and observers can watch through Google Earth.

BIMStorm is a social technology that accesses advanced collaboration capabilities that involve participants from all over the world who are working in real time. Kimon describes it as Cloud Computing BIM. Using the Onuma Planning System, BIMStorm is a wild, 24-hour design playground for architects and engineers from around the world to gather virtually and practice building as far as they can within the time limit. Teams self-select members needed for the project they chose to build. Much of the exercise is working out interoperability challenges. The platform allows everyone to touch the data directly. The process is almost magical to watch as it takes shape on Google Earth. Observers can link to www.bimstorm.com and log in to view a live event or see the completed work of previous events.

According to one observer, "The range of software in play is comprehensive enough to go from site plan (large-scale) to pro forma (building-by-building economic performance) and through a range of designs in a 24-hour period, resulting in the equivalent of an astonishing 2.8 million pages of documents. It allows planners, designers, builders, elected officials, and the public to review the implications of

Figure 10.5   BIMStorm Boston Results

Courtesy of Onuma, Inc.

design and policy decisions as they would appear on the site. A process that was once extremely time consuming, and potentially controversial, can now be advanced in a fraction of the time."[6] (See Figure 10.5.)

THE FUTURE OF BIM

Arol Wolford envisions BIM's capability for providing precise automated quantities and cost estimations. The time, errors, paper, and shipping costs this would save would cut 10 percent out of the cost of a project. It would have a secondary benefit of lowering the sales cost for subs and manufacturers who have to take the time to count and estimate five projects to win one. The more significant benefit allows analysis and comparison of different solutions, by comparing directly the performance of one piece of equipment to another or one material over another.

Kimon's focus has been on the front-end planning side, but his future vision is that BIM will tie predesign, design, and construction and operations together in a seamless loop of information. Construction Operations Building Information Exchange (COBIE) focuses on tying equipment information to the BIM model for operations and facility management. Along with this, Arol Wolford points out that the building's information will now have an ongoing life. Traditionally, once a building was completed, all the project binders and plans disappeared to a warehouse. Even if someone wanted to access the information, the stacks of binders and rolls of plans made it impossible to retrieve. "The building is like a first-run movie," he explains, "but after that, there are derivative products that provide value and offer additional revenue streams. Someone is going to have to manage that information, and architects are in a great position to take on that stewardship role and be paid well for doing it."

Since they're located in California, Swinerton sees the new opportunity to expand their service offering related to BIM. They have set up a real estate consulting division to manage the information platform and interoperability for large projects. An airport hired Swinerton to manage the BIM process for a large expansion being constructed by another firm. Swinerton's role is to integrate the many different BIM software platforms used on the project, work out the interoperability and data exchange between the platforms, and leverage its analytics and simulation capabilities. Swinerton also manages the handover of BIM data from construction to commissioning through life-cycle operations.

Dan Gonzales described a new software package Swinerton is testing that provides pinpoint labor scheduling. The software takes all the locations, quantities, and phases and calculates productivity based on RSMeans data. It will use the schedule and workforce assignment, and report on whether crews will finish faster or slower than projected. If a crew finishes too soon, they stand around, but if they are too slow, they hold up work. The software indicates their deviation from the optimum schedule using an angled line. The direction and angle of its incline or descent indicates how far off the optimum path the work will be. Leveling the lines adjusts the workforce to fit the proposed schedule.

McGraw-Hill's Steve Jones sees a future of construction moving down the same path as the aerospace industry, with the fabrication of integrated subassemblies of a building called "chunking." He described how a $7 billion MEP contractor, EMCOR, is rapidly moving in the direction of prefabricated sections of plumbing and HVAC components that can be brought to site and attached and assembled instead of constructed. He believes that a team will soon be able to take a rapid prototyping tool like Beck Technologies DProfiler (labeled a macro-BIM product for quick modeling and feasibility) and design a building to 30 percent of its requirements; they can then go straight to the subcontractors and allow them to model the rest of the details. With extensive fabrication the site shifts to assembly rather than construction.

Steve is also surprised and encouraged to see that in McGraw-Hill's research for the SmartMarket Report on BIM, 57 percent of the firms indicated they needed training on the soft skills of working with others in a collaborative environment, the cultural transition. This recognition of need can turn into the driver that pushes BIM into its "2.0" phase of growth.

In the future, human resource data will be tied to the kind of office a person has, and assessment software, which now exists, will profile a work team and then track their performance against other teams using different space archetypes.[7] Multinational corporations will be able to track the air or light quality from building to building and track sick days or turnover and correlate how buildings compare to one another.

Future BIM tools will use a gaming engine to drive their software. Gaming engines provide a more powerful means for modeling and simulation, but they have not been adapted to provide analytics. Design may take on the form of an interactive 3D game. As BIM continues to translate the design process into rules, the threshold lowers at some point—and the interface between the user and the software allows anyone to use it. If you think of design as a set of problems to define and solve in spatial terms, then it is not too difficult to see how this might translate into an architectural game. The Serious Games Initiative has several games that frame sustainability challenges, global conflict, public policy, and poverty within an interactive game medium to learn the tradeoffs of decision making within different complex scenarios.

As BIM moves from adding intelligence to architecture, there will be a future drive for the architecture of intelligence. Derrick de Kerckhove, director of the McLuhan Program in Culture & Technology at the University of Toronto, describes the meaning of and opportunity for living in virtual space in his 2001 book, *The Architecture of Intelligence*. "The architecture of intelligence is the architecture of connectivity. It is the architecture that brings together the three main spatial environments that we live in and with today: mind, world and networks."

Finally, imagine Kimon's BIMStorm in the future. The top teams in the world will assemble virtually. Each member's profile, role, and areas of expertise will be listed—much like a BIM Facebook. The team will begin to organize itself through a strengths profiling assessment to identify where there are good personnel matches and flag those that will need to receive a facilitated session to establish clearer rules of engagement.

The team will then begin a site review through Google Earth, using Geographic Information Systems (GIS) for analysis. An online programming survey will help collect the data for an initial needs assessment. Each of the teams will then submit additional questions for the owner to clarify intent. This data will export into a parametric pro forma that allows multiple financial and performance feasibility scenarios. The data used to establish space requirements can then be exported into a modeling software to develop a massing model. The client will have full access to the process in real time and can compare the progress to the targets by viewing her dashboard. At anytime she can drill down to a deeper level.

This approximates Kimon's vision for low-carbon collaboration.

McGraw-Hill describes the difference between lonely and social BIM as a metaphor for BIM in the mindset of the old model of silos of excellence versus BIM as part of collaborative design. The title of Finith Jernigan's book, *BIG BIM little bim*, reinforces the importance of not fixating on BIM as software application, but instead as a collection of tools, processes, and a cultural mindset. To use BIM to its full advantage implies teams, collaboration, and the removal of waste and errors by building it virtually before building on site.

Though BIM is rapidly growing, it's still in an early adoption phase. The big advances will come as the different elements of planning, design, implementation, operations, and broader analytics link and then integrate.

Chapter 11 Key 6: Integrating Project Delivery

"In Sutter's brave new world of Lean construction, the traditional 'command and control' mentality of project management is gone. Gone are most lump sum, low-bid contracts. Gone are guaranteed maximum prices. Gone are inflated bids to cover risk. Gone are the adversaries. Gone are most requests for information. And, so far, gone are costly claims."

—Nadine Post, *Engineering News*

The headline in the local paper forced Jim's hand: "New City Hall Uncertainty Threatens New Commercial Development." As city manager, Jim could no longer avoid facing the council. Rumors were now front-page news, and delays on the project would soon back the city into a corner. A large developer planned to buy the old building site, tear it down, and build a mixed-use town center that combined retail, business, and townhouses. Continued delays with no end in sight caused the developer to send a letter to the mayor, each city council member, and the local paper with a clear message: "If the city is not capable or willing to keep its promised hand-over date of the old City Hall for demolition, we will have no choice but to select an alternate site in the neighboring town."

Stan, the construction manager, spent a blurry weekend reworking the critical path for the project and running scenarios to see if and where they could make up time. He needed to brief Jim before the city council meeting. The polite veneer of this small town had cracked. This would be a tough meeting with one question on the table: "What's the recovery plan?"

"How in the world did this thing get so off track?" Stan was weary and frustrated. He had helped to sell their firm to Jim and the city council. "Our size and expertise will make the difference for a project of this importance to the community," he'd said. They were selected over two local firms who had a long history with the city.

His firm tapped Stan because he was one of their best. A former Marine and expert in logistics, he was allowed to handpick his subs. A project of this stature would open a new and growing market for the contractor—or so it had seemed. Now it looked like the firm would likely take a big loss and have to contend with several lawsuits as well.

Stan had begun the project four months earlier with a thorough analysis of the design, schedule, trades, and constraints. He broke the job down into its individual elements and knew every aspect inside and out. He crafted a strategy for deploying resources and was ready to map out a clear plan, which took shape in an elaborate critical path. The master schedule listed more than 6,000 activities defined and linked, each with its predecessor and successor. He worked closely with the point person for every firm after the contracts were awarded to make sure that everyone bought in to their schedule. Stan had built-in buffers at potential pinch points in the schedule. He felt that the project contingency of 5 percent for the architect and 7 percent for their portion would be more than adequate.

Jim and several members of his department were impressed with Stan's forethought and planning at the kickoff meeting. He knew this was the right team to bring in, even though he caught heat for not selecting one of the local contractors.

But then a particularly hard winter delayed breaking ground. Stan thought that if he could gain some time getting the structure up and expedite the curtain wall, he might be able to double up crews on the interior and align back with the schedule—maybe. The structural fabricator promised to rush their order, but the engineer missed his hand-off and they lost their production slot by a day. That cost Stan's team a critical two weeks in the schedule. When the structure was finally erected, the curtain wall was ready to go. But then a problem in coordination showed up. The curtain wall contractor called out for a $\frac{1}{8}$ inch tolerance to attach to the frame, but the structural contractor left $\frac{1}{4}$ inch. Stan pressed for the recovery date. The best guess was a three- to four-week delay to fabricate new attachment brackets.

At this point, the schedule was broken. There was no way to keep up with the day-to-day problems and update the master schedule to provide some kind of order to the project. Stan had to improvise daily and assign whatever subs he had where he could. He lost coordination of the schedule, and the owner lost confidence that Stan and his team could keep their promises.

TRADITIONAL PROJECT MANAGEMENT

Stan's approach followed a textbook project management process: reduce everything to its elements and reconstitute those elements back to the whole. From there, Stan identified the logical phases, determined individual tasks for each phase, sequenced them, allocated the time required, and then linked dependent tasks to prior ones. Stan was using the latest software, which allowed quick adjustments in case a task finishes faster or is delayed and shifts all the successive tasks linked. Stan's approach was rational, orderly, and made sense, which was certainly confirmed during the kickoff meeting as he went through the intricate details of how he arrived at a plan. When Stan opened it up for questions or concerns, there were only a few; most simply wanted to clarify their part in the puzzle. During the entire meeting, whenever Stan looked up, he saw everyone nodding in agreement. Stan would look back to the master schedule and point to the blueprint, and after another phase was explained, he looked up and everyone still nodded.

What went wrong in Stan's airtight plan? The same thing that goes wrong with the 70 percent of projects that exceed their budget and bust the schedule. Traditional project management just *doesn't work* in today's world. This approach to planning and project management consistently produces unreliable outcomes. According to the Lean Construction Institute, "Normally only 50 percent of the tasks on weekly work plans are completed by the end of the plan week."[1] That figure is well documented.[2]

We can trace the problem to assembly-line thinking adapted for management by pioneers like Fredrick Taylor.[3] Assembly-line thinking does not reflect what really takes place when constructing a building. Yet its attraction is hard to deny; it's part of our Western, rational, Cartesian DNA. Within that paradigm, we have come to believe that the world is divided by knowers and doers. The knowers figure out what, how, and who; the doers perform the specific task assigned. If everyone does his or her job, then everything goes according to plan; at least, that is the theory. KlingStubbins's Scott Simpson sums up the situation: "Conventional execution, even if flawlessly carried out, can only achieve conventional results."

So how can the construction industry keep its schedule and price promises? As we'll see, the answer lies in another major mindshift and, yes, another revolution. It's called Lean Construction.

LEAN CONSTRUCTION

Like most of us, when Stan approaches a project, he sees a collection of elements (material and labor) assembled to produce a building. His job is to bring order to all of these moving parts.

Stan knows that getting the most out of his effort will require him to make each specific element as productive as possible. That typically means completing each activity in the shortest amount of time for the least cost. He can see the linear cause and effect along a stream of tasks, but it begins to break down when multiple sequences run into obstacles or collide. There's just no way to play through all of these different possibilities and then reconstruct a master schedule.

Stan has to lock down on one or possibly two schedules and then do his best to realign the work and force the crews to line up with the new plan. But at this point in the project, the activity seems to have taken on a life of its own, and reining it back in will be no easy feat.

A NETWORK OF COMMITMENTS

Some of Stan's buddies in Michigan have told him about a process they follow called Lean Construction. When he heard them say, "We focus on the relational interactions between the trades," he had to laugh. That just seemed like chaos; they were asking for trouble. One friend described a project as a "network of commitments."

"What does that mean, a network of commitments?" Stan laughed. "That's no different than what I do. It just sounds cool and New Age-y."

This fluffy phrase, "a network of commitments," was like a needle in Stan's mind. It would not go away. He went home that evening and crashed in his recliner, looking for some good music to listen to. Music was his refuge. It was like another language and world that he loved to explore.

"Now there's a familiar sound." He stopped on a channel, "An Evening at the Kennedy Center with the Marine Corps Band." The band stirred up memories of his days as a Marine—the precision, the dedication, and the loyalty to one another. He loved to watch the conductor, standing tall like a stick and waving his arms toward one group and then another. "Perfect coordination and harmony, I love it!" While listening to the music with its clarity and harmony, his thoughts drifted back to the project. Stan didn't wear his Marine pride on his sleeve, but he *did* bring that pride to the work he did. If the crews with whom he was working could show just an ounce of that kind of discipline and pride in their work, things would be better.

He clicked through a few more channels and ran across another show, "The Legends of Jazz" with Ramsey Lewis as host. He watched bass guitar player Marcus Miller begin with a few quiet and simple chords and then shift to an up-tempo syncopated rhythm. Within seconds, the drums, guitar, and piano entered at the same time. Stan brought his recliner forward and now sat at the edge with elbows on knees and staring directly into his television. Stan was having what he called "a music moment."

Stan watched the way the musicians looked at each other for cues, the way they leaned toward one another during transitions. He noticed the way in which the lead switched from player to player. Suddenly, the idea of a project as a "network of commitments" took on a whole new meaning. Stan realized that he was trying to run projects like that Marine drill sergeant; there *was* no network of commitments. The only commitment was to learn your part and follow the leader. Jazz, on the other hand, now that was all about commitments to one another— from tight interaction to listening, *really* listening. Music wouldn't work at all if one guy tried to take charge, but it sounds fantastic when everyone is working to synchronize with the other musicians.

Could this really be what his buddies in Michigan meant? Can a project really flow like a jazz session? Stan promised himself that if he managed to survive this project, he was going to call his buddies to find out more.

DESCRIBING THE ELEPHANT

Hal Macomber, a principal for Lean Project Consulting, Inc., uses the parable of the three blind men describing an elephant to explain why, when it comes to large, complex projects, we are unable to grasp the big picture: because people see only the part of the project they are touching directly.

Breaking projects into knowers and doers, therefore, is inherently flawed. Central planning fails. The revolution turns the entire situation upside down, to one where the traditional doers provide the collective intelligence to tackle large and complex tasks. The rub, however, is that distributed collective intelligence does not behave according to Cartesian logic.

Lean Construction provides a framework with tools to capture the big picture, tools that are proving highly effective. The hurdle is giving up the illusion that a clearly laid out plan, with assigned tasks and milestones, represents anything more than one blind man's take on the elephant. Once over this attachment, the rest becomes amazingly simple and, in retrospect, common sense.

Co-author of *Swarm Intelligence* Eric Bonabeau reinforces the nature of the shift and the challenge making it in an interview for O'Reilly Media. He explains that, "Human beings suffer from a 'centralized mindset'; they would like to assign the coordination of activities to a central command. With self-organization, the behavior of the group is often unpredictable, emerging from the collective interactions of all the individuals. The simple rules by which individuals interact can generate complex group behavior.

"My experience trying to 'sell' the concepts of swarm intelligence to the commercial world is that managers would rather live with a problem they can't solve than with a solution they don't fully understand or control. So the mindset is a big barrier to adoption."[4]

Bonabeau describes several features of self-organization: flexibility to adapt to changing environments; a group's ability to perform a given task, even if one element of it fails, and the absence of need for external source or force of control. The hardest feature to embrace is the notion that various paths may emerge along the path to the solution, instead of following a predetermined (critical) path.

IF IT CAN WORK WITH GM . . .

In 1984, General Motors and Toyota entered into a joint venture, New United Motor Manufacturing, Inc. (NUMMI). By all accounts, the original GM plant had been a failure, while NUMMI was a success.

Toyota used its unique management approach—Lean—to transform the same workers using the same equipment into an award-winning factory.

NUMMI has become a famous case study that is often cited to highlight the contrasting mindsets. That contrast is perhaps best captured by this quote from a worker in Matthew May's *The Elegant Solution:*

"Never in a million years would I tell you this work is creative. Then Toyota took over twenty years ago. They teach us their system and say to us, 'We want you to tell us how to make it better.' We went from 'just do your job' with GM to 'no one knows the job better than you' with Toyota."

GM was so impressed with the results that they created a Global Lean department. Yet several Lean experts to whom we spoke note that GM's results still lag far behind that of Toyota. They offered the explanation that, "Toyota has no department for Lean, no central program. Toyota develops their 'masters,' called Sensei's, through a non-directed mentoring process and new masters seek to develop others. It's simply a part of their culture, not a department."

The lesson for commercial real estate? In the absence of a new paradigm, Lean might as well be just another bag of tools. Leadership's biggest challenge is to transform its legacy management system and culture.

IS IT WORTH THE EFFORT?

Keeping promises requires more than good intentions. It requires rewiring 500 years of Western rational breeding and a lifetime of habit. And this rewiring calls for transformational leadership. However, being an expert within a bad system seems to trump the discomfort of being clueless in a good system. The payoff to let go may be enough to cross over, or the cost for not changing may one day force your hand.

Here are some numbers that may make it easier to decide to cross over:

- McGraw-Hill's Steve Jones says that they typically estimate labor for a construction project at 50 percent—10 percent for overhead and 40 percent for materials.
- Glenn Ballard and Greg Howell, who run the Lean Construction Institute, have tracked numbers that indicate only 50 percent of promises made for the week ahead are delivered.

- Clive Thomas Cain, in *Profitable Partnering for Lean Construction*, reports that "Overall, the ineffective utilisation of labour and the wastage of materials put total unnecessary costs at around 42 percent."

Cain goes on to explain the improvement that he found by employing techniques similar to the ones that Toyota developed: "[The] Improving M&E Site productivity study and other similar studies . . . puts labour efficiency at the industry average of 40 percent . . . and materials wastage at 30 percent . . . " In another report, the effective utilization of labor ran between 30 to 40 percent. On top of all this, there is a large disconnect among the knowers, those who plan and manage these projects, who overoptimistically estimated labor efficiency at 85 percent.

To go back to an earlier point, Cain argues that instead of looking for project cost reductions by decreasing profit margins through competitive bidding there is more to gain by changing to a system that uses collective intelligence to reduce waste and inefficiency.

Projects that adopted the Lean mindset and techniques were able to raise their "labour efficiency levels to around 70 percent and reduce material waste to around 4 percent. This gives a saving of around 30 percent which is then available for increasing profits and wages, reducing prices, improving research and development and developing training." On a $10 million project, that savings equals $3 million. What could you save on *your* next project?

WHAT DO YOU TRACK?

Keeping promises assumes keeping track of the things that routinely interfere with delivering on those promises. However, Cain found that "virtually no firms within the industry have an improvement program based on measurement and elimination of unnecessary cost." He provides owners with a series of questions for their teams to better uncover which hidden areas drain efficiency.

- Do they know how often materials arrive late?
- Do they know how much rework regularly occurs (including design)?
- Do they know how much regular disruption occurs on site?
- Do they know how often cluttered or unorganized work areas cause delay and disruption?

- Do they know how much of the raw materials are wasted?
- If the answers to any of these questions are no, Cain then asks: "How can they know their performance is improving?"

GETTING USED TO NEW THINKING

Moving into a world where trust is the governing principle supported by a system to enable keeping promises will demand a new understanding of the nature of a project within this different context. DPR's Dean Reed defines projects as "networks of commitments." The role of leaders is to "bring coherence to these networks of relationships in the face of uncertain paths." They identify the work clusters, bring the right people together, set the stage to work collectively, and help each team choose the right tools to understand and rehearse the work before them. Leaders invest more effort developing healthy team dynamics and have to exercise restraint from stepping in and directing efforts. This is a paradigm shift away from managing activities and toward improving the relational interactions.

A paper issued by the AIA describing *Target-Value Design* defines design as a social activity: "The notion that one person sits alone and is inspired to design misses both the nature of design and the countless contributions of others." Value in this world is not determined up front; it evolves as the client's understanding of the project grows. They are brought to make decisions that trade one value for another. Dean Reed explains that value surfaces in his group's projects as they work against the constraints of time and money. For example, "Our client desires a marble floor, but [after] exploring that option, [finds that] it is more expensive than she had planned. Now there is a choice to be made. Choices [raise the issue of] priorities, and allow the project team to gain deeper insight into the client's unscripted values." In this context, you will never hear these words from a client: "You gave us what we asked for, just not what we wanted."

The client must take an active role as part of the team, one that is vital to the collective mind. The role that traditional third parties have played—as a buffer to and agent for the owner—must also be redefined. They can take a more significant part by bringing key partners to the table. They may be able to wear the leadership mantle that provides cohesion to the team if they can adapt to the new mindset and acquire new skills. They can no longer justify their value through adversarial bidding practices that only reduce profit margins and create a context that needs a sheriff to maintain order.

This is a world that searches for fundamental causes, and realizes that those causes lie hidden beneath layers of consequences. Removing those layers requires a different mindset toward problem solving. Trust is the only context for those closest to the root problem to come forward and share what they see. Candor is the barometer of trust. Now is the only time to see the problem within its context, and the collective mind is the only way to see the elephant in its entirety.

Simply put:

- Trust aligns relationships.
- Early collaboration aligns the team with the business case.
- Sustainability aligns vision.
- Transformational leadership realigns paradigms.
- BIM aligns design.
- Lean thinking aligns process.

These are all facets to a prism, and each contains the light of the other components. For example, Lean practices seek to define value through the client and assume trust, and it is collaborative These descriptions, however, help to call out a particular strength as we attempt to understand the elephant.

THE ESSENTIALS

We now find Stan doing some homework on the Internet and finding information on The Lean Construction Institute. The institute had a considerable amount of material on its website, and it was a bit overwhelming to Stan. So he called his friend and asked, "Where do I start?"

His friend said, "Let me step back a bit and explain some of the changes taking place in the industry.

"There are two primary frameworks that provide a guide for this new paradigm and process: the Lean Construction Institute, led by Glenn Ballard and Gregory Howell, adapting Toyota's production process for construction; and the American Institute of Architects guidelines for Integrated Project Delivery.

"Lean Construction embodies a paradigm shift from conventional project management expressed as a philosophy for delivering value, a theory of project management, specific techniques, tools, workshops, and resources. The LCI website is www.leanconstruction.org. The site offers links to research, audio and PowerPoint presentations, and useful books."

Stan was scribbling notes madly as his friend continued.

"The American Institute of Architects issued their guidelines for Integrated Project Delivery (IPD) in April 2006, which they followed up with a practical guide collaborating with CURT and the Associated General Contractors in July 2007.[5] The AIA provides a broader conceptual framework supported by contracting practices. It does not provide strategy or tools, and it's not a philosophy. Markku Alison is the AIA's resource architect supporting their IPD initiative.

"The two models complement each other. If your firm is interested in the framework and thinking behind keeping promises through trust and integration, but you want to develop your own approach toward projects, the AIA resources will best serve those needs. If you're looking for a system to support that shift, I recommend exploring what the Lean Construction Institute offers."

"It looks like I've got my work cut out for me, then," said Stan. "Thanks for your help."

"No problem," said his friend. "Enjoy the journey!"

Throughout our own journey, Mindshift attended workshops, conducted research, and tapped into the experience and knowledge of several experts, like Dean Reed (DPR), George Zettel (Turner Construction's Lean champion), Gary Hamor (president of Lean Practices, Inc.), to help us get our arms around Lean and its potential to transform project management.

We liked the idea of breaking a project into its component systems so that we could wrap our minds around it. Matthew May notes in his book describing Toyota's management, "A given system is broken down into its component systems and designed in a modular fashion, enabling individual parts to develop before being integrated into a single system."[6] This scales the project down to a doer level of understanding. Sutter Health divides projects into systems of eight clusters, each of which is led by a cluster manager: structure, site improvements, landscapes, material handling, vertical transportation, interior finishes, building envelope, and mechanical, electrical, and plumbing.

We also found that Lean becomes a continuous process for the elimination of waste, because it trains people to identify the common forms and causes for waste. And more important it identifies these signs of waste as symptoms for deeper systemic issues. If workers were waiting, that would lead to an immediate inquiry to trace the roots: Do they not have the tools or materials? Are they unclear of their task? George Zettel pointed out that their studies showed that 50 percent of a construction worker's time is waiting. Taking too much material or more-than-needed components to the site "just in case" is waste. Staging and restaging materials is waste, and it's commonly done. Rework is a major source of waste, and can account for up to 10 percent of the cost for a conventional project.

Here's an example.

Would we rather have a master plumber doing actual plumbing work or walking across the site to get more materials? The idea behind eliminating waste is to keep this plumber busy 90 percent of the time or better. Retrieving parts or tools is not plumbing work; it is not adding value and therefore is waste. Keeping the plumber plumbing is Lean's objective.

Some will ask, "Who is going to retrieve the materials. They have to be moved." The first goal is to stage the materials to minimize the movement and then secondly assign the task to a lower paid laborer so the plumber can focus on where he adds his value. This example deals with three of the seven sources of waste: waiting (for materials), unnecessary movement, and an inefficient process.

Lean thinking allows a team to develop a deeper understanding of value, rather than simply focusing on delivering a project on time and within budget. Values are those benefits that the client and different project stakeholders desire and gain on the project. The understanding of these facets grows and clarifies as the project evolves.

The goal of the Lean journey is to achieve minimal waste and maximum value. Meeting that goal requires the ability to build quality by not allowing variations on the front-end and during implementation. This is yet another shift in thinking. Under the old model, the work is completed, inspected, and then corrected. This system treats a component of work as if it were unrelated to the rest of the project. Lean thinking doesn't just build in quality because it sounds good or it's a principle. It is a principle because any deviation from this practice hinders relationships—either by waiting or taking additional time to fix or work around the problem. It also hides the root of the source of that problem.

Lean thinking is built on mutual respect. It embraces the practice that everyone brings value, has a stake in the outcome, and has an equal voice in deciding direction. Respect enables self-organization and candor. One of the most appealing elements of Lean thinking is its search for simplicity. This is manifested in the drive to root causes, establishing value as defined by the client, communicating visually, and breaking complex things down to the doer level of understanding.

Gary Hamor says that up to 30 percent of Lean thinking and processes deal with communication. He claims that we all know where assumptions lead, and Lean's strength makes the invisible visible (processes) and the intangible tangible (value). Traditional project management tends to be highly abstract: timelines, tasks, checklists, RFIs, and change orders. Lean goes in the opposite direction.

Behind each of those abstractions are people. If the process is designed around people improving their interactions, then much of these abstractions shrink or disappear entirely.

GETTING STARTED

Stan did his homework for almost a year before he was finally ready to get started. Lean was still a bit of a mystery to him, but he kept hearing about the incredible results—projects routinely completed ahead of schedule and frequently 10 percent under budget. Two things stood out even more than cost savings: Many of these projects had just a handful of change orders, and there were no claims at the end of the job! In fact, each of the people to whom his buddy had introduced him spoke about Lean with the same kind of enthusiasm they might have for their favorite car. One project manager that he talked to on a hospital site in Tennessee even said, "I'm having fun again, and the results are awesome."

Still, Stan was frustrated. There seemed to be some code, some fraternity that all these people were in on, the meaning of which had not yet come together for Stan. He could see that simply overlaying some of the tricks he had read about, like value-stream mapping, might improve some of his project, but not to the degree he was seeing take place on the Lean projects.

So when Stan heard about a training seminar that the Lean Construction Institute was holding at Texas A&M, he immediately signed up. He read a little more and learned that Texas A&M was developing a center of excellence around Lean, Green, and BIM. "This ought to be interesting," he thought to himself.

At the seminar, Stan met many Lean veterans, people from DPR, Turner Construction, Linbeck, and Swinerton, and he heard about others, like Boldt and Herrero. There were a few architectural and engineering firms along with some of the sub-trades. The session facilitators spent a little time covering theory and a few case studies, but they then quickly divided the room into tables of six people for an exercise called the Airplane Game.

THE AIRPLANE GAME

Stan sat down at the table and introduced himself to the other five players. The goal was for each team to build as many Lego airplanes as possible in six minutes. Stan frowned; he remembered playing Legos with his son when he was a kid. But he didn't say anything. By now, he'd learned that his preconceptions didn't really get him anywhere. The group's job was to simulate three different scenarios. The first was a fairly conventional process. Each person would take part in adding a few blocks to the plane, and pass their work down to the next station. That seemed easy.

The policy for the first exercise seemed straightforward. Just do your job without talking back and forth. You can't pass along work until you complete your batch of five. If there are any mistakes, they get passed along and caught by the inspector at the end. For the logistics, they were allowed to look at a highlighted picture of their part of the plane. The scale was small and all the lines were the same color. It was a bit confusing, but Stan figured he could do it. Each person from the team went to the material bins and selected the number of pieces they thought they might need. Each person was rewarded by the number of pieces they completed.

When the timer went off, Stan's adrenaline started pumping. He was second in line and had four pieces to attach. The first station only had two, the main fuselage and the beam of the wing. Stan could feel his fingers fumble a bit, especially when he was just more than halfway through and there was a new batch of five sitting in the queue. At about two minutes into the exercise, their first plane—and batch—was completed. The last guy raised his hand and the facilitator noted the time. Stan looked up from time to time and saw some of the others fumbling and attaching a Lego block just off of its mark, remarking to himself, "Nothing I can do about it."

When the timer sounded the end, everyone looked up, tense from the competition. Stan glanced around the table. He had passed along all the work he could, but the station before him had three batches of five that could not get passed forward because it took Stan longer to add his four pieces.

It was time to measure everyone's performance. Stan's team over-estimated the number of planes they could finish by three times. About 25 percent of the finished planes had defects. The most eye-opening count were the number of incomplete subassemblies at the different stations.

"Wow," Stan thought. "That's a lot of wasted work. We didn't even come close to our target."

The facilitator debriefed the group, and there was a lot of active chatter. Several examples were thrown out comparing the problems to a live job; drywall and the MEP portions came up a few times. He then laid out the changes for the second exercise. This time, instead of building batches of five, one plane was to remain in the queue. The team was allowed to point out problems, but it was not permitted to fix them once they passed the station that created them. "*Now* how many planes do you think your team will build, and how fast will you put that first plane together?"

At the end of this phase, the first plane was completed in under a minute. The number of completed planes doubled, and the number of mistakes dropped as well. And while the estimates were still off, they were a lot closer.

"What are some of the lessons we can learn from this change?" the facilitator asked. The answers came at him rapid-fire:

"Reducing the size of each batch streamlines things."

"We could communicate a little more, and we caught some mistakes as soon as they happened."

"We were much more realistic in what we said we would do, and almost dead on in our projections of when we would finish that first plane."

"Excellent," encouraged the facilitator. "Our final exercise will modify the process even more drastically. This time, each team member will have his own diagram with color-coding of the blocks that you are responsible for assembling. We are also going to give each person an even number of pieces to attach. The biggest change, however, is communication and the ability to help one another."

When the timer buzzed, the room was buzzing too, because just about everyone had the same epiphany.

"So what happened this time?" asked the facilitator.

"Our first plane was completed in less than 20 seconds!"

"That's a big improvement over your two-minute plane in round one."

"We doubled our output again."

"We had no defects."

"We had a lot of talk going back and forth and a little help if one of the members was getting bogged down."

"We were one plane off our estimate. Not bad!"

The facilitator instructed, "Okay, now each of you look at your tables. How many subassemblies are sitting in each station?"

Stan looked and laughed with disbelief; not a single piece remained at their table and only a few were at some of the others.

MAKING CONNECTIONS

"No waste, no defects, and more than tripling your output! That's what we call optimizing the whole."

Stan sat back in his chair and thought, "If I could go into each section of a job and restructure how we attack an area, I can see how we would turn this thing upside down! But for me to get all the trades to sit down and even look at a section—let alone work out this kind of give and take—a lot would have to change."

While some of what Stan had learned began to make sense to him, it also elicited deeper questions about how to achieve the cooperation. He felt that he had turned a corner; but he was not yet solidly heading down this Lean path.

Stan played a few more games at the seminar that illustrated ideas and spurred deeper discussions that clarified what distinguishes Lean from traditional project management.[7] Stan finally got the point that Lean was as much a mindset as it was a set of tools. Once he began to see that a project was a network of commitments, the other pieces began to fall into place.

PIECES TO THE PUZZLE

Stan heard a lot about those other pieces at the seminar, and his interest was now definitely piqued. Two of these tools—value stream mapping (a technique used to analyze the flow of work and information required to complete work) and last planner system (a tool for collaboratively managing a network of relationships and the conversations required for . . . coordination, production planning, and project delivery[8])—seemed particularly interesting to him. Stan wanted to know more about them, so he invited his buddy out for drinks after the seminar.

VALUE STREAM MAPPING (VSM)

"Tell me more about value stream mapping," Stan asked his buddy. He'd heard that VSM was one of the key tools, and he'd seen pictures of people standing along a wall placing Post-it Notes all over the place. "I don't get it," he said. "How in the world do you map out every step on a construction project?"

"We don't."

"Then what's all of that commotion that takes place with half a dozen people sticking Post-it Notes everywhere?"

"I typically map the areas that are complicated or where we have some problems. You have to remember that most of this is about inciting good communication between people. If members of the team are going to have meaningful exchange on these topics, then they need to be comfortable with one another. So we create some kind of social structure among the people who will form into a team.

"I still don't get it."

Figure 11.1   Value Stream Mapping

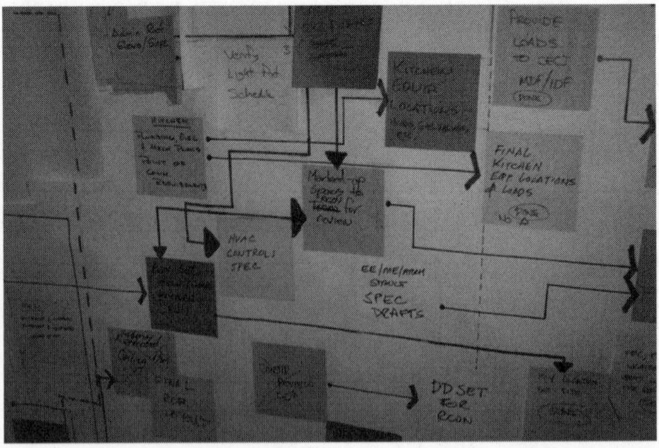

Courtesy of DPR.

"Let me give you an example. We were having trouble getting paid in a timely way, and it was creating friction between our billing group and the client's accounts receivable group. We brought them together for a lunch and then went back to the project room to meet. The first thing we did is break the ice and get each group to talk to one another.

"Our facilitator asked the client's team to map each step they take in order to pay a bill: who receives it, where it goes next if there are no questions, what happens if there are, and so on. And we followed each trail through until it gets paid.

"The facilitator then asked our team to go up and do the same with our process: to map out each step that it takes to generate an invoice. Once both were up on the board, we ran through both processes while each team explained their own. The facilitator then asked both groups to go up to the map on the wall and begin looking for gaps, overlaps, or places that create delays or problems. Within 30 or 40 minutes, the buzz, light debates, and problem solving allowed a new map to emerge.

"The facilitator has the group stand by the map and walk through the process as a whole. As they discuss the procedure, a few more steps are removed, linked, or renamed. But like the airplane game we played this afternoon, we restructured the work and gave everyone a say in the process—with a very clear understanding from everyone on how to make it as smooth as possible."

"So what happened?" asked Stan.

"Our turnaround for payment went from well past 60 days to under 20," his buddy said, smiling. "We also kept the group together as a social network, had a few lunches, and revisited the map to improve it further."

LAST PLANNER SYSTEM

Stan and his friend had time for one more round of beers before they called it a night. "How do you deal with so much flux from week to week?" asked Stan. "It's a killer trying to keep up with the changes and hold the master schedule together. When I get promises from each of the crews at the beginning of the week, I'm lucky if half of the work is completed."

"Stan, here's what we found using the old system. Our crews never had a real say in the schedule. So we started off without any buy-in. Sometimes a crew knew upfront that it would be a stretch to make, but nobody wants to admit that in a public forum. We also had the superintendents in the room and no one from the crews doing the work. So we got many heads nodding but no one really looking up or speaking up. The superintendents were also coming in with their agenda—how to make money and get in and out as quickly as possible. There was no interest in coordination. The site too often became a competition, with people getting in each other's way and making a general mess."

"Yep, that's it," Stan agreed.

"So we adopted a tool that really pulls this together; it's called Last Planner. I don't set the schedules anymore the way I used to building my master schedule. We pull the doers together and set the plan collectively. It's called Last Planner because the last ones who plan out the work are also the ones doing the work."

"Good idea," said Stan.

"Yeah, it's really simple when you think about it. We take the crews that have work that week; we know the goal, and we begin walking backwards. If, for example, our drywall crew is going to complete their work, they need a full set of plans and a 3D model posted to see what the product will look like when finished. In order for them to have the plans, the architect has to get the owner to sign off. To get the sign-off, the architect has to have the full specs and pricing completed. To have the full specs and pricing, they need to have reviewed the options. And so we just keep going backwards until each step is covered and handoffs are made clear.

"This works on a larger scale too. We set our milestones with the master schedule, work through the phases, and discuss the handoffs. These set our targets. Then we look out six weeks at what we think we can do, figure out what work has to be prepped, and look for any constraints that need to be removed. Once we get down to the week's plan, we're tackling work that we are confident can get done with the teams that have to directly coordinate with one another. They begin committing to the work, and then making promises to one another regarding handoffs (see Figure 11.2).

"We make the handoffs clear, measure results at the end of each day, and post those results in each area. We keep track of the amount of commitments that were made, and divide that by the number that we completed. Any promise not kept is identified in one of the many categories we track. Just like the airplane game, our accuracy projecting work starts out a bit shaky but quickly improves. After a few weeks, we'll start seeing some patterns show up. There are usually one or two reasons that we find more often than others that the work hasn't been completed as promised. We can then attack that category with some of the other tools that we have with Lean." (See Figure 11.3.)

Figure 11.2   Planning Windows for the Last Planner System

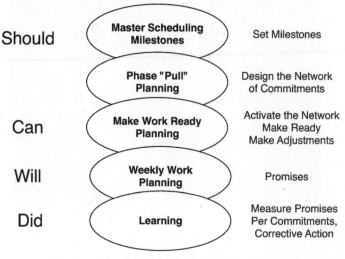

The Last Planner System of Production Control
5 - Connected Conversations

Should — Master Scheduling Milestones — Set Milestones

— Phase "Pull" Planning — Design the Network of Commitments

Can — Make Work Ready Planning — Activate the Network / Make Ready / Make Adjustments

Will — Weekly Work Planning — Promises

Did — Learning — Measure Promises Per Commitments, Corrective Action

www.leanconstructioninstitute.org

Adapted from a presentation by the Lean Construction Institute

Figure 11.3   Metrics for Unmet Promises

Reason	ocurrence
Unclear information	✗✗✗✗✗✗✗✗✗✗✗✗
Too few operative(s)	✗✗✗✗✗✗✗✗✗✗✗
No promise to deliver	✗✗✗✗✗✗✗✗✗
Client/Design change	✗✗✗✗✗✗
Overrated capacity	✗✗✗✗✗✗
Late request	✗✗✗✗✗
Unclear requirement/CoS	✗✗✗✗
Prerequisite work	✗✗✗
Failure to request	✗✗
CoS not made clear	✗✗
Rework	✗✗
Other	✗✗
Absent operative(s)	✗
Unplanned work	✗
No customer	
No performer	
No due date	

Figure 11.4   The Big Room

Courtesy of DPR.

NO MORE SILOS

Stan felt like the two big mysteries that had been holding him back were on the verge of being revealed. He asked his friend, "How do you get away from the silos when planning a project? And how do you schedule work with any degree of confidence?"

His friend said, "Well, Lean has several tools built on the essentials we were talking about today. Target value costing and visual management are two really good ones."

We agree with Stan's friend. Target Value Costing provides a collaborative tool for arriving at the target cost on projects that usually involve an open-book approach by each of the stakeholders. Once costs are determined, managers create incentives meant to reward the outcome of the project- and not the individual stakeholders. Dean Reed gave an example where his team placed all of their profit for a recent job at risk and would only make a profit if they met the target number. They met that number, and the project achieved additional incentives.

Visual management recognizes that a picture is worth a thousand words. Whenever possible, Lean projects attempt to use visual tools to map processes, providing 3D images for the way the work is to look when completed. Turner's George Zettle says that they use BIM to create a sequence of steps for how an area will come together. They will either have a laptop on site to play the animation or take screen shots several steps along the animation and show the crew. Tocci Construction sets up a poster-size 3D model on an easel for crews to see a greater level of detail. Part of visual management, however, is building the awareness that visual cues on the site have an underlying story. A pile of material sitting out is a symptom of a problem that needs to be explored, as is a messy work area.

Lean has a wide range of other tools with resources to walk you through the big idea or principle and explain how to use them.

STAN GETS A FIRST-HAND TASTE

Stan's buddy called to invite him to spend a day with one of their teams involved in a Target Value Design exercise for a university physics lab. Stan arrives at the "Big Room" with 40 people or so (see Figure 11.4). He didn't see his friend, so Stan sat in the back and kept quiet. When the day was over he could hardly believe what he saw and the positive energy he left with. His friend called and asked how the day went. Stan was eager to replay the day.

"The team broke the project down into each cluster (sitework, structure, interiors, etc.) and took an in-depth look at each member's pricing. At one point in the meeting, the mechanical design engineer spoke up: 'The cost of my work is above the target.' So far, he is the only one out of line."

"How did it play out?"

"Certainly not what I expected. The engineer presents in front of all 40 or so people and describes the status of his work and the measures he is taking to get within the budget. At the end of the presentation one of the members begins to question him, with some tough questions. He was asked what kind of new ideas he was bringing to the job and whether or not he was pulling out all the stops to get his work in line. I just assumed it was the GC, the architect, or maybe the owner. When the session was over and each cluster team broke off to meet, I went up to one of the guys who I knew was with the contractor and asked, 'Who was the guy putting some solid pressure on the mechanical engineer?' When he told me it was the concrete frame subcontractor, I was blown away, but then it clicked. When everyone has a shared interest in the outcome of the project, anyone can step up."

"Stan, I think you've put it together. Our common incentive pool creates genuine transparency, and Lean provides a way to handle what in the old days would have turned into finger pointing, or worse never brought up in the first place. When everyone has skin in the game then everyone looks after one another in a positive way."

This meeting actually took place, and one of our Mindshift members was there to observe. The specific technique of Target Value Design was useful, but the process and the behavior that was witnessed made a bigger impression.

LEAN ARCHITECTS

Lean is slowly working its way into the offices of architects. They too have their internal processes, silos, and handoffs that can benefit from the same disciplines. Set Based Design is one tool firms like HGA Architects and Engineers on the Sutter Health projects are currently using. George Zettle describes how this works (see Figure 11.5).

"The architect will create a set of design solutions early in the project and carry those solutions forward until there is a clear 'winner.' For example, we may consider two or three structural framing systems, and as we get further into the design, the architect will better define the interior space and the floor circulation. This may change the bay sizes and favor one solution over the other. It sounds counterintuitive, but it really does

Figure 11.5   Set Based Design

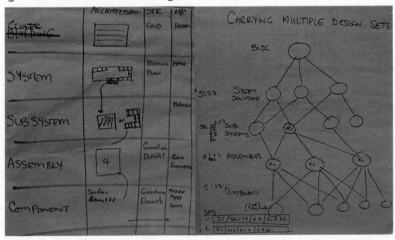

Courtesy of DPR.

save time and cost. If we lock in too early on a particular solution, and we find out it's not the optimal one, then the client either has to live with a less-than-desired outcome or pay for a major rework of the design. This way, we haven't exhausted one solution all the way through."

LEAN: TALKING POINTS

Stan went back to the office filled with plans. "Janet," he said to his assistant, "call a meeting for Monday. I think we're ready to get this thing going for real."

It had been a long journey for Stan—more than a year, in fact. During that time, he had to accept that the old way of doing things really wasn't working, and then he had to learn a whole new way of seeing—a completely different world view. But once he got it, he *got* it. And he was ready to run with the ball and show others exactly how to work within this new paradigm.

Stan's story is common among other Lean advocates. Here's why:

- Lean aims for predictability of workflow and not for optimizing productivity of each component.
- Lean works to improve relational interaction to reach outcomes; it does not focus on outcomes as a means to drive activity.
- The customer determines value, and that value clarifies through the project. Value is not fixed at the outset. Lowest upfront price does not equate to lowest final cost or best value.
- Doers determine how and when work is done, instead of centralized planning pushed through a critical path.
- Quality is built-in at the front end instead of inspected and repaired at the back end.
- Lean focuses on variability throughout the process. Traditional project management is only concerned about it at key milestones.
- Lean creates an environment of transparency, whereas conventional projects don't ask, or worse issues are ignored and/or covered up.
- Incentive is based on the outcome of the project and not on individual completion of tasks.
- Lean projects are networks of relationships built within an environment of people who feel committed to one another; and these commitments are not abstractions, like timelines and task lists.
- Because incentives are shared, money can be shifted to changing priorities without penalizing anyone.

- The client plays an active role in the project and does not delegate their role to a third party.
- Sub-trades are recast as flexible players to the overall project, which leverages talent and skills where they can make the best effect.
- Design is an iterative process and requires options; it is not a predetermined path.
- Design is a social activity that includes key stakeholders, and is not the exclusive activity of "experts."
- Lean teams co-locate and interact regularly, not just when meetings are scheduled.
- Work is a group endeavor, not a collection of independent efforts.
- Lean uses systems theory to understand the nature and dynamics of a project instead of breaking a project into its individual parts.

THE FUTURE FOR LEAN

Lean is still in its early adopter phase. There are strong regional areas that are using Lean practices and several individual firms. Similar to the adoption of BIM, some of the larger firms' field offices are practicing Lean, but have not migrated to Lean as a culture. That migration takes time.

Healthcare was one of the first industries to adopt Lean Construction, and Sutter Health is perhaps still the best example. This number is growing rapidly. The future of Lean, however, may already be unfolding. At the time of writing this book, we identified 49 hospitals or healthcare systems adopting Lean to improve their internal operations. Several of the firms we interviewed are developing a consulting side to their business, as they recognize the broader applications for Lean thinking and large demand within organizations for improving efficiency and removing waste.

In Lean, Stan discovered a life-changing world built on trust, participation, and a new kind of common sense. We heard the same sentiment expressed over and over when we talked to construction managers using Lean and the owners whose projects have been transformed.

In the next chapter, we describe the Integrated Form of Agreement and AIA's Integrated Project Delivery Guidelines. The chapter will provide the rationale behind these radical departures from traditional contract structures and provide examples of how they are being used.

Chapter 12 Key 7: Trust-Based Agreements and Client-Centered Incentives

"Trust goes hand in hand with, and is dependent on, a perceived risk. Without risk, there's simply no need to talk about trust."

—Matthew May, *The Elegant Solution: Toyota's Formula for Mastering Innovation*

President of Solidus Mark Charette sits down with Harry, the president of a regional bank, to review the contract details prior to the final award for the construction and full interior finish out of their new headquarters. Solidus has already walked the bank through their process: three phases of analysis, with the principals for each of the consultants and suppliers on Mark's team in every meeting. The bank compared Solidus' proposal with submissions from two other firms and found Mark's price just slightly less than the highest firm's offer. And so, this meeting is the final step.

When Mark lays the contract on Harry's desk, the banker looks it over in surprise. It's just one page, guaranteeing the price for the project, the move-in date, and doesn't have any change orders. "Where's the rest of the contract?"

"That's it," Mark replies. "One page."

"And your lawyer's okay with that?"

"We actually do quite well with this," Mark explains. "We've used it for 10 years, and our clients really like it. Our lawyer wasn't crazy about it at first, but when he reviewed our whole process with the client, he too became a believer. Are there any details you think we need to cover or add? We've included the guarantee on our price, your move-in date, and no change orders. You've got a two-year warranty on all of our work and longer for the furniture. The contract is based on the final proposal with all of the details. But let me know if you see something else we need to cover."

"No, this is everything, Mark. I just didn't think it was going to be this easy."

With that, the two men stood up and shook hands. Deal done.

Harry carried a copy of that one-page contract with him for the next two weeks; he simply couldn't get over it. He displayed it with pride to several colleagues and to all of his direct reports. For Harry, it served as a trophy and restored some of the trust he had lost long ago during a difficult series of projects with people who built buildings the traditional way.

When owners put their trust in architects and builders to complete a building on schedule and on budget, they are generally taking an enormous risk. And every time that trust is broken, it's eroded a little more. Eventually, both owners and builders become cynical: Fool me once, shame on you; fool me twice, shame on me." The Sarbanes-Oxley Act of 2002 represents a low point in trust toward American business: just another example of a bad law attempting to cope with bad behavior. According to an article by Michael Malone in *Business News*, "The new laws and regulations have neither prevented frauds nor instituted fairness. But they have managed to kill the creation of new public companies in the U.S."[1]

But wait a minute. The very next year, 2003, CEO of Berkshire Hathaway Warren Buffet completed his purchase of McLane Distribution from Wal-Mart for $1.5 billion with a handshake. This deal was based on trust;[2] so it *can* happen. And, as we'll see in this chapter, it is beginning to happen more and more. The idea of trust-based collaborative teams—enabled by tools like BIM, Lean, and new contract formats we'll look at in this chapter—is gaining momentum.

Of course, most businesspeople are unwilling to base a deal on a handshake without a legal document to back it up. We're not quite *there* yet! Although we're slowly stepping out of the toxic paradigm of using the courts to settle disputes, we don't want to swing to the other extreme and presume that handshakes mean the same thing to everyone. However, these new documents strike a balance in our evolving understanding of trust-based and relational contracting. The three common references for these agreements are:

- The AIA's "Integrated Project Delivery Guidelines" (IPD)
- Sutter Health's Integrated Form of Agreement (IFOA)
- *The Project Alliancing Practitioner's Guide* out of Australia. We will draw from their resources and some of the work of Chuck Thomsen, a fellow with the AIA, and many conversations with those using these agreements.
- Some firms simply use a Memorandum of Understanding (MoU).

This chapter is meant to be both a primer and an attempt to uncover the source of the incredible effectiveness that these agreements enable.

THE CONTRACT MINDSHIFT

In the mid-19th century, construction liability issues were pretty simple: Under the concept of the Master Builder—where design and construction was conjoined—builders were held liable for work. But as the industrial revolution evolved, factory and other buildings became more complex. Architects began to specialize in design, leaving construction to builders. The Master Builder concept, and its simple standard for liability, fell apart.

The new measure of liability became "Standard of Care," which stated that a professional is not liable if they can demonstrate using the same level of care as would be expected among their peers. Architects, as advisors and consultants, were not in a position to guarantee results; so they were therefore not liable.

In 1918, contractors reached a similar position of protection with the United States Supreme Court *Spearin* decision. Spearin had been awarded a bid to replace a six-foot section of storm pipe for a Navy dry dock. The pipe failed, and the Navy sued. It turned out that Spearin had built the section according to the plans and specs provided by the Navy, and the Navy had approved the work. Neither party knew that the storm pipe would later be impacted by a dam failure, which forced more pressure than the pipe was designed to handle. The court ruled that as long as the contractor builds according to the plan, and the owner or owner's agent approves the work, the contractor cannot be held liable.

Although these explanations greatly oversimplify the issues related to project liability, they do illustrate why we are in our current mess: Architects and contractors have more than 90 years of finding ways to insulate themselves against liability and implicate the other.

It's a no-brainer that there *must* be a better way, and some have already found that in the form of strategic alliances. The roots of collaboration and teaming in the construction industry begin in 1990 with the Andrew project—a failing oil rig project for BP in the hostile North Sea. It was initiated in 1974, and didn't get far for the next 16 years. The conditions were complex and unpredictable, and BP could not find qualified firms willing to go through a traditional bid process and take on that level of risk. In this case, necessity became the mother of collaboration. BP changed the rules, shared the risk, selected partners that they treated as partners, and opened the books to collaboratively create a solution.

The results were spectacular. The project came in 45 percent below the target cost and six months ahead of schedule!

A 1994 BP report concluded that under the traditional procurement model, existing contractors are short term and adversarial, project objectives are unaligned, accountability is unclear, risks are placed on parties unable to influence or control them, and the skills and knowledge of contractors are unrecognized and underutilized.[3] Sound familiar? This approach found its way to Australia and morphed into public works projects.

In 2006, The Society of Construction Law in the UK presented results on 34 alliance projects in Australia. They found that 88 percent completed under budget, and 73 percent ahead of schedule. Projects that followed traditional delivery averaged 10 percent over budget, and 90 percent were late. Similar practices have been adopted in other industries. Many have taken place within the aerospace and automotive industries—most notably, Boeing and Toyota—in the form of integrated supply chain management.

Throughout this book you've read about projects completed under budget, early, and with few or no change orders. All of these use tools like BIM or Lean Construction, and a trust-based team formation like Will Lichtig's integrated form of agreement (IFOA), which distinguishes between transactions and relational agreements. In a traditional (and transactional) contract, the owner defines the requirements, breaks that down into each component, gets a price, and then attempts to shed risk for the outcome. The project is, ironically, left out of the loop in this kind of thinking. Lichtig therefore asked himself, "How can we break the mold to do what is in the best interest of the project?" His answer was based on the insight that *a project is a collective enterprise*. The owner is forming strategic relationships required not just to deliver a building, but also to define the value and risk associated with the enterprise.

Some in the industry feel that the rise of integrated, trust-based teams is really the return of a collective Master Builder (tying design and construction into one mind). Sutter Health's David Long says that the trust-based contract "abandons, as a document, the idea of preparation for litigation. Instead, it is based on focusing the team to concentrate on how to deliver a successful project. It's a very basic concept, but a paradigm so difficult to shift to because of a century of construction contracting."

This paradigm shift that Long cites moves construction contracts from arm's-length agreements to an interdependent relational framework; from adversarial to collaborative; from protectionist to mutual benefit; from risk allocation to shared risk; from separate contingencies to combined; from separate agreements to one; and from a standard of care criteria to striving for zero defects.

That does not mean, however, that teams and managers should move forward with blind trust. The hard work is transforming your company's attitudes through your own mind shift and then finding partners who are making—or want to make—the same shift. Remember, it's not the form of the contract that draws the team together. Instead, *the contract is a reflection of the quality of relationships sitting around the table*. Projects are a network of relationships—a highly social enterprise. Owners are not buying a product but rather a service to improve their company's performance.

WHAT OWNERS NEED TO KNOW

If owners now play an active role as an equal stakeholder, exactly what are they supposed to do? If you're going to share the risk, what do you really need to know?

The following case studies are composites of various situations, both of which are based on the experiences of actual owners. The Global Foods case shows how an owner who is new to the process walks through a trust-based approach to a sophisticated, complex relocations project. The second shows how trust-based teams are formed, and what they look like from the inside. Together, these should give you a more holistic—and *realistic*—look at what to expect when you enter into the world of trust-based teams and shared risk.

A NEW HOME FOR GLOBAL FOODS: TRUST-BASED AGREEMENT FOR A LARGE PROJECT

Ben received the call from his CFO: "The acquisition is final. Ben, I need you to find a new home and pull together the four companies that now make up our division."

Ben, vice president of real estate for giant conglomerate Global Foods, was already on top of it. Their division, Selective Foods, serviced high-end restaurants and organic grocery stores worldwide. The culture of high-end food service was much different than their sister divisions. They sold to mainstream retail, which was a business model built on high volume and low margins. The Selective Foods division was rapidly growing, and with more than 500 people now spread across the Houston Metroplex, it was time to bring them together.

Ben had some new ideas for this building, and he needed to find a creative way to build a five-star environment with a two-star budget, since the parent company, located in Germany, kept a tight rein on spending. Mark, one of the principals from a national architectural firm, told him about an "A Team" approach called Integrated Project Delivery. He also gave him Will Lichtig's article on IFOAs[4] and some case studies of Sutter and GM. Ben was intrigued and set up a meeting with Mark to learn more.

Ben, Mark, and developer Renee met for almost two hours at a small, quiet coffee shop not far from downtown. Mark explained the new thinking behind the relational approach, and emphasized that trust-based thinking was core to the results that Ben had read about and the structure he was about to review pulled it together.

Renee was quick to ask how the teams would be selected. "What do we do with our project manager? He's ready to go. Our next step was to begin a bid process to select that architect and contractor. His fee is already built into our contract. . . ."

It quickly became apparent that Renee had some concerns about this approach. "Ben," she said, "here's our first test. Are you going to approach this as a team, or is everyone going to have clear roles and contracts that stipulate those roles? There seems to be a place for everyone in this new arrangement, and everyone stands to come out better, but we may need to back up a step or two before moving forward."

Mark smiled. "Renee," he said, "let me tie this together by sharing how Sutter Health developed its agreements."

SUPPORTING CHANGED WORK

"We called Will Lichtig," Mark explained, "who developed Sutter's Integrated Form of Agreement (IFOA). Once we began applying some of the Lean principles for reducing waste on projects, we saw how projects really do come together as a whole, not piecemeal. Lean provided the ability to restructure work and roles to optimize the outcome of an area instead of playing traffic cop between the trades. By using the Value Stream Map, we found times when spending an extra dollar on a structural solution saved two dollars installing the MEP. You can immediately see the problem of trying to reduce the contract for the MEP and give that money to the structural guy using the old contracts; you'd have a war on your hands. The contracts prevented us from moving money around these commercial boundaries. We used to say that leaks happen at the intersection of contracts because of these barriers. We asked Will how they got around the problem, and he gave us a great explanation."

Mark told Ben and Renee about the IFOA, a multi-party agreement that each key stakeholder signs that eliminates each party's tendency to work off of different terms and incentives. Each firm is compensated for their direct costs on the project. Those costs are developed in the team forum when establishing the target costs. Each firm provides those costs in an open book manner that's exposed for audit. The design and construction contingencies are placed into a single risk pool along with each company's direct profit and direct overhead for the project. That structure provides the flexibility to shift money from the contingency pool if necessary. It also allows the team to reduce the scope and direct cost for one area, without penalizing that firm and adding it to another area.

Renee brought this back to her question regarding their project manager and his fees. "We're willing to play nice in the sandbox; that's not a problem. But if we start over and sign-on with this new multi-party form of agreement, how do we make our fee?"

"Good question. I'm going to assume that you have a cost associated to your CM's time and direct overhead costs for the project?"

"Correct." Renee nodded along.

"Well, that fee is compensated for in the agreement along with the direct cost for each stakeholder."

"What about our profit and general overhead? We have a built-in load on this cost, as we do with all of our costs."

"That profit and overhead is put into a pool along with the other stakeholders," Mark explained. "The team puts that pool at risk. If the project hits its target cost, then you make your normal profit and overhead for the project. If there are cost overruns, those are paid first out of the agreed-to contingency and then out of the pool. This is sometimes called the 'pain incentive.' It aligns everyone's financial interest to make sure the project is successful—all for one and one for all."

Ben looked puzzled. "I can see how that shifts the focus away from each person taking care of themselves and hurting the project. I can also see that it frees us up to move money around to take advantage of a savings opportunity, or to cover for an overrun on a part of the project. This is great for me as the owner. But why would my suppliers be willing to sign up for this? They're just stepping up to more risk by tying their compensation to one another."

"Great question!" said Mark. "So you don't think you can find a team that will sign up for this just to make you look good?" Everyone laughed, including Renee.

"Ben, there's a shared gain side to this too. You and your team will establish a target price for the project, along with a contingency. If the project comes in below, either, we recommend that a portion of that be paid out to the team. We leave the amount or the percentages up to each team to work out ahead of time. But believe me, this is a strong motivator. We have seen teams double their net profit on a project and—as of this date, knock on wood—every project that has used this approach has finished below its target cost."

"I'm starting to like the sound of this!" Renee said. "I can see that by pulling the right team into this project and developing a collaborative dynamic, we could really make it sing."

Mark looked at his watch. "I've got an appointment back at the office. Ben, I'll send you a proposal for leading this effort and copy Renee. Look it over. If you like what you see, then we can begin with the next step: team selection."

TEAM SELECTION BEGINS

Mark received his signed proposal the next morning, along with a note that said, "Be here by 2 P.M., and let's get this thing moving!"

He arrived with a list of firms for Ben and Renee to review. "These firms are familiar with or have participated in an integrated project. Ben, the first thing we'll do is issue an invitation. It will include the general scope of the project, of course. But more important, it will outline the trust-based principles and guidelines for expected behavior. There's nothing unique for this project. I'm borrowing from the work Sutter's done and the AIA's documents; we've adapted the two. It shouldn't be a surprise; these firms are familiar with the expectations. I've also outlined the compensation approach we discussed yesterday."

"I'm glad you mentioned that," said Ben. "Could you explain target costing? I wasn't sure if you meant the team sets the price for the job. If that's how it works, then we've got to talk, because I'm not real comfortable with the fox building the chicken coop!"

SETTING THE PROJECT TARGET COST

"Great questions," said Mark. "I'm assuming you've created a business case for making this move, and that a new building is part of that larger business case?"

"Absolutely."

"Okay. Then once we have a team in place, we start with your business case. This is quite different than having a budget for the project, because a business case is not tied to any market value for a building. It's simply your rationale for consolidating your four units. It asks what your project consolidation will mean to the division and how much you plan to spend to make it happen."

"So what's the team going to do with that information?"

"They validate it."

"What do you mean? I'm the one who validates the thing!"

"No question. What I'm talking about is that the team provides you with a detailed study broken down into the trade divisions for projected costs. Not what you typically get, which is a generalized cost per square foot estimate. No offense, Renee."

"None taken," she smiled. "I'm a sponge at this point."

"Ben, the value of working out in detail what the team thinks you can get for the cost you've planned to spend flushes out key assumptions. Are we thinking clear story for the interior walls or full sheet rock, side lights, or solid doors?"

"So basically, you're saying it takes a village to create a cost estimate?" Ben chuckled.

"Sort of. Can you see the value of this business plan validation?"

"Darned right. But how do I know that your team's numbers jive with the market? It still feels like this is the fox building the chicken coop, but a better behaved fox, maybe?"

"We search out some benchmarks. At this point, we've got what we call 'expected costs'; and we can do this one of three ways. You can ask the team to bring in cost breakdowns from previous projects to see if they are in line. You can pay a firm to develop a full pre-construction estimate. Or, you can bring in a construction manager or a Quantity Surveyor to review the numbers."

"I'm okay with that. I'd probably appoint someone who I've worked with in the past and hire them to audit the results. So now we're ready to start?"

"Almost. This is the part you are going to like; this is where we set a target cost."

"About time," Ben laughed.

"Ben, you and the team will set a target below the expected costs. This step is intended to drive innovation from the team. We sometimes say that we pressurize the system to force people to rethink their assumptions. During the business case review, we focused our attention on helping define your needs through preliminary programming. You can see how that interaction helps clarify what is valuable to you on this project, and that's hard to do in a vacuum. At this point, there may be some requirements that we set aside earlier, but target cost analysis provides a vehicle to focus that innovative effort toward achieving some of those desires.

"You may want to place those high-paid tele-chefs you keep telling me about closer to their gourmet kitchen. But we can think about that in a few weeks, when we actually go through the validation process live.

"If the project completes under the target cost, we recommend that a percentage of that gain is used as a performance incentive. Some of our clients take 50 percent of that gain and proportionately divide it among the team."

"That's it?" Ben asked.

"Yep. The firms I've listed are familiar with both the IFOA and the new contracts from the AIA. I'll handle any of the questions that may come up, just in case. Once we receive responses to the invitation, we'll be set for tryouts."

Mark briefed Ben and Renee on the difference between this form of team selection and the more traditional manner. "Ben, we'll invite the three teams to our office. I've set aside our brainstorm room for the next three days to meet with one firm per day. I've asked that each team include an architect, contractor, and any of the key subs whom they feel will play a critical role for their group. This will be more like a tryout than a standard presentation/interview. Our BIM specialists have developed a series of three early-stage concept models that we'll be able to use to spur dialog and problem solving. I've set up several scenarios with key objectives that firms will work through, and then we'll see what they come up with. We'll engage in an hour of dialog with each team and then let them work on the first exercise for an hour, with 30 minutes to debrief. We'll finish this portion in the morning and then work through two more problem-solving sessions in the afternoon. These will be long days, but exciting ones."

NEEDS AND WANTS

The home office in Germany didn't give Ben as much money for the project as he would have liked. That meant reusing the existing furniture, some of which was 10 to 15 years old.

One of the units, The Food Concierge Group, included an intense but unique call center. These individuals were on the phone with high-paid chefs from around the world, answering questions about the food, its preparation, and trouble-shooting problems. These employees had strong culinary backgrounds, were among the highest paid in the division, and were hard to replace. Ben was hoping that the new facility would go a long way in reducing the turnover they had been experiencing recently. His plans included a small lounge and a gourmet kitchen that the call center staff could use to research questions. The Food Concierge Group was a major revenue source that not only developed chef loyalty, but also expanded sales.

Another challenge Ben faced was reducing the cost of moving people around. Every time a group restructured or introduced a new product, it required relocating people, offices, and equipment. Tearing down and reconstructing a private office cost almost $15,000. At 50 to 70 private offices a year, they were spending close to $1 million for just two units. With all four units in one location, that would only increase the amount of churn.

Ben thought about what Mark had said about "needs and wants" affecting their team selection process. His curiosity was piqued, and he wanted to see if he could actually put some of his *own* desired wants back into the job.

THE TRYOUT

The first team—an architect, contractor, structural engineer, and tax consultant—arrived promptly and were escorted to the brainstorm room. Ben, Renee, and Mark greeted them as they entered. Mark introduced the format.

"We take the first hour to listen and talk. We're interested in your team structure, how it works, and especially any previous projects upon which you have taken this kind of approach. We made it clear for the interview that we're not looking for presentations; so if you brought a PowerPoint, you can use it for another prospect. Any questions? No? All right, then I have one. I've never seen a team bring in a tax accountant. I've seen a lot of other specialties, but not this one."

"She's our secret weapon," said the contractor. "You'll see later what she can do."

"*Now* I'm curious," said Mark. "Let's get started."

At the end of the first hour, they stopped for a break. When they returned, Mark set up the first exercise.

"We have provided you with three concept models, along with our assumptions and some preliminary programming information. It's currently 9:30 A.M. You have until 11 to work through the models and choose the one that you think is best. We'll take about 30 minutes to debrief and then go to lunch together. We want to hear your reasons for picking the model, your assumptions behind the selection, and what advantages you think it has over the others. Good luck, and we'll see you in 90 minutes."

Ben, Renee, and Mark knew that there was obviously no right or wrong choice among the three models. The only information that they wanted to uncover when the debriefing began was how the team worked together, their rationale, and the questions they presented. They wanted a team that saw the process as an open-ended conversation, not just an assignment to follow through with.

The first team chose the second model, which Mark's group had developed to show a high-performance green building that included underfloor air, the potential for co-generated power, and a very open and highly flexible interior. Mark's team called this scenario "the German" option. It followed many of the European trends to create a more human-centered environment. It took advantage of natural light, had a higher quality of air distribution, was easily adaptable, and focused on green construction. It was probably the highest cost option, and Ben considered it to be outside his budget. He was disappointed to see the team take this route; after all, cost constraints were one of the problems stated for the exercise.

Then the team presented their ideas. "Option two provides the greatest long-term payback. It offers the highest LEED rating, and that rating is consistent with the image and client base to whom Selective Foods markets."

Another member added, "A high-performance sustainable building aligns with the parent company's values and their own statements regarding their position toward the environment."

Then they closed with the attention getter: "And we believe we can provide this solution for the same cost or less than conventional construction."

Ben put his fourth cup of coffee on the table and sat up attentively. "Run that last statement by me one more time."

"We believe option two can be built for the same or less cost than conventional construction."

Ben was clearly surprised to hear this—even the second time. "I know we don't get into value and cost until this afternoon, but I need to understand how in the world you're going to pull off something like this. Unless you know something I don't know, that building will cost a premium to construct!"

"Perhaps, Ben, but here's where our team is coming from. We're assuming that you have estimated these models at market prices. We did a quick calculation for each of the three based on the programming you gave us, and its looks like we have a good, better, best set of options. There is a 15 to 20 percent delta among the three options, give or take."

"That's pretty close. If I hear you correctly, you're proposing that our 'best' option can come in for the same cost as our 'good' scenario?"

"Pretty much."

"Okay, so give me the short take on this."

"We've worked on a half-dozen integrated projects as a team. Most are completing at about 10 percent less than market costs for traditional construction, and some are close to 20 percent ahead. In many cases, we're adding features with no additional costs that are not included in that reduced cost. We have also finished each project 5 to 10 percent ahead of schedule."

Ben pulled out a calculator. "That's pretty impressive. I can see that if your claims are true, you could get close to that 20 percent reduction. That's still too tight to consider taking this route. I know you haven't been given a chance to provide detailed estimates, but you understand that a lot has to go right for an aggressive strategy like you've proposed to work. Did you consider a buffer?"

"Actually, yes. We'll now bring out our secret weapon, Jill."

Jill smiled. "Thank you," she said. "I'm a certified CPA specializing in Construction Tax Planning (CTP). I'm also a licensed architect; I practiced for about 10 years, until I came over to the dark side." Everyone laughed.

Ben jumped in: "Our tax department follows a cost segmentation approach for all of our purchases at the end of a job and looks for items we can classify as personal property."

"Correct," said Jill. "And you are probably overlooking more than half of the opportunities available by taking this approach *after* the job is over. If it's done properly beforehand, you could reduce your cost by about 6 percent for the core and shell and up to 17 percent on the interiors, net present value. Do you know if your tax department is recouping that much on capital projects?"

"Not even close," said Ben. "It's maybe 1 or 2 percent. In fact, our CFO rejected a proposal from a firm to do that on our last project because he said it wasn't worth the hassle for 1 or 2 percent."

"CTP follows a more in-depth analysis than conventional construction tax planning. To get the maximum advantage, potential areas for reclassification should be reviewed as early as possible with other key stakeholders like your tax department and legal team—even in the pre-design stage," Jill continued. "Once a strategy is identified along with the possible areas to reclassify, the architect has a map when working through different design scenarios. Without that map, the architect might make a choice that could just as easily be reclassified using another solution.

"We then work with the architect to make sure those items are properly marked on the plan, segregated for what might be considered normal operational use, and documented. Every dollar you can shift from a capital item to personal property results in a 20-cent savings. We estimated that you could recoup between $2.5 million and $4 million on this project. That's your buffer."

Ben was impressed. "I see why she's your secret weapon. But can you give me a few examples of what you spotted in the scenario and programming data we provided? I'm curious."

"Sure. The co-generated power, for one thing. It's not your main power source. Your raised floor is being used as a technology platform, is not attached to the building, and is not essential to the building's operations. Your gourmet kitchen may also qualify. That's just a few. But to make this work, you have to coordinate it during planning. It would be impossible for your tax department to go through a floor plan, a spec list, and the invoices *after* the fact and figure this out."

Mark jumped in. "Ben, are you beginning to see the benefit of bringing these teams in early to help you flesh out the business case? We're not even halfway through the day, and we're already seeing the kind of creative thinking that comes from teams who work together regularly. If we set up our selection process around a problem-solving workshop, we're going to find out who can really deliver."

The group broke for lunch and walked over to Zydeco Diner. This, too, was part of the tryout—getting a feel for how everyone interacts and beginning to build that relational context for working together.

Ben, Mark, and Renee saw two other teams that week, and chose the first team that presented—the one with Jill, the secret weapon. After working through the business case, estimated cost, and now target cost, Ben was able to get closer to his five-star solution.

ACHIEVING A FIVE-STAR SOLUTION

An important shift in the paradigm is a team's ability to look at the whole job instead of focusing on line items. This allowed Ben to evaluate not only the cost of a proposed solution, but to consider all of the trade-off savings. Similarly, taking an integrated design approach allowed the New York Times Corporation's David Thurm and Compuware's Larry Fees to incorporate higher-performing solutions that in a traditional delivery model appear to be more expensive. The offsetting costs to other areas of the project provided measurable cost justification for the choices.

If the team is on top of its game, it may have a secret weapon like Jill, the construction tax consultant. By using a raised floor as a technology platform, Selective Foods is able to reduce the cost an additional 20 cents on the dollar, which includes the cabling under the floor and the carpet on top of the floor.

Tim McGinn, principal at Cohos Evamy, an integrated AE firm in Canada, shared several examples of clients who were able to gain significantly higher performance through an integrated design approach. He explained it in the following way: "Integrated design, in contrast [to traditional design methods], is essentially lateral. Its power lies in its ability to stimulate meaningful collaboration. Multiple perspectives are brought to bear early on; synergies are identified, creative solutions developed, dead ends avoided, schedules accelerated, and communication and coordination enhanced. All stakeholders contribute to the design through an iterative process that considers each of the building's major components and systems. The approach is holistic, inclusive, and creative."[5]

When it came time to spec out Ben's furniture, the team brought in a logistics expert to do a complete cost comparison for tearing down the existing furniture, moving it, ordering necessary replacement parts, analyzing downtime to the groups, and assessing the limitations that the existing product would have on an improved layout and interior scheme. The hard costs for moving the furniture, the significant discount they would receive from a manufacturer for a purchase of 500 offices, and some added tax depreciation brought the cost difference down to a point that it was worth considering if the project could afford new furniture. The team's integrated approach allowed them to work through the trade-offs with Ben and his HR person to go forward with new furniture.

The team also presented a movable wall solution to handle Ben's churn and the $1 million he was spending annually to tear down private offices and rebuild them. Ben could reduce that annual cost to under $200,000 with this solution. A corporate move, however, is a capital expense, and future reconfiguration comes from the operational budget. Ben could only deal with his capital budget if he wanted this solution. Originally, he had asked a contractor with whom he had a long-time relationship for his thoughts on this topic. This contractor told Ben that it would be double the cost of drywall; so Ben was ready to write it off, even when his new team asked him to reconsider. He protested, "I don't understand why it's so doggone expensive. You would think that if it were made in a factory, it should be at least *close* to what we're doing inside our building. Where does the additional cost come from?"

Here again, the paradigm gets in the way. The team showed Ben that his contractor took a simple run of drywall and provided a lineal foot estimate. They told him that a better comparison would be to look at the cost when it is fully integrated with the other trades. The movable wall is a fully integrated wall system that includes the electrical, the doors, and the glazing. It reduces the labor rate for the carpet and ceiling by up to 40 percent, because installers do not have to cut around the walls. When these savings are added to the picture, the gap narrows and could even be equal to conventional drywall. This solution also qualifies for accelerated depreciation—resulting in a reduced cost of up to 20 cents on the dollar.

The particular solutions are secondary to the opportunity for owners to engage in a new kind of dialogue and search for performance improvements. With traditional bids and traditional project teams, these kinds of explorations are rare and only find the low-hanging fruit. These examples illustrate how value is redefined in this new context as something that grows and clarifies.

In the end, Ben not only got what he had hoped for, he got much more than he expected. That is the common message we heard from the owners who shifted their paradigm.

CHOOSING THE CONTRACT

Once the team is chosen, a variety of tools can govern the relationship. We followed Will Lichtig's IFOA structure in the story above because it's a flexible document that defines the relational nature of the enterprise.

The IFOA is a single contract signed by the key stakeholders—most typically the owner, architect, and contractor and may include key sub-trades or suppliers. A developer can also play an important role. But again, the owner decides which essential core members will sign and assure the performance of the project.

According to Lichtig, "The parties recognize that each of their opportunities to succeed on the Project is directly tied to the performance of other Project participants. The parties shall therefore work together in the spirit of cooperation, collaboration, and mutual respect for the benefit of the Project."[6]

The AIA created contracts to support their Integrated Project Delivery Guidelines. One of the forms is called a Single Purpose Entity (SPE), where a project is treated as if it were a limited liability partnership. This builds on the relational nature of the IFOA and formalizes the governance for a project. It takes more work to set up, but some feel that it addresses risk and liability more clearly.

One of the companies we interviewed stated that the relationships with their partners are strong, and the approach they have evolved has worked; so they use standard contracts and a Memorandum of Understanding (MoU) to explain conditions or expectations that fall outside the contracts. It is their version of a handshake agreement. The principal for the firm with whom we spoke said they did not feel that the additional work to set up an SPE was justified for a single project, given the strength of the relationships they had with their partners.

Alliance Partnerships are adapted out of the United Kingdom and Australian experience of creating long-term strategic relationships and keeping those intact over several projects. *The Project Alliancing Practitioner's Guide*, referred to earlier, offers a thorough examination of how to set up and run a successful alliance. President of Westbrook Air Conditioning and Plumbing Owen Matthews shared at a Construction User's Roundtable conference the alliance that his firm established with several others. He describes their team as follows:

"All of the design and construction team members are equal shareholders in IPD^{TM}, Inc.[7] We have all been working together on major projects for years and have come to respect and appreciate one another's abilities. Moreover, we have formed professional friendships that have streamlined the business process. In many ways, we have been a team for a long time and have only formalized the relationship with the formation of IPD™, Inc."[8]

Our purpose in reviewing these options is to provide an overview of the kinds of structures available; however, there are others to choose from. The AIA has several variations in their new contracts that address the different kinds of integrated teams. The AGC issued its Consensus Docs designed from the contractor's role in a project. We encourage you to consider the value an agreement brings to the team's ability to interact freely and work on behalf of the owner while exploring these options. Scott Simpson summarizes the objective when choosing an agreement that best fits: "Architects should concentrate on leadership rather than ownership, on design rather than avoiding risks."

INSURANCE AND LIABILITY

A few years ago, while leading Sutter Health's efforts, David Pixley claimed that "the insurance and legal [industries] haven't caught up, and we're not waiting." Solidus's Mark Charette and Scott Simpson said that their approach is to build trust and provide complete transparency. We wanted to hear something more concrete, so we asked Will Lichtig, "What do you tell your new clients who may not be as bold and big as Sutter? We have had questions raised that shared risk and collaborative design blur the lines of ultimate responsibility. Or are we misinterpreting how the IFOA works?"

"There have been no claims to date," Will explained, "so in that sense, it is working, but [it's] still early. Some have the misperception that the IFOA stipulates no claims against one another, and that is not the case." He went on to explain that each firm is at risk for the money they put in the profit pool, which does not affect the insurance companies; they are only at risk for anything that falls outside of the "standard of care." If design is a collaborative effort, it is still possible to assign a "responsible designer" who ensures the accuracy of their model.

We talked to some of the lead insurance spokespeople to hear their comments on this trend. They openly acknowledge that insurance companies are behind, but they also point to the fact that the nature of their business is to deal in proven track records and clarity. At this point, neither of these exists to the degree necessary for insurance companies to fully endorse. There are still a variety of contracts in use and no real consensus as to which will set the standard. The people we spoke to believe IPD reduces risk and stated that, as more projects complete, their ability to assess risk will improve. For now, as one executive stated, "Bring me a contract, and I'll tell you if we can insure it or not."

Though the subject of insurance and liability remains unsettled, it is rapidly evolving, like so many of the other revolutions throughout the industry. One thing is clear: The form of agreement an owner chooses can enable or gut the inner power that makes trust-based integrated delivery so effective.

FURNITURE DEALER: A TRUST-BASED PROJECT WITHOUT THE BELLS AND WHISTLES

It's not just large owners like Ben who are working with trust-based teams. Smaller owners, and suppliers themselves, are showing an interest in this new kind of working relationship.

Meg owns a furniture dealership in the Carolinas. Her firm is mid-sized and serves a secondary market. A few Fortune 100 companies have call centers in the area, but most of the companies in the market are regional and local firms. There is a growing state university, and the area is healthy. It's attracting more companies that want to compete for business.

Meg saw this trend and wanted to take advantage of her local roots and the relational way business is still handled in the region. Bigger firms would like to take a share of her pie, and she, in turn, wants to expand her business. If she had a network in place of design and construction people she could trust, together they might be able to generate some good-sized projects.

Meg heard about IPD at a local AIA luncheon at which an IPD resource architect from Washington, D.C. spoke. During the session, she heard references to BIM, and someone in the audience asked if IPD was anything like Lean Construction. She knew that neither she nor any of her suppliers were quite ready for BIM, and she had never heard of Lean. She did see very clearly that she could recruit a team and could develop their own way to streamline the process and make the experience a lot more predictable for the owner and a lot less contentious for everyone involved.

Meg knew just about every decision maker in town, including a particularly progressive construction manager named James. He had once mentioned handling a project as an alliance manager, so she called him.

"James, this is Meg. Have you got a minute? I'd like to run something by you." Meg outlined her idea, and James told her there was no reason it shouldn't work.

"Great!" exclaimed Meg. "Can you send me a proposal for helping to pull this together?"

A few weeks later, Meg invited several business owners with whom she had worked for more than 20 years, including an architect, contractor, developer, MEP engineer, and advertising principal. Some had worked together before; a few were new. But they had one thing in common: the fact that Meg knew and trusted all of them. Meg made her case and outlined the benefits she thought they could all gain by forming an alliance and creating a team approach "just like a sports franchise," she explained, "or a movie crew." The entire group agreed that the idea made a lot of sense. It was simply taking the way they had worked together on past projects and creating an "A" team. She handed it over to James to explain how they could get started.

THE EXECUTIVE PRODUCER

"Meg is like an executive producer pulling this team together, and I'm like a director," said James. "The governance for this alliance will actually be a mutual and equal partnership between each person in the room who chooses to participate. We can make this as buttoned-up as we want, or as open ended; that really becomes your decision. I will put together a proposal for my role as the alliance manager, and I'll explain what that is in a minute. And even though I described Meg as an executive producer, please know that when it comes to decisions everyone has an equal say. Part of my role is to help you determine how to make decisions as a team: consensus, majority, or unanimous. Our decision-making will evolve as we become more familiar with each other's businesses and gain more confidence in our process.

"Another part of my role is to help you find ways to deliver projects more efficiently. I'm pretty good at that. When we dig into where the waste and mistakes are typically made, I think you'll be surprised at just how much we'll be able to streamline our efforts. Every percent we find in waste means another percent to your bottom line or a more competitive bid."

They all liked that idea.

GOING TO MARKET

James walked the team through a strategy for going to market. It would be slow at first. The idea of hiring a turnkey team—take-it-or-leave-it—would take time for decision makers to become comfortable with. So he outlined some practical steps they could use when approaching owners and responding to requests for bid.

Once they had met and worked through their delivery approach, they became convinced that they could remove enough waste to make it attractive for a potential owner. Of course, they needed the right kind of owner. James outlined two kinds: early adopters and those who are fed up with the old system.

First, James told the team, they would need to find an independent means to validate that the pricing they offer is truly less than if the owner openly bid it. "Owners will not simply trust the concept, no matter how good it sounds—not even those who are fed up."

If the owner is comfortable with the team, they can offer to provide a complete pre-construction analysis using traditional project assumptions. The owner may hire a construction manager to test the numbers, or he may bid the job but allow the team to compete as a single entity. Each approach has it pros and cons, James told them, "but I recommend that you all be willing to go that extra mile until there are enough projects and happy customers to use as references."

It took Meg and her team almost a year to meld and better understand each other's process. One of the members turned out not to be very committed to the idea, and sent a mid-level manager to most of the meetings or missed meetings altogether. After a few months, James recognized the pattern. As alliance manager, he found a way to provide that firm with a graceful exit. With recommendations from other team members, they soon found a replacement.

It was almost nine months before they found the right kind of owner to whom they could present the story. The owner was very interested; he fell into the "fed-up" category. There were no immediate projects, but several that they could begin planning halfway through the year. The group remained enthusiastic about their story and continued to get comfortable with explaining it. They improved their own under-standing of the process in trying to answer the new questions that came up in just about every presentation.

Finally, they received their first opportunity: a 20,000-square-foot regional bank office. James walked them through a form of business case validation with the owner, and at that point, they were asked to put together a pricing proposal. The bank decided to also let their regular construction firm bid the job. The team recognized that the other firm would not let this go without a fight. They turned to James to manage the process of putting together the pricing and rooting out as much waste and inefficiency as possible.

The team's price was almost 10 percent less than the other bid. That surprised both the team and the bank, because they knew the other firm would reduce their price as much as possible. Meg's team submitted their pricing in an open-book manner. The direct costs were shown, as were the profit, overhead, and contingency. Their proposal stipulated a split of the remaining contingency—50 percent for the owner and 50 percent for the team. The team also felt confident enough to guarantee the move-in date, but not the price.

According to Clive Thomas Cain, author of *Profitable Partnering for Lean Construction*, a certain UK study tracked the improvement among teams using Lean Construction as an integrating tool. Initial projects achieved a 5 percent reduction in cost. After three to five projects, that improved to 30 percent.

The bank project went well, much better, in fact, than the bank president had expected. It was a bit awkward for the team, and there were miscues working through their first project. James used some of the mistakes and bumps to learn and improve. However, no one could argue with the results. They finished under their target cost and only used 30 percent of the contingency. There were change orders, but less than half of what normally takes place. There was no conflict, and the tenor of the work was cooperative and upbeat.

This project affirmed Meg's and her colleagues' value of their trusted relationships, and it took a common sense approach to streamlining the process. Meg knew that this taste of success would spur the desire to keep working to reach that 30 percent level of cost reduction. She also knew that the journey of improving with a group of people whom you like and respect would lead to further growth.

The developer was not directly involved in this project, but partici-pated in every meeting. Once the project was completed, he approached the team with a significant opportunity. He saw the power of creating a unified team along with the right kind of incentives. He showed Meg and the others several scenarios of what constructing a building for 15 or 20 percent below the market might mean for a developer to lower rents or add performance to a building. With that overview, he presented his business case for a LEED Platinum building in a new development area of downtown.

CREATING VALUE THROUGH LONG-TERM RELATIONSHIPS

The idea of trust-based collaborative teams enabled by integrating tools like BIM, Lean, and new contract formats is gaining momentum. It provides opportunities to form specific teams like Meg's, and provides owners like Ben with a turnkey approach. It will permit brokers to create a series of teams and allow them to compete as teams that move more toward alliance management and away from traditional construction management. It gives developers the chance to create their "A" teams and build better quality buildings for less cost. Large AE firms or design-build firms will be able to migrate to a larger team configuration built on high trust and collaboration.

As firms build greater comfort with their team members, and become intimately familiar with the different business models and the drivers behind those models, they can begin to step outside their traditional roles and create new forms of value. A supplier may partner with a developer to provide materials at cost and share in the equity of the building. Suppliers may partner with an owner and offer an alternative means of financing the solution provided. Interface, for example, developed an Evergreen lease for their flooring systems that transformed the transaction of buying floor covering to a life-cycle relationship of use and service.

When our paradigm changes from providing value through transactions to creating value through long-term relationships, value is allowed to—and inevitably *will*—evolve over time. Protecting that quality lies at the heart of crafting new kinds of agreements.

Chapter 13 Key 8: Offsite Construction

Architecture has over the past century finally become a machine, with as much as fifty percent of the cost embedded in systems, not structure, walls, and roof. Developments of lightweight, high-strength, and high-performance materials offer the prospect of economy, efficient transport, reuse, and less waste all of which streamline the process cycle. The result is a more sustainable architecture.

—Stephen Kieran and James Timberlake,
refabricating Architecture

Offsite or "manufactured construction" is an invisible revolution, really, a revolution in waiting. Offsite construction is here, it is pervasive within every construction project, and it is making many things easier, but few people are aware of it. In fact, there's really only one book that talks about the incredible revolution of *thinking* that offsite construction represents. In *refabricating Architecture*, authors Stephen Kieran and James Timberlake provide a fine argument for a shift from looking at a building as a constructed object to an assembly of a highly sophisticated system with multiple subsystems. This is really a paradigm shift in the way we think of buildings and how they are built.

A GLIMPSE INTO THE FUTURE

It's the year 2020, and Manny and Stu have just completed a day of work on a new 30-story high-rise going up in Chicago's Loop. They head over to O'Brien's for a beer to recap the day and talk about tomorrow. At the pub, they run into the integrated wall techs who are working on the same job.

Manny and Stu are "slab techs" for Ready Fit Integrated Floors, a high-precision design and fabrication shop. The company builds a prefabricated slab that looks like it is upside down when manufactured. The flat surface is on the bottom. Four vertical sections create long channels that are the length of the slab, and extend a foot in height. The slab includes built-in plumbing, electrical, and data, and it acts as a plenum for the air-conditioning and heat to the building.

The new floor is called an Integrated Modular Slab. The new slabs are lighter weight but much stronger, which allows for longer runs. A combination of the channel design and new carbon fiber nanotechnology have reduced the concrete content by two-thirds and made the process much faster and safer. The pipe, cable, and conduit are delivered to the shop, bar-coded and matched to a specific slab. When these are snapped in place, the slab is closed up using concrete access floor tiles laid over the channels and tightened. The Integrated Modular Slabs are delivered to the site and easily set in place.

All that Manny and Stu need are a drill and a number of quick connect pipe fittings sorted and identified in clear plastic bags with barcodes. Their job is to go to the junction of each slab, remove the floor tile with the drill, and then connect the cable and conduit with a flexible quick connect and the plumbing pipe from slab to slab. Each junction takes about five minutes, and there are 50 per floor; it takes a little more than half a day to complete a floor.

Five trades are combined into one integrated system. It takes a day for the slabs to be inserted into the floor plate, and then a half-day to make all the connections. Ten years ago, that same floor would have taken a few months and involved 30 or more people on site. In 2020, it takes a crane operator, two slab handlers with a slab dolly, and Manny and Stu.

HOW GOOD CAN IT LOOK?

Architects and designers are sometimes skeptical about how a manufactured solution will look. The answer from offsite fabrication is simple: "How good do you *want* it to look?"

Frank Gehry's work is one extreme of how attractive a manufactured solution can look. On a similar level, the interior finish for the Kimmel Center in Philadelphia (Figure 13.1) offers a more traditional image of beauty.[1] All the woodwork was cut and shaped in a factory in China, and it was assembled like an enormous, magnificent three-dimensional puzzle. These are examples of what Kieran and Timberlake might identify as "artistic expressions," where the impression of a master's craft presides. But is that impression diminished because Gehry's design technique used a sophisticated BIM tool originally developed for aircraft manufacturing? Not at all. The tool allowed Gehry to extend his craft and more accurately turn his vision of smooth curvatures of form into architecture. One would also be hard pressed to imagine an attempt to build a facility like the Kimmel with crews of traditional mill workers. The cost and time to take this approach would prohibit a designer from even thinking of this solution.

Figure 13.1   The Kimmel Center for the Performing Arts

Figure 13.2   Stealth Fighter

Kieran and Timberlake describe another form of beauty: function so well translated that the object itself is beautiful. They offer an image of the Stealth Fighter as one example (Figure 13.2).

Figures 13.3 and 13.4 show a fully integrated interior wall system called Enclose[2] that changes the notion of manufactured walls. This product is fully integrated both in function and architectural aesthetic, blurring the lines between traditional roles of architect and

Figure 13.3   3D Model of an Offsite Fabricated Office

Courtesy of Haworth.

Figure 13.4   The Actual Offsite Fabricated Office

Courtesy of Haworth.

manufacturer. Gensler worked with Haworth to develop the detailing and function.

Manufactured solutions are breaking the choice barrier between utility and aesthetic. This is one example combining both high-performance adaptable interior space with a refined aesthetic arrived at by a form that fitly follows its function.

There are certainly tradeoffs in the manufactured world, but they are the same kind of sacrifices made in switching to a different medium. An artist who attempts to replicate an oil painting in watercolors, for example, will get bad results, and will likely blame the medium.

Similarly, some of the first underfloor air projects suffered from poor installations. If the tiles were not properly seated, air leaked through the plenum into the envelope and robbed the underfloor diffusers, which directed that air into the space. That created uneven cooling and heat. Some firms handling the early installations experimented with the volume of airflow compared to overhead systems and got it wrong, usually by having too much air pushed through the floor. The most common mistake was their failure to take into account what is called "perimeter loads." In other words, the temperature from the exterior fluctuated more than the air in the middle of the floor. If not compensated for, the exterior area stays hotter or cooler than the interior of the space.

The federal government was one of the first large owners to adopt underfloor air solutions. Their research showed the same results that companies like the New York Times Corporation, Compuware, and the Dearborn Center found: underfloor air provides higher quality airflow, significantly lowers energy costs, and offers more user control—three decidedly significant benefits. The General Services Administration issued a report on the advantages of underfloor air and recommended it for GSA projects. The federal government was also the guinea pig for firms to learn how to design and install these systems, and had many of the first—and worst—performing floors. That led to a moratorium on these systems that lasted several years. They have only recently (and cautiously) returned to recommended use.

At this point, however, the benefits of offsite construction are just too good to ignore:

- Manufactured solutions can achieve 50 to 75 percent less waste than the equivalent site-built building.
- The controlled environment and precision equipment provide higher and more consistent quality.
- Offsite construction allows several systems of the building to be created simultaneously, which shortens the schedule.
- Production provides greater control of the schedule to produce product on a just-in-time basis.
- The reduction of cutting tools, welding, sharp edges, and caustic and toxic chemical reduces injuries. Fewer people required onsite—and less competition for access—also diminish the amount of injuries.
- Moving the skill to the shop or factories allows lower-cost labor on site. Transitioning from trade-specific skills to assembly techs also allows more people to work on a variety of systems.
- Readymade units and systems that arrive on site when needed decrease the loss, theft, and damage of raw materials.
- Many manufactured systems lower the energy requirements, which enhances a building's green performance.
- Modular systems that are reusable significantly lower the cost of change, reducing the waste created by conventional demolition and disposal.
- Modular systems lessen the time needed to turn over a space for reconfiguration or new tenants.

STICK BUILT NO MORE

The story of Manny and Stu presents a radically different picture of a day in the life of what used to be trade craft workers. The Integrated Modular Slab is not the radical shift; a variation of that product is actually available today. The *real* change comes in moving from trades to technicians, and from fabricated objects like ductwork or plumbing to integrated systems delivered as chunks. The craft is replaced by computer-controlled equipment in a sophisticated shop or factory. It no longer makes sense to have different people for air-conditioning, plumbing, electrical, data, and access flooring.

The industry is at an intersection. BIM and offsite construction have run into market demand for higher performance and quality, along with demands for lower cost. However, the paradigm and process for design, cost estimating, and working through various trades still imagine a building as a location where the raw materials are brought to the site and numerous specialty trades fashion, form, and construct. This is called "stick building." One person described the model as hundreds of ants who each take their grain of sand and add it to the pile.

The industry requires a massive culture shift to take full advantage of offsite construction's potential in the way that other industries have. At the moment, offsite construction remains below the sight lines of the industry and is still actively resisted in many quarters. Owners who want offsite construction have to swim upstream and, in many cases, fight passive resistance, misinformation, and lack of sophistication through the sub-trades. They have to work through the artificial cost premiums that trades add, either out of ignorance or to protect their scope of work. Owners have been victims of trades learning on the job and installing solutions like underfloor air without understanding how to properly balance or seal the system.

But resistance doesn't come just from the sub-trades. Architects sometimes protest for perceived aesthetic limitations. They also defy suggestions because they think integrated systems carry a higher cost than each solution delivered separately by its trade. They do not have the tools to disaggregate an integrated system and compare its components to separate individual functions. That kind of thinking makes no sense in the first place, but with the lack of tools to compare function and cost decision makers are lost.

Local codes, especially in some of the major cities, are also obstacles, and these tie directly to union requirements that still delineate work according to old trades divisions. Developers and landlords hesitate because integrated systems don't fit easily into pro formas that contain one line item for electrical, and one for HVAC. Some of the solutions blur the tax line between real property and personal property.

We have frequently found that when a manufactured solution is said to be more expensive as an upfront cost, further analysis found that not to be the case. In Chapter 8 David Thurm told his story about the DALI lighting system, which consultants originally explained was far too expensive. When he went back to discover the reasoning behind this—following the money—he found several intermediaries in the process that added no value. He challenged some of the pricing assumptions, and with a little homework and clarity regarding functional requirements and manufacturing capabilities, the cost was very much in line with expectations.

The same exercise takes place with prefabricated interior walls, HVAC, plumbing, and raised floors. When all the stakeholders are brought together (including the trades whose scope of work reduces or is simplified as a consequence of the new solution), costs fall in line with conventional construction and significantly add new performance capabilities that conventional construction cannot address.

The reason for this roadblock is an outdated worldview about construction that gets in the way.

Figure 13.5   Novartis Modular Lab Equipment

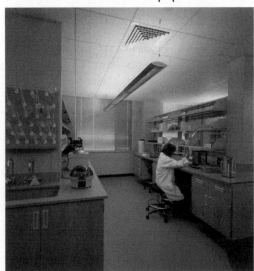

Courtesy of KlingStubbins.

Figure 13.6   Pierson College—Kullman Modular Building Units—
provided by Kieran and Timberlake, Architects

Courtesy of Kieran and Timberlake, Architects.

Figure 13.7   Cutaway of a Raised Floor System

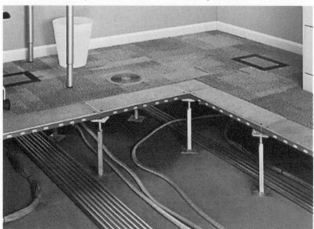

Courtesy of Haworth.

Figure 13.8   Autodesk Custom Fabricated Ceiling

Courtesy of KlingStubbins.

THE ESTIMATING ROADBLOCK

Estimators are the librarians for the construction industry, and the Construction Specifications Institute's (CSI) MasterFormat[3] is its Dewey Decimal system. Until 2004, the MasterFormat described a project through a hierarchy of 16 divisions and multiple subdivisions. The MasterFormat laid out the chronology and its sequences approximately: General Requirements, Site Construction, Concrete, Masonry, Metals, and so on.

Here is a sample of how items are categorized:

- 03 41 16 Precast Concrete Slabs
- 07 92 00 Joint Sealants
- 23 07 16 HVAC Equipment Insulation
- 09 91 00 Painting

The 28-page MasterFormat was designed and introduced in 1963. Almost 50 years later, the MasterFormat worldview has not changed; it has only expanded. Today, just the list of Division Numbers and Titles is 170 pages, not including descriptions or explanations.

The MasterFormat presents the current construction worldview, wherein jobs are understood as a parade of trades and priced accordingly. It expanded from 16 to 50 divisions in 2004, in an attempt to handle increased specialization, but that only makes it less responsive to new ideas in construction. Any attempt to combine solutions from different trade divisions (integrated subassemblies) short-circuits the machine. For example, if an estimator tries to compare the construction of a section of drywall to a complete pre-engineered wall that only needs to be set in place, then something like the following will take place.

The estimator will ask the following trades and suppliers for a price on a section of drywall, which falls into Division 9 of the Construction Specification Institutes (CSI's) MasterFormat:

- Metal stud supplier
- Drywall board distributor
- A survey layout specialist
- A sheetrock installer
- Rough carpentry and blocking
- Insulation
- Caulking
- Taping
- Painting

The doors, glass, electrical, data, and plumbing that may be part of this wall system all fall under different divisions and trades. The industry simply thinks in terms of dividing a job into its trades.

The trained thinking and the software estimating tools to support this parade of trades approach are unequipped to take an integrated system like a wall or raised floor and reverse-engineer it for comparisons. Manufacturers of integrated solutions recount story after story of presenting to contractors or architects and receiving blank stares. They will even receive strong negative reactions—something akin to listeners sticking fingers in their ears repeating out loud, "La, la, la, la, la . . . I can't hear you!"

In *Everything Is Miscellaneous*, author David Weinberger compares a fluid and highly adaptable digital world to the rigid and restricted world of physical classifications systems. The construction world reflects the inflexible and controlled paradigm expressed in its classification, pricing, and organizing system. Until this system migrates fully to both the technology and worldview expressed in tools like BIM, offsite construction will continue to run into this wall.

"If we want to see how the physical world has silently shaped how we put together our ideas about the world—and why *any* traditional classification scheme is bound to embarrass somebody—there is no better example than the Dewey Decimal system."[4] A close runner-up has to be CSI's MasterFormat system. Like Dewey, the CSI system, "is caught in a problem endemic to large classification systems tied to the physical world." There is no end to the expansion and shifting around of categories—to the point that the system finally collapses.

BIM, for example, has not just improved the efficiency of design, but also changed its very nature. BIM deals in whole integrated objects, not a parade of trades. The CSI system is unable to cope with that. Offsite construction has evolved beyond making things like ductwork and cutting and shaping pipe more efficiently and toward delivering whole, integrated systems.

THE OWNER'S ADVANTAGE

Fortunately, owners are not encumbered with the construction subculture and its worldview. Consequently, when they see a solution that makes sense to a broader world, they understand it.

Owners want solutions that perform better, have more predictable pricing, and make life easier. We found an interesting coincidence in our interviews with David Thurm, Compuware's Larry Fees, and Paul Beitler of Beitler Commercial Real Estate. Each one built the first high-rise building in their city to use an underfloor air system: New York, Detroit, and Chicago, respectively. Each leader researched the different systems and became convinced of its many benefits. One went so far as to take his team to Europe to view what is common practice there. All three had to fight and push against the project's architect, contractor, or a key consultant who was locked into that Master-Format worldview—all of whom expressed objections like, "It will be too expensive" or "It will complicate and delay the project."

None of the objections proved valid; in fact the opposite turned out to be true. The solutions were cost effective on the front end and simplified each of the projects. The systems also lowered energy costs and improved air quality, both providing more consistent heating and cooling and generating cleaner air.

THE NEW MASTER BUILDER

As the Master Builder metaphor gave way to DBB, the architect became isolated in design. Today, architecture and construction are reuniting—not on the physical job site, but in the factory and on the virtual job site through BIM. Consider again David Thurm's group's development of the Digital Addressable Lighting Interface system with their engineer, consultant, architect, and manufacturer. "Designers and producers are members of a team that comes together to solve specific problems."[5] Sutter Health and other projects referenced are receiving lower-cost projects delivered faster, at a higher quality, and with added capabilities.

And Ghafari's Bob Mauck claims, "If you are not doing stick building, then you can phase and sequence a project differently." While working on one of the GM facilities, Bob's team was able to ship assembled portions of the project straight to the job site using just-in-time scheduling because they had no lay down areas to stage parts or materials. Scott Simpson recommends that we "think of construction as offsite assembly, factories for offices."

Offsite construction is a tool that goes hand-in-hand with the mind shift this book advocates: to solve the cost, quality, and time tradeoff.

THE FUTURE

Commercial real estate is quickly evolving to the point where the sheer number of manufactured solutions will tip the industry into a completely different model and mindset. The 2008 AIA national convention in Boston was filled with small companies offering a variety of manufactured solutions: from new kinds of precast concrete, exterior walls systems, and MEP solutions, to many other companies with a seemingly endless variety of options. We were also struck by the fact that no one has pulled all of this together—either to provide a comprehensive picture of how much of a building could be assembled using manufactured solutions, or tools to help architects and contractors make true cost comparisons with conventional construction.

Most manufacturers use CAD/CAM (computer-aided design/computer-aided manufacturing), but have not converted their catalogus into architectural BIM objects. One hurdle, however, is the perceived cost of converting the data. One firm estimated the price tag for this at about half a million dollars. However, we found that using a firm like SmartObjects (a Reed Construction Data company) to convert the data can cost a fifth—or even less—of that estimate. We heard of a recent project where an architect approached a large manufacturer and told them that if they wanted to participate, they would need to convert their catalogue to BIM objects. SmartObjects was able to make the conversion within a month and for a fraction of what they had originally estimated.

The point, however, is that BIM provides a tool for architects to easily bypass the old CSI straitjacket and offer owners integrated or manufactured solutions. We see sub-trades increasingly stepping into BIM and mass customized solutions. We also see some of these firms moving upstream in the value chain and providing design and engineering expertise to architects and engineers. The picture will look like the one that McGraw Hill's Steve Jones paints: An owner will work with an architect or contractor to develop a model that provides the clear concept, 30 percent of the project (to the point of the traditional design development phase), and then bring in sub-trades with sophisticated BIM capabilities and CNC equipment.

We can see large AE firms providing complete integrated design and fabrication of buildings as systems. Some of these large firms already use a similar approach for large industrial projects. We also see some of the furniture manufacturers who provide interior building systems expanding further and leveraging their engineering sophistication and equipment capacity. Some of the larger national construction firms might explore partnering with a furniture manufacturer as part of their integrated supply chain, and using BIM to deliver precision ductwork, plumbing, millwork, access flooring, and interior walls—and, oh yes, furniture—as part of an integrated and modular interior system.

Today, the industry is waiting for architects to approach buildings more like an engineer integrating various systems. It is waiting for construction to talk about buildings in common sense language, where a wall is a wall and not a parade of trades. It is waiting for an integrated pricing approach. It is waiting for contractors who can pull all of this together into an integrated delivery model.

The technology is ahead of the process, format, and culture, yes. But that is changing quickly.

Chapter 14 Key 9: Workplace Productivity

"Your environment produces your experiences. Your experiences stimulate your convictions and opinions, and these convictions, in turn, help to reinforce values. Values are the ideas in which you really do believe and for which you are willing to take action."

—Michael Vance, former dean of Disney University

Barbara is vice president of real estate. While planning her company's corporate relocation, she goes over the numbers with her broker. So far, there has been no announcement to the employees of a corporate move. Too many details remained undecided, and it was not worth the distraction and speculation that would occur.

The selection was narrowed to three locations, all of which were in the target area. Barbara's mandate is to reduce the real estate cost by 10 percent. The developer's architect created some test fit drawings, simple plans with boxes to represent offices drawn in the space. Now the exercise was to see which option would allow for the most efficient number of offices per square feet. Barbara and the broker compare the plans and the features of each building. "Option two will fit 20 offices more than the others with a slightly smaller floor plate. With all things being equal, this looks like the building to choose."

The broker closes the deal and secures an increased but average build-out allowance. He sits down with Barbara to begin the process of selecting an architect, then a contractor. Barbara has a nagging feeling that something had been left out of the equation, but she and the broker have been through this drill before: take the puzzle of a new space and try to give each group as much as possible within the constraints of available space and working within the corporate standards, and of course, the budget. No, everything was in place. She shrugged off her doubts and went back to work.

Way back in Chapter 2, Vice President of Worldwide Real Estate for Cisco Systems Mark Golan[1] had this to say: "About 60 percent of the office space that companies pay so dearly for is now a dead zone of darkened doorways and wasting cubes." And although Barbara doesn't know it yet, that's exactly where her project is headed. The element she left out of her equation was a big one: the effect that her building would have on the human performance of the people who would work there.

This story brings us to the final element in the commercial real estate revolution: workplace productivity. It is the enormous iceberg that lies beneath all the effort that goes into the design and construction of a building and its interior space. It's strange but true: With all the talk about innovation and workplace performance and with all of the courses in productivity that architects and engineers take in design school, in real life the design and construction of buildings and spaces seldom *really* uses human performance as the driving criteria. Why? Because the system for building and leasing is only tied to this bigger picture through a spreadsheet.

A PRODUCTIVE WORKPLACE DOES NOT HAVE TO COST MORE

The idea should be simple: We create buildings to improve the work and life that goes on inside. Many companies even have mission statements that tell the world, "Our people are our greatest asset." However, when it comes to the most important tool that helps people perform, we change our tune. Not intentionally, it's just that the system of real estate transactions causes good people to make bad decisions. The capital expenditure that we want to minimize is disconnected from the people it is meant to empower. It is the same kind of disconnection that led Barbara to bid the project and select a team of strangers to design and build it. She won't see the quality of the team relationships or their individual capabilities; yet these will determine the success of her project.

This is no way to run an industry.

Tim Springer, president of Hero Inc., is recognized as one of the top experts in the world on issues of work behavior and the professional environment. He explains that according to general accounting practice, buildings are classified as "sunk cost," something to minimize. One developer on our team shared how a global client measures the productivity of their real estate: "By the cost per square foot per employee." If that is the measure, then what is the objective? To reduce cost.

Corporate real estate executives often talk the talk about productive work spaces, and they know some of the template approaches toward popular thinking about productive work spaces: open spaces, more meeting area, good lighting, and making sure that the word "collaborative" is thrown in. But real estate decisions always get down to the same thing: reducing cost and speed to market.

Years ago, Robert Probst, the father of open office systems, had this to say about offices: "Today's office is a wasteland. It saps vitality, blocks talent, frustrates accomplishment. It is the daily scene of unfulfilled intentions and effort." His words still ring true today.

Ironically, Gensler's 2008 *Workplace Survey* reports that high-performing companies score much better on their facilities than average companies, showing increased profits of 37 percent to 75 percent (Figure 14.1). The survey also shows that higher scores on their facility assessment correspond to stronger employee engagement, based on Gallup's Q12 survey.[2] So what's holding everybody back?

The same paradigm straitjacket that afflicts design and impedes smooth construction prevents most companies from getting the most out of their greatest asset: their people. The quality of the work environment is disconnected from factors that drive real estate decisions; in other words, the tail wags the dog. Buildings follow pro formas, spreadsheets, and hard numbers, and the employees fall by the wayside.

The truth is that buildings today are not, ultimately, designed for people. They are designed to produce a return on investment. Once that is secured, it is *then* up to the people who work inside to make the best of it. But this kind of swap is a false choice. The tradeoff between

Figure 14.1   Gensler's Work Place Index Measure of
Profit Increase

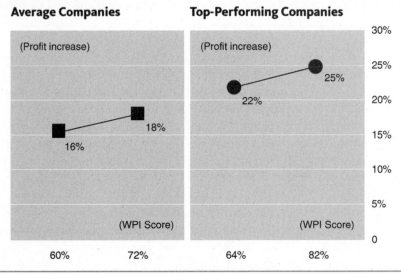

cost, quality, and time is another false choice when working within a
trust-based paradigm. Creating a work-enhancing environment does
not equal a sunk cost to the company.[3]

We've described buildings in this book as networks of commitments
and a social enterprise. Is it possible to import this same kind of
thinking when we approach designing the space in which people
will work and live in? Vivian Loftness, professor of architecture at
Carnegie Mellon University and senior researcher at the Center for
Building Performance and Diagnostics, explains the challenge that the
industry meets when speaking to corporate decision makers. "Ask an
executive why they would buy a $30,000 car when you could buy a
$10,000 car, and they could list off the reasons. Similarly, if you ask
them why they would invest in a $3,000 laptop when they could easily
buy one for under $1,000, and again, they can list off the reasons.
But that same executive will choose a $100-per-square-foot building
over a $300-per-square-foot building because they don't have a similar
means for comparison." Location, location, location—and rent, image, and operating costs—drive the decision.

The workplace is also a network of commitments. The design of that
space is a social enterprise. The same paradigm that creates more than

50 percent waste in the design and delivery of buildings carries over into our work and workplace. The opportunities for change based on the keys we've outlined in this book have implications for truly transformative opportunities (see Figure 14.2).

THE BIG IDEAS

As a business owner, your biggest investment is people. Compared to what you will spend on your building, how big *is* that investment?

Tim Springer draws this picture: "For every dollar businesses spend, about 85 cents is on people. . . . For every dollar spent on people, about a dime is spent on the work environment. So there's a clear choice: You can spend time and resources shaving pennies off that dime, or invest that dime to get a greater return on effort for the seventy-eight cents you spend on your people."[4] Like construction, workplace performance is a story of waste. Waste is a big idea that reflects the same old thinking at work. The office wasteland that Probst decried is due to the old paradigm that creates the spaces and perpetuates the practices.

When we view the workplace as a network of commitments and different interlocking systems, we begin to see how this relational model for streamlining and improving quality fits. Here are some

Figure 14.2   Carnegie Mellon Study of Cost Distribution

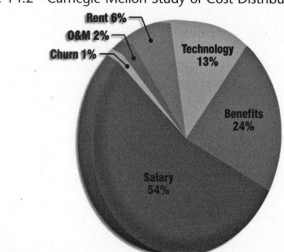

parallels we found when applying Lean thinking to identify sources of waste in the workplace: too much information, redundant, out of date, over specialized, low quality, requiring rework, waiting in the queue, loss in translation, and more effort than needed.

It doesn't have to be this way, and in some industries, it isn't. Today, healthcare systems are beginning to take ideas from the Lean Construction revolution and adopting Lean thinking for their internal operations. We identified 49 healthcare systems with Lean initiatives.

Some other big ideas, we hope, will also influence the future of how we think about workplace productivity.

COGNITIVE ERGONOMICS

Neuroscience is a big idea that is rapidly changing our understanding of how people work and the many modes in which they operate. It combines biology and psychology, revealing how the brain works best and under what conditions. The application for the work environment is called cognitive ergonomics. In a chapter entitled "Cognitive Ergonomics" for Kimball International's book *Minds at Work*, author Jan Lauwereyn[5] frames the opportunity ahead: "I think what you can do for the mind in a work setting is to understand its strengths and its weaknesses, its constraints, and make sure that you present things, and stimuli and tasks and whatever, in a format that is most suitable for the brain or mind to work in."

Brain science tells us that there are distinct thinking patterns for different generations: the reading generation (the Boomers' parents), the television generation (the Boomers), and now the iGeneration (the Boomers' kids). Two recent books by neuropsychologists, *iBrain*[6] and *Proust and the Squid*,[7] discuss how distinctly these different minds work and see the world. Traditional strategies for melding and harnessing different generations have never considered that the people who occupy an office might speak the same language but live in genuinely different worlds.

VISUAL RICH ENVIRONMENTS

The concept of "visual rich environments" is a big idea that follows the same tributary fed by Lean thinking and the new neuroscience. Lean uses visual tools to simplify complex processes and to bring the invisible dynamics within processes to the surface. The iGeneration is coming of age immersed in a multimedia and multimodal environment. They will not only be comfortable working within this context, but will work best with a variety of ambient visual cues. But those of us who were raised first to read or to watch television will find such environments stressful, intrusive, and disorienting. Organizations like Yahoo! are experimenting with more visual versus text communication, and finding that it is more inclusive for a global organization.

ASSESSMENT TOOLS

Assessment tools are another—though hidden—substantial new idea. Organizations like Gensler, Haworth, and Gallup offer user-friendly online tools for organizations to better understand the effectiveness of their facility, the dynamic between different internal subcultures, and the extent to which people are tapping into their natural strengths to accomplish their work. It is hidden because—again—the old paradigm gets in the way.

These tools answer questions that real estate executives don't ask. They are also considered an add-on cost. Because of denominator management, real estate decision makers cannot correlate how spending the money will change the output of the organization (even though surveys say they believe it will).

When assessment tools *are* used, however, they are often neutered because of the way organizations apply them. These tools are most effective when developing the business case, not simply as a programming tool once the building is selected and most of the parameters are already defined. Earlier, Swinerton's Dan Gonzales described how BIM's usefulness is neutered when they are brought in at the design phase. Jill, the CPA, described the same obstacle related to optimizing the tax strategy for a project. The principle of early collaboration includes workplace performance.

Furniture manufacturers with similar tools confront an additional set of challenges. Manufacturers have studied the workplace and the way in which people work and live in the environment since open-planned systems were introduced more than 40 years ago. Some have published insightful studies, and some have developed software to survey, analyze, and aid planning. These assessment tools examine workflow, communication flow, work culture integration, and effective use of space and recommend the best use of their equipment (furniture). Some of their tools have evolved into a rich knowledge base that few companies tap into or even know to tap into.

The system of vendor selection and bidding prevents most manufacturers from ever presenting this option. It may be included as a footnote service, or it may be used as a loss leader with the hope that the client will see it as a value-added service. The current paradigm, unfortunately, puts the wrong people in the decision chair to see its value. Like architects, the service is viewed as a line-item expense. If brought in early as one tool for developing the business case, they could easily prove their worth and set metrics to measure that worth.

The old system creates a false choice, because it views planning interior space as a transaction. Without partners that trust each other and the process of early collaboration, there is little chance of making any significant difference in workplace performance. Architects and manufacturers will try their best to improve a company's work environment, but they must do so blindfolded and with one hand tied behind their backs.

There are early adopters in this arena similar to the owners we cite throughout the book who have changed their paradigm for construction. These early adopters do see dramatic tangible results. We will provide a brief review of those who are leading this field of work and some of the companies that are benefiting. Assessment tools, if used in the context of trust-based teams and early collaboration, will not result in higher costs.

THE OWNER'S MIND SHIFT

Improving workplace performance—just like all of the other revolutions described in this book—requires a mind shift. In fact, it requires several shifts.

Mind Shift: Tools Enable Collective Design

The first is a shift away from seeing workplace performance as something that focuses on tools and moving toward adopting a mindset of an entity that is *enabled* by tools. It begins by viewing the process as a collective enterprise among strategic partners, not a transaction that is ordered off of a menu of services.

Mind Shift: Work as a Whole

It's also a shift away from viewing tasks as a measure of productivity to seeing work in its entirety. We discovered that lesson in the construction process. Optimizing individual trades at the expense of an area—or the project as a whole—turns counterproductive. Tim Springer has developed a context-based method for measuring performance that is similar to the way Lean Construction approaches outcomes. He shifts the paradigm from productivity as a mechanistic way to measure output over input, to one of performance instead. "Performance is more about outcomes, and less about outputs. Every company can measure performance. If you don't know how, ask the people who do the job and they'll tell you the best way to measure their performance. They know what it takes to perform." This sounds very similar to Lean Construction's Last Planner approach. Springer goes on to describe performance as task- and situation-specific, using an operational definition rather than an equation.

Mind Shift: A New Definition of Value

A third shift will create a new definition of value in addition to measuring the number of people per square feet or the cost per person per square feet. Vivian Loftness, of the Center for Building Performance Diagnostics, speaks to this point. Her organization helps companies measure the tangible data points to evaluate the relationship of their space to performance. When a company begins to decide where they can get the greatest return for their investment, Vivian points out the relative cost of energy, rent, and employee productivity: $2 for energy, $20 for rent, and $200 for productivity. Once companies understand how to decode the makeup of the $200-per-square-foot cost, then they can begin to shift their focus to leveraging productivity, where the return is exponentially greater.

Tim Springer describes the need for businesses to radically change their paradigm of a building from one of rigid, fixed cost that resists organizational change to one of a flexible, adaptable tool that continually realigns the environment to the changing realities of the marketplace. "Business today is focused on what's new, fast, flexible, changing, independent of time and place, and able to do more with less. This is juxtaposed to the characteristics of traditional facilities— very long life cycles, aging inventory, difficult to change, place dependent, and costly."

Tim goes on to describe the need for adopting a process that abandons the old method of taking a snapshot of a particular moment's need and then carrying that quickly aging snapshot through the 12- to 18-month cycle of planning before move-in. Collaborative teams, in contrast, are able to remain flexible and not lock in to a particular solution until far later in the process because of the nature of iterative design and tools like BIM.

Mind Shift: A Flexible Platform for Change

Viewing interior space as a flexible platform for change is another key mind shift. Some of the Mindshift members describe how using parametric pro forma tools and rapid prototyping allow planning to occur closer to the time of need and provide flexibility to quickly respond to changes in requirement. One of the important tools for making this kind of flexibility possible is moving away from traditional fixed-wall construction and above-ceiling utilities.

Companies invest months in planning a new space and attempt to address change by using cubicles where they can. Some change is tolerated before ordering furniture and awarding the construction contracts. At some point, however, the owner tells their users that no more modifications are allowed until after move-in. Cubicles tethered by data cabling and electrical connections may be movable, but not without some hassle and cost. Fixed-wall private offices and conference rooms are inflexible and, therefore, costly and disruptive to change.

However, there are solutions available to create a fully adaptable interior with pre-manufactured movable wall systems, raised floors that accommodate air, data, and electrical, modular millwork, and modular programmable electrical infrastructures. Each of the major manufacturers provides solutions for this new paradigm of space. Herman Miller describes a common goal:

• Enable people who use buildings to be active agents in the creation and evolution of the spaces that support their activities.

- Preserve and improve the economic equation for people who build and own buildings.
- Lessen the environmental impact of the built environment—from construction through continuous use.[8]

Design firms are working collaboratively with owners and the manufacturers, both to design solutions (as we found with David Thurm at the New York Times Headquarters) and to coordinate the different platforms offered. Be prepared, however, to have to swim upstream against the old paradigm block of landlords, developers, and brokers. The best strategy is to take a strong stance and work to develop that strategic partnership early. The team will be able to address these hurdles if brought in early.

Mind Shift: A New View of Work

A final mind shift addresses an outdated view of work. Futurist and Mindshift Thought Leader Rex Miller says, "The problem is that a lot of work styles and approaches were invented more than 50 years ago, and they are not in synch with what's going on today."[9] He describes seven conditions that redefine the current business environment:

1. **Interconnection.** Instead of living in a domino world, where one change logically causes the next, we have entered a chain-reaction world of exponential outcomes. In this brave new world, interdependent relationships can exhibit extraordinary cohesion or, if destabilized, spiral out of control.
2. **Complexity.** Complex systems behave not as a collection of separate parts but as a whole. When you cut down a forest, divide a family, change a line of computer code, or protect a threatened industry with tariffs, you set in motion a ripple effect. Scenario planning and parametric modeling is replacing spreadsheet analysis and insular strategic planning to better understand the impact of decisions within a market, among stakeholders and within an organization.
3. **Acceleration.** Change accelerates with each new technology and concept, and these changes have a compounding effect. As our lives become more interconnected, our actions get cycled back through our living and technological networks, and become amplified and accelerated.

4. **Intangibility.** We're moving away from a tangible world we can touch and hold to a world that operates on intangibles like information, potential, innovation, and reputation. We are moving away from tangible and rational measure of value.

5. **Convergence.** Convergence is an inherent property of our digital medium of communication. Print, graphics, sound, and data can all reside in a single medium that is reproduced through a common digital language of bits and bytes. That means that we will no longer process these sensory experiences separately. It also means that past boundaries of knowledge and organizations blur, crumble, and eventually integrate.

6. **Immediacy.** The time it takes to absorb and adjust to digitally paced activities grows shorter. How do we function in an environment where reality leaves us little time or no time for reflection but "changes ceaselessly, unfolding in an irregular, disorderly, unpredictable manner despite our vain attempts to ensure the contrary?"

7. **Unpredictability.** Complex and highly interactive systems are unpredictable. Kenneth Boulding, renowned economist and scholar, says, "the search for ultimately stable parameters in evolutionary systems is futile, for they probably do not exist." In the old physics, every action has an equal and opposite reaction. When you drop a rock from a window, you can predict with accuracy when it will hit the ground and with what impact. But each factor, player, condition, issue, or option, when interconnected, exponentially multiplies the number of outcomes. Within complex systems, actions often create unintended outcomes.[10]

Companies that are actively dealing with these realities are asking their people to work differently, to adapt, to continually learn, to innovate, and to take initiative. Unless that vision and mandate filters down to transform the environments in which people work, however, companies are asking their troops to take the battlefield using conventional weapons against a fluid marketplace that favors agility and rapid deployment.

Many of the new solutions manufacturers provide —both in decision-making and as products—"enable people who use buildings to be active agents in the creation and evolution of the spaces that support their activities."

The leaders in the field of workplace performance and productivity are relatively few, but they are very important to this transformation. Together, they offer a surprising breadth and depth of information.

Their efforts are deeper than we can cover in this chapter, but resources are listed in the appendix.

MAPPING WORKPLACE IMPROVEMENT

There is no lack of research and case studies showing that better facilities improve an organization's performance and bottom line, as evidence by the following:

- The Rocky Mountain Institute tracked productivity gains of 6 percent with improvements in thermal control, lighting, acoustics, and indoor quality.
- Johnson Controls reports that indoor environments affect human performance from 5 percent to 15 percent.
- Citibank reduced their space by 23 percent and reduced churn costs by 76 percent and reduced the average cost of a workstation by 20 percent.[11]
- The USGBC provides the case study of West Bend Insurance that documented a 16 percent increase in productivity moving into a new 150,000-square-foot green building. The increase represents more than $2 million a year.

And then there's the Aardex story we promised earlier. The book *User Effective Buildings* shares the following:

In the early summer of 2003, the Albuquerque Office of Hearings and Appeals moved into their new User Effective® facility, developed by Aardex. Because the realized increases in productivity and overall savings in salary expense, the cost per square foot of combined resources (facility plus personnel) fell from $228 per square foot to $187 per square foot. The overall cost to process each case fell from $995 per case to $912 per case.

Although this is a case study in a public sector business and we do not have the profit side of a traditional free market business model, we can apply conservative cost/revenue ratio and recognize a 28.6 percent increase in output (revenue) at a 9.1 percent decrease in cost.

A second case study from the book references a 7.5 percent increase in productivity with the redesign of an improved lower-energy lighting system.[12]

In a Gallup report, results from New Century Financial reflected that those employees who did not feel engaged (or felt disengaged) with the company performed 23 percent and 28 percent lower than employees who did feel engaged. Gensler tracked the profit gap between companies scoring over 72 percent on their Work Place Index compared to those scoring 60 percent and below, and found that the profit for these the higher-scoring companies ranged from 37 percent to 75 percent more.

The numbers from the research and case studies that show improved productivity would fill a volume or two. In connecting the dots, however, we found some common area headings upon which these studies focused. This framework will help owners and professionals develop their strategies, create meaningful metrics, and track performance.

CATEGORIES FOR IMPROVEMENT

This section provides some of the generalized categories from the research above that can and *should* be included when planning a new building or space. It not an inclusive list, but you will find that it covers a range. We found that organizations that successfully applied these categories took a simple, though not easy, approach. They set benchmarks by taking a pre-move assessment of how they rated in each of the categories important to them. A strategy for how to use the design of new space to improve these factors was developed. Post-occupancy surveys were then administered and used to see if targets were reached and if adjustments were needed.

> **Health and well-being** includes factors like improved and natural lighting, air quality, acoustics, and thermal control. Testing for sick building syndrome (SBS)[13] is a real and underestimated threat to health related to air quality. The World Health Organization reports that up to 30 percent of new buildings worldwide suffer from SBS, and older buildings are more likely to have inadequate air systems. This also includes proper ergonomics (seating and adjustable work areas).
>
> **Process improvement** considers the flow of work. It applies tools like Lean thinking to improve that flow.
>
> **Cognitive ergonomics** attempts to identify the strengths of employees through a wide range of assessment tools, and it considers

how to redesign work and team configurations to allow people to perform through their natural strengths.

Work dynamics looks at different modes of work to assess how well a facility supports those modes: social, focused work, learning and collaboration. It also reflects on how well a facility provides zones for people to work in proximity, both casually and in a broader public context. We saw on the construction side that "projects as a social enterprise" provided co-location for an ongoing project, visual tools for group communication, and helped to create a sense of cohesion.

Cultural effectiveness deals with cultural clarity, integration, and helping each subgroup in a company take advantage of their unique identity. Cultural effectiveness includes understanding and working with the distinct orientations of the reading, television, and digital generations.

Effective space addresses the right kind of space, the proper amount of space, and the flow and efficient interaction with the space. It helps companies find the right balance between each of these different kinds, and it also deals with the integration of technology. The most important factor to consider is how easily the space allows for change.

Human resource factors for effective space include reducing absenteeism, workers' compensation, turnover, and improving recruitment.

Sustainability has become a key driver for facility effectiveness and is tied to workplace performance. We have already covered this topic in detail in Chapter 8.

CASE STUDY: HIGH-TECH TELECOMMUNICATIONS FIRM EXPANSION

A large high-tech telecommunications firm set a goal to reduce turnover and improve recruiting by experimenting in a new expansion facility. They researched the market to compare the work environment they were providing with two major competitors. The firm had hired 2,000 people the previous year, and 1,000 were replacing people who left. Their churn rate was 20 percent.

Further research led the company to contact some Wall Street analysts and ask how they could compare the relative strength of one firm in their sector to another. They learned that since talent was a major competitive advantage, these Wall Street analysts kept tabs on some of the major recruiting firms in their industry. The recruiters told the analysts that new recruits based about 50 percent of their decision on the total compensation package, about 25 percent on their direct supervisor, and about 25 percent on the facility. From its own survey, this telecom company also discovered that its facilities ranked the lowest between the two other competitors, but its compensation was in line, and its front-line managers also received high marks.

The end of the story went counter to what the firm's consultants and suppliers had anticipated. While their competitors were going to smaller, more open spaces, this firm chose larger, adaptable private spaces. The reason? The employees in this space were programmers and engineers. The company surveyed similar employees in private offices, and it found that those in open-plan offices were interrupted at a much higher rate and that it took a programmer 20 minutes after the interruption to mentally rework back to where they were when they were interrupted. These programmers were losing two to three hours of productivity to their counterparts, and they showed a higher level of dissatisfaction with their office setup.

Homework pays off.

JOIN THE REVOLUTION!

The *Commercial Real Estate Revolution* is, in essence, a simple concept: The old design-bid-build paradigm had its day, but it has outlived its usefulness and is getting in the way of the kind of real change that can transform the way we build buildings and the way we live and work in them. The revolution begins with transforming our behavior and relationships.

The new paradigm, based on trust, collaboration, and sustainability, creates buildings that go up on time and within or under budget; are healthy to build and healthy to use; save money up front and over the long run; and create workspaces where people not only survive, but thrive. The transforming potential behind these principles and displayed in the many stories is real and available to anyone—today! In fact, these lessons are applicable to many businesses and industries struggling with similar challenges. Mindshift is not offering a quick fix or a silver bullet. We are offering a different set of assumptions and examples of those who are disrupting the status quo with extra-ordinary results.

We hope this book has provoked your thinking and provided you with the ideas, tools, and motivation you need to begin exploring how you want to do business, and to join in the conversation. If you would like to find more materials, support, and join the conversation you link to www.thecrerevolution.com.

Individuals can make a difference. We look forward to seeing you along the journey.

Appendix 1: Mindshift Core Team

Ben Weeks—Principal
Aardex (303) 327-4458
ben.weeks@aardex.com
Developer

Craig Janssen—Principal
Acoustic Dimension (972) 239-1505
cjanssen@acousticdimensions.com
Acoustic, Sound and Lighting Engineering

Markku Allison, AIA—Resource Architect
American Institute of Architects (202) 626-7487
mallison@aia.org
Association

Marilyn Archer—Principal
Gensler (713) 844-0000
marilyn_archer@gensler.com
Architect

Dean Strombom—Principal
Gensler (713) 844-0000
dean_strombom@gensler.com
Architect

Bill Black—National Director Strategic Business Solution
Haworth (403) 203-6158
bill.black@Haworth.com
Manufacturer

Mabel Casey—Vice President Global Marketing and Sales Support
Haworth (616) 393-3343
mabel.casey@haworth.com
Manufacturer

Lydia Knowles—Marketing/Project Management Specialist
Haworth (616) 393-1415
lydia.knowles@haworth.com
Manufacturer

Jabir Al-Hilal—Director Construction Tax Planning Services
KPMG (713) 319-2236
jal-hilali@kpmg.com
Construction Tax Planning

Kyle Davy—President
Kyle V. Davy Consulting (510) 525-7737
kyle@kylevdavy.com
Leadership and AEC Practice Consulting

Ray Lucchesi—Principal
Lucchesi, Galati (702) 263-7111
lucchesi@lgainc.com
Architect

Rex Miller—Thought Leader
Mindshift (214) 498-3055
rex@rexmiller.net
Futurist, Author, and Consultant

Susan Szenasy—Chief Editor
Metropolis Magazine (212) 886-2531
sss@metropolismag.com
Magazine

Mark Charette—President, C.E.O.
Solidus, Inc. (860) 257-4900
mcharette@gosolidus.com
Design, Build & Furnish Contractor

Ric Nelson—Vice President of Development Services
Transwestern (214) 446-4543
ric.nelson@transwestern.net
Developer

Mark Iammarino—Vice President/GM
Turner Special Projects (312) 327-2010
miammarino@tcco.com
General Contractor

Les Shepherd—Chief Architect
U.S. General Services Administration (202) 501-1888
les.shepherd@gsa.gov
Architect/Owner

Kurt Young—Principal
Walter P Moore (713) 630-7300
kyoung@walterpmoore.com
Structural Engineering

Appendix 2: Mindshift Advisors

The following individuals were important contributors and advisors to our research. They represent individuals who are early adopters and experts. We appreciate their advice, stories, and insight.

Andrew Fisher—CAD Manager, LEED AP
Anshen + Allen (617) 451-6990
andrew.fisher@anshen.com
Architectural Firm

John Paul Beitler III—Vice President
Beitler Properties LLC (312) 654-4456
jpbeitler@beitlerproperties.com
Developer

David Kievet—Group President
The Boldt Company (920) 739-6321
dave.kievet@boldt.com
Consulting, Technical, and Construction Solutions

Deke Smith—Executive Director
buildingSMART Alliance (202) 289-7800
dsmith@nibs.org
Non-profit Organization to Coordinate Industry Transformation Initiatives

Vinson A. Chapman—Principal
CCM Consulting Group (972) 304-0888
vchapman@ccmcg.biz
Construction Auditing

Vivian Loftness—Senior Researcher
Center for Building Performance and Diagnostics (412) 268-2350
loftness@cmu.edu
Research Institute

Larry Fees—former Vice President of Real Estate
Compuware (248) 320-1643
larry.fees@glrg.biz
Owner and Commercial Real Estate Consultant

David Dillard—President
CSD Architecture (214) 220-1800
ddillard@csdarch.com
Architect

Tim McGinn—Principal
Cohos Evamy (403) 541-5462
mcginnt@cohos-evamy.com
Mechanical, Electrical, and Plumbing Engineering

Randy Thompson—Area Leader, Client Solutions
Cushman Wakefield (972) 663-9740
randy.thompson@cushwake.com
Global Real Estate Solutions

Doug Harden—Principal
Douglas R. Harden, AIA (469) 939-8018
drharden@msn.com
Consulting, Client Representation,
    Program-Project Management

Dean Reed—Lean Construction Coordinator
DPR (650) 474-1450
deanr@dprinc.com
General Contractor

Bob Mauck AIA, PE—Vice President, Virtual
    Design and Construction
Ghafari (313) 441-3000
rmauck@ghafari.com
Architectural and Engineering

Tim Springer—President
Human Environment Research Organization,
    Inc. (630) 761-2665
tim.springer@hero-inc.com
Research and Consulting for High Performance Workplaces

Greg Wilkinson—CEO
Hill & Wilkinson, Ltd. (214) 299-4311
gwilkinson@hill-wilkinson.com
General Contractor

Scott Simpson—FAIA, LEED AP, Senior Director
KlingStubbins (617) 491-6450
ssimpson@klingstubbins.com
Architect

Gary Hamor—President and CEO
Lean Practices, Inc. (970) 535-9230
garyh@leanpractices.com
Lean Process Consulting

William Lichtig—Attorney
McDonough Holland & Allen PC (916) 444-3900
wlichtig@mhalaw.com
Law Firm

Stephen Jones—Senior Director Business Development
McGraw Hill Construction (212) 904-3755
steve_jones@mcgraw-hill.com
Construction and Architectural Resources

David Thurm—Senior Vice President of Operations
New York Times Corporation (212) 556-1714
thurm@nytimes.com
Owner

Andy Fuhrman
Open Standards Consortium for Real Estate, Inc. (831) 458-3346
andy.fuhrman@oscre.org
Deliver global standards for exchanging
    electronic real property information
    and drive their adoption

Kimon Onuma—FAIA, President
Onuma, Inc. (626) 793-7400
kg@onuma.com
Architect and BIMStorm Creator

Arol Wolford—SmartBIM
Solutions Group Reed Construction Data (770) 417-4243
arol.worlford@reedbusiness.com
BIM Expert, Industry Consultant and former Revit Board Member

Dan Gonzales—Corporate Manager of Virtual Design Construction
Swinerton (925) 689-2336
dgonzales@swinerton.com
General Contractor

James Timberlake and Stephen Kieran—Partners
Kieran and Timberlake (215) 922-6600
timberlake@kierantimberlake.com
Architects and Authors

George Zettel—Construction Manager/Lean Champion
Turner Construction (916) 554-7919
gzettel@tcco.com
General Contractor

MINDSHIFT CONTRIBUTORS
We would like to thank the following individuals for their support providing articles, proofing our chapters, contacts with individuals, and their opinions on what we were thinking.

Larry Canfield—President, Canfields
Tyler Adams—Project Manager, Centerpoint Builders Ltd.
Julius Gombos—Executive Managing Director, Cushman & Wakefield LePage
Monte Chapin—Architectural Consultant, Graphisoft
Kevin Kampschroer—Director, Research & Expert Services, GSA
Carl Chinn—Project Manager, Long Building Intelligence
Bob Theodore—Director of Dealer Development, Kimball Office Furniture
Andy Fuhrman—CEO, OSCRE Americas, Inc.
Wes Garwood—Senior Associate, Page Southerland Page
Peter Papesch—Principal, Papesch Associates
Steve Fridsma—Worship Environments Architect, ProgressiveAE
Cathy Hutchison—Random Thought Connector, Strategic Dimensions
Raymond Kahl—Principal, Urban Design
Clifford Bourland—Architecture & Design Editor, Urban Design

Appendix 3: Recommended Reading

Leadership

Bonabeau, Eric, Marco Dorigo, and Guy Theraulaz. *Swarm Intelligence: From Natural to Artificial Systems (Santa Fe Institute Studies in the Sciences of Complexity Proceedings)*. New York: Oxford University Press, USA, 1999.

Brown, Tim. "Design Thinking." *Harvard Business Review*: 84–92.

Christensen, Clayton M. *The Innovator's Dilemma: When New Technologies Cause Great Firms to Fail*. New York: Harvard Business School Press, 1997.

Cramer, James P., and Scott Simpson. *The Next Architect: A New Twist on the Future of Design*. Atlanta: Greenway Communications, 2006.

Davy, Kyle V., and Susan L. Harris. *Value Redesigned: New Models for Professional Practice*. Atlanta: Greenway Communications, 2005.

Greenleaf, Robert K. *The Power of Servant Leadership*. San Francisco, CA: Berrett-Koehler Publishers, 1998.

Kim, W. Chan, and Renee Mauborgne. *Blue Ocean Strategy: How to Create Uncontested Market Space and Make Competition Irrelevant*. New York: Harvard Business School Press, 2005.

Merrill, Rebecca R., and Stephen M.R.Covey. *The Speed of Trust*. New York: Simon & Schuster, 2006.

O'Reilly, Charles, and Michael Tushman."The Ambidextrous Organization." *Harvard Business Review*: 1–8.

Rogers, Everett, and Everett M. Rogers. *Diffusion of Innovations* (5th ed). New York: Free Press, 2003.

Schrage, Michael. *No More Teams!: Mastering the Dynamics of Creative Collaboration.* New York: Currency Doubleday, 1995.

Schrage, Michael. *Serious Play: How the World's Best Companies Simulate to Innovate.* New York: Harvard Business School Press, 1999.

Story, Derrick."Swarm Intelligence: An Interview with Eric Bonabeau | O'Reilly Media." OpenP2P.com www.openp2p.com—bonabeau.html (February 21, 2003).

Tapscott, Don. *Grown Up Digital: How the Net Generation is Changing the World.* New York: McGraw-Hill, 2008.

Thurm, David. "Master of the House: Why a Company Should Take Control of Its Building Projects." *Harvard Business Review*: 1–9.

Green

Anderson, Ray. *Mid-Course Correction: Toward a Sustainable Enterprise: The Interface Model.* White River Junction, VT: Peregrinzilla Press, 1998.

Burr, Andrew."CoStar Study Finds Energy Star, LEED Bldgs. Outperform Peers – CoStar Group." CoStar—Commercial Real Estate Information Company. www.costar.com—Article.aspx (April 26, 2008).

Davis Langdon."Cost Benefits of Going Green." http://www.davislangdon.com/ANZ/Research/Research-Finder/Info-Data-Publications/CostofGoingGreen/ (April 1, 2007).

Cassidy, Robert (Editor in Chief) "Green Buildings and the Bottom Line." BDC Network. http://www.capitalmarketspartnership.com/UserFiles/Admin%20Building%20Design%20Construction%202006%20White%20Paper.pdf (November, 1, 2006).

"Green Building Smart Market Report 2006." McGraw-Hill. www.construction.com—default.asp.

Hawken, Paul. *Blessed Unrest: How the Largest Movement in the World Came into Being and Why No One Saw It Coming.* New York: Viking, 2007.

Hawken, Paul, Amory Lovins, and L. Hunter Lovins. *Natural Capitalism: Creating the Next Industrial Revolution.* New York: Back Bay Books, 2000.

Kats, Greg. "Cost and Benefits of Green Buildings. A Report to California's Sustainable Buildings Task Force." California: 1-134.

Laur, Joe, Sara Schley, Peter M. Senge, and Bryan Smith. *The Necessary Revolution: How Individuals And Organizations Are Working Together to Create a Sustainable World.* New York: Currency, 2008.

Integrated Delivery

Elvin, George. *Integrated Practice in Architecture: Mastering Design-Build, Fast-Track, and Building Information Modeling.* New York: Wiley, 2007.

The American Institute of Architects. *Integrated Project Delivery Guide.* Washington, DC: American Institute of Architects, 2007.

The General Services Administration. *The Integrated Workplace: A Comprehensive Approach to Developing Workspace.* Washington, DC: GSA, 1999.

Lichtig, Will."The Integrated Agreement for Lean Project Delivery." McDonough Holland & Allen PC. www.mhalaw.com—ABA_IntegratedAgmt.pdf (June 1, 2006).

Thomsen, Charles. *Program Management*. Washington, DC: AIA, 2008.

Lean Thinking

Ballard, Glenn, and Gregory Howell."Competing Construction Management Paradigms." *Lean Construction Journal 1.1* (2003): 38–45.

Cain, Clive Thomas. *Profitable Partnering for Lean Construction*. Malden, MA: Wiley-Blackwell, 2004.

Kennedy, Michael N. *Product Development for the Lean Enterprise: Why Toyota's System Is Four Times More Productive and How You Can Implement It*. Richmond: Oaklea Press, 2008.

May, Matthew E. *The Elegant Solution: Toyota's Formula for Mastering Innovation*. New York: Free Press, 2006.

Mossman, Alan. "Last Planner: Collaborative Production Planning, Collaborative Programme Coordination." *Lean Construction Institute UK* (Nov. 16, 2007): 1–6.

Workplace Performance

Brinkley, Ian. "Defining the knowledge economy: knowledge economy programme report." Home—The Work Foundation. www.theworkfoundation .com—publicationdetail.aspx (3 July 2006.).

Buckingham, Marcus, and Donald O. Clifton. *Now, Discover Your Strengths*. New York: Free Press, 2001.

Cameron, Kim S., Jeff Degraff, Robert E. Quinn, and Anjan Thakor. *Competing Values Leadership: Creating Value in Organizations (New Horizons in Management)*. London: Edward Elgar Pub. 2007.

Corporation, Aardex. *User Effective Buildings*. St. Paul, MN: Aardex Corporation, 2004.

Horgen, Turid H., Michael L. Joroff, William L. Porter, and Donald A. Schön. *Excellence By Design: Transforming Workplace and Work Practice*. New York: Wiley, 1998.

Loftness, Vivian, Volker Hartkopf, and Beran Gurtekin."Building Investment Decision Support (BIDS): Cost-Benefit Tool to Promote High Performance Components, Flexible Infrastructures and Systems Integration for Sustainable Commercial Buildings and Productive Organizations." Pittsburgh, PA. 1-30.

Minds at Work. Jasper: Kimball Office, 2008.

BIM

Jernigan, Finith E. *BIG BIM little bim* (2nd Ed). Salisbury, MD: 4site Press, 2008.

Jones, Stephen. "Introduction to BIM." *SmartMarket Report Design and Construction Intelligence, 2009*: 1–45.

Smith, Deke, and Alan Edgar."Building Information Modeling (BIM) | Whole Building Design Guide." WBDG—The Whole Building Design Guide. www .wbdg.org—bim.php (July 24, 2008).

Smith, Dana K., and Michael Tardif. *Building Information Modeling: A Strategic Implementation Guide for Architects, Engineers, Constructors, and Real Estate Asset Managers.* New York: Wiley, 2009.

Off-Site Construction

Kieran, Stephen, and James Timberlake. *Refabricating Architecture: How Manufacturing Methodologies are Poised to Transform Building Construction.* New York: McGraw-Hill Professional, 2003.

Industry Review

Lepatner, Barry B. *Broken Buildings, Busted Budgets: How to Fix America's Trillion-Dollar Construction Industry.* Chicago: University of Chicago Press, 2008.

Products and Players' Trends—Outlook 2009—Research & Analytics— McGraw-Hill Construction. Welcome to the McGraw-Hill Information Center.construction.ecnext.com—summary_0249–295662_ITM_analytics (October 23, 2008).

Thaler, Richard H. *The Winner's Curse.* Princeton: Princeton University Press, 1994.

Appendix 4: Website Resources and Links

Mindshift Resources

The Commercial Real Estate Revolution Website
www.thecrerevolution.com

Mindshift Wiki—Free Resources and Downloads
www.mindshiftwiki.com

Mindshift Blog—Current News and Trends
www.mindshiftblog.com

Website for Rex Miller—Mindshift Thought Leader
www.rexmiller.net

Sustainability

United States Green Building Council (USGBC)
www.usgbc.org

Architecture 2030
www.architecture2030.org

AIA's 50 to 50 Initiative
www.aia.org/fiftytofifty

Rocky Mountain Institute
http://bet.rmi.org

Energy Star
www.energystar.gov

Green Wikia
http://green.wikia.com—Wikia_Green

Noe 21
www.noe21.org—joomla

Green Building Initiative
www.thegbi.org

Green Building Services
www.greenbuildingservices.com

American Society of Heating, Refrigerating, and Air-Conditioning Engineers
(ASHRAE)
www.ashrae.org/

World Changing
www.worldchanging.com

Tree Hugger
www.treehugger.com

Center for Sustainable Systems
http://css.snre.umich.edu

John T. Lyle Center for Regenerative Studies
www.csupomona.edu—~crs

The Institute for Market Transformation to Sustainability
http://mts.sustainableproducts.com—index.html

Interface Raise
www.interfaceglobal.com—InterfaceRaise.aspx

Natural Resource Defense Council
www.nrdc.org—default.asp

Deconstruction Institute
www.deconstructioninstitute.com—calc1.php

Integrated Project Delivery
Australia Project Alliance Guide
http://omswiki.pbwiki.com—Trust-Based+Agreements

American Institute of Architects Integrated Project Delivery Resources
www.aia.org—AIAS078435

PD Guidelines
www.aia.org/ipd

Podcasts
www.aia.org—pod_default

AGC Consensus Docs
www.consensusdocs.org—index.html

Architectural Record—IPD
http://archrecord.construction.com

Strategic Forum—UK
www.strategicforum.org.uk—home.html

Team Focus Group
www.teamfocus.org—partnering.html

4SiteSystems
www.4sitesystems.org

Lean Construction
International Group for Lean Construction
www.iglc.net

Lean Construction Institute
www.leanconstruction.org

BIM
AEC Bytes
www.aecbytes.com

American Institute of Architects—Preparing for BIM
www.aia.org—AIAS077631

Change the World 2008
http://changetheworld2008.ning.com

bimx
http://bimx.blogspot.com

Center for Virtual Architecture (CVA)
http://cva.ap.buffalo.edu

Wikitecture
www.studiowikitecture.com—index.php

Workplace Performance
Lawrence Berkeley National Laboratory: Commercial Building Ventilation and
Indoor Environmental Quality
http://eetd.lbl.gov—viaq.

Lawrence Berkley National Laboratory: Building Technologies Department
http://btech.lbl.gov

The Future of Work
www.thefutureofwork.net

New Ways of Work—New WOW
www.newwow.net—public

CoreClarity
www.coreclarity.net

Human Environment Research Organization (HERO)
www.hero-inc.com

The Workplace Foundation
www.theworkfoundation.com

Prefabrication and Modular Construction
Project FROG
www.projectfrog.com

fabprefab
www.fabprefab.com—home.htm

Kullman Offsite Construction
www.kullman.com/index.html

Build Offsite
www.buildoffsite.com/

Life Cycle Building Management
Softlandings
www.softlandings.org.uk

Whole Building Design Guide
www.wbdg.org

Construction Operations Building Exchange
www.wbdg.org—cobie.php

Building Life-Cycle Interoperable Software
www.blis-project.org

Athena
www.athenasmi.org

Research and Standards Organizations
Constructing Excellence in the Built Environment
www.constructingexcellence.org.uk

FIATECH
www.fiatech.org

Center for Integrated Facility Engineering (CIFE)
www.stanford.edu—CIFE

Open Standards Consortium for Real Estate (OSCRE)
www.oscre.org

buildingSMART alliance
www.buildingsmartalliance.org

National Institute for Building Science (NIBS)
www.nibs.org

Construction Specification Institute
www.csinet.org

Construction Industry Institute (CII)
www.construction-institute.org

National BIM Standards
http://nbimsdoc.opengeospatial.org

International Council for Research and Innovation in Building and Construction (CIB)
www.cibworld.nl—website

Construction Institute (CI)
www.constructioninst.org

Construction Institute
www.construction.org

Buildings Futures Institute
www.bsu.edu—bfi

Open Building Strategic Studies (OBOM)
www.obom.org

Publications
Metropolis
www.metropolismag.com—cda

Building Design and Construction
www.bdcnetwork.com

McGraw-Hill Construction
http://construction.ecnext.com/coms2/analytics

Engineering News Record
http://enr.construction.com—default.asp

Building Energy Performance Info
www.bepinfo.com—default1.aspx

McGraw-Hill Construction—Dodge
http://dodge.construction.com—analytics

Today's Facility Man
http://todaysfacilitymanager.com

Greenway Group
www.greenway.us

Reforming Project Management
www.reformingprojectmanagement.com

Impact Assessment—A Technology Research News Column
www.trnmag.com—Impact_Assessment.html

Media Architecture
www.mediaarchitecture.org

Professional Organizations
Construction Users Roundtable (CURT)
www.curt.org

American Institute of Architects
www.aia.org

Lean Construction Institute (LCI)
www.leanconstruction.org

Associated General Contractors of America (AGC)
www.agc.org

CoreNet Global
www.corenetglobal.org

Industrial Asset Management Council
www.IAMC.org

International Facility Management Association (IFMA)
www.ifma.org

International Interior Design Association
www.iida.org

Construction Owners Association of America, Inc. (COAA)
www.coaa.org

Building Owners and Managers Association (BOMA)
www.boma.org

Construction Managers Association of America (CMAA)
www.cmaanet.org

Design-Build Institute of America (DBIA)
www.dbia.org

Associated Builders and Contractors (ABC)
www.abc.org

American Subcontractors Association (ASA)
www.asaonline.com

American Council of Engineering Companies (ACEC)
www.acec.org

American Society of Civil Engineers (ASCE)
www.asce.org

American Institute of Steel Construction (AISC)
www.aisc.org

ASQ Design and Construction Division
www.asq.org—design

Networks and Alliances
Global Design Alliance
www.globalda.com

Discovery AE
www.discoveryae.com

Mindshift
www.mindshiftwiki.com

Design Futures Council
www.di.net—the_design_futures_council

National Builders Alliance
www.nationalbuildersalliance.com

Blogs and Wiki Sites
Collaborative Construction Blog
www.collaborativeconstruction.blogspot.com

Archiplanet Wiki
www.archiplanet.org—Main_Page

designreform
http://designreform.net

Software
BIM Modeling Tools
Revit by Autodesk
www.revit.com

ArchiCAD by Graphisoft
www.graphisoft.com

Vico Constructor
www.vicosoftware.com

Vectorworks by Nemetschek
www.nemetschek.net—architect

Microstation by Bentley
www.bentley.com

Gehry Technologies
http://gehrytechnologies.com

Early Collaboration and Planning Tools
Onuma Planning System (OPS)
http://onuma.com—products

BIMStorm
http://BIMStorm.com

DProfiler by Beck Technologies
www.beck-technology.com

Trelligence Affinity
www.trelligence.com

dRofus
www.drofus.no/index.php?page=en&lang=en

Analysis Tools: BIM Coordination (Clash Detecting)
Navis Works by Autodesk
www.nemetschek.net—architect

Solibri Model Checker by Solibri Inc.
www.solibri.com

ProjectWise by Bentley
www.bentley.com—projectwiset+project+teamt+collaboration

Synchro
www.synchroltd.com

3D Modeling
Sketchup by Google
www.sketchup.google.com

Form-Z
www.formz.com

Moment of Inspiration (MOI) 3D
http://moi3d.com

Visualization, Rendering Tools
Artlantis
www.artlantis.com

Piranesi by Informatix
www.informatix.co.uk—piranesi

3D Studio Max by Autodesk
http://usa.autodesk.com—index

Cinema 4D by Maxon
www.maxon.net—cinema4d_e.html

Maxwell Render
www.maxwellrender.com

Green Analysis
Ecotect by Autodesk
www.ecotect.com

Integrated Environmental Solutions (IES)
www.iesve.com—default.asp

Energy Plus
http://gundog.lbl.gov—ep_main.html

Advance Modeling
Vico 5D Presenter
www.vicosoftware.com

Rhino
www.rhino3d.com

Subtrade Modeling
Tekla—Structural Steel
www.tekla.com

Revit Structure
http://usa.autodesk.com—index

Graitec—Concrete
www.graitec.com—ac.asp

Revit MEP Suite by Autodesk—Mechanical, Electrical, & Plumbing
http://usa.autodesk.com—index

Ardis by Graitec
www.adris.co.uk—acad_revitmep.html

BIM Model Server
Jotne EPM
www.epmtech.jotne.com—products.41332.en.html

Onuma
http://onuma.com—BimDataApi.php

Laser Scanner Spatial Imaging
Faro—As-Built Documentation
www.faro.com—content.aspx

Leica—Geosystems
www.buy.leica-geosystems.com

Trimble Spatial Imaging
www.trimble.com—spatialimaging.shtml

Geospatial
Google Earth
http://earth.google.com

Open Geospatial Consortium
www.opengeospatial.org

Appendix 5: Mapping the Future

These are three charts that provide a shorthand view of the shift taking place in culture and business.

What The Next Architect Will Look Like:

Issue	Past	Present	Future
Delivery	Design-bid-build	Emerging design-build	Integrated delivery
Fees	Percentage	Fixed/hourly	Value-based
Process	Linear	Overlapping	Simultaneous
Technology	Paper	Mixed media	3D, 4D, BIM
Role	Artist	Design technician	Team leader
Management	Undervalued	Emerging	Prerequisite
Structure	Single firm	Multi-firm teams	Virtual team
Market Reach	Local	Regional/national	Global
Business Model	Standard AIA Services	Modular services	Results-based

(*Continued*)

(*Continued*)

Issue	Past	Present	Future
Construction	Fragmented	CM-based	Integrated
Services	Generalist	Specialist	Blended
Management	Practice-focused	Profession-focused	Entrepreneur
Risk	Conflict Avoidance	Structured accountability	Embraces risk

Adapted from the book *The Next Architect,* James P. Cramer, Scott Simpson. Greenway Communications.

The Shift from Traditional to Integrated Practice

Traditional		Integrated Practice
Fragmented assembled on a just-as-needed or minimum-necessary basis, strongly hierarchical, controlled	Teams	An Integrated team entity composed of all project life cycle stakeholders, assembled early in the process. Collaborative.
Linear, distinct, segregated; knowledge gathered on a just-as-needed basis; information is hoarded	Process	Concurrent, multi-level, integrated; early contributions of knowledge and expertise; information openly shared.
Individually managed; transferred to the greatest extent possible	Risk	Collectively managed; appropriately shared.
Paper-based; 2-dimensional; analog	Communications/ Technology	Digitally based, virtual 4-dimensional. Building Information Modeling (BIM).
Minimum effort for maximum return; minimize or transfer risk; don't share	Agreements	Encourage, foster, promote & support open sharing & collaboration; full integration.
Individually focused; emphasis on composition	Education	Team-based, integrated, collaborative; technologically inclusive; a materials and methods focus in addition to composition.

Shared by Christine McEntee, executive director for the AIA, at the June 2007 Mindshift gathering in Chicago.

	Print Culture 1500–1950	Broadcast Culture 1950–2010	Digital Culture 2010–
How We Work and Trade			
Manager	The Manager	The Leader	The Catalyst
Metaphor for Work	Factory	Office	Network
Value	Productivity	Quality	Innovation
Marketing	Improve condition	Create wants	Tailored fulfillment
How We Know			
Sense of Time	Past/History	Future/Novelty	Virtual Time Travel
Sense of space	Nation	Global Village	Flat World
Knowledge	Law of Identity	Uncertainty Principle	Chaos Theory
Collective Memory	Book	Documentary	Database/Cloud
How We Live Together			
Authority	Credibility and position	Relevancy or influence	By example or catalyst
Influence	Credentials	Impression	Connections
Ethics	Ethics	Pragmatics	Reciprocity

Adapted from Rex Miller's *Millennium Matrix*, published by Jossey-Bass.

Notes

INTRODUCTION
1. "The industry we work in is estimated at $4.5 trillion dollars and some estimates identify the waste in the industry at over 50%." Dianne Davis, heading Economic Programs for the buildingSMART Alliance. The buildingSMART alliance operates within the independent nonprofit National Institute of Building Sciences (NIBS). http://www .buildingsmartalliance.org/programs/economic_issues.php.
2. Clayton M. Christensen, *The Innovator's Dilemma*. Perseus Distribution Services, 1997.

CHAPTER 1
1. The Bureau of Economic Analysis states the U.S. GDP reached $14.08 trillion in 2007. The *Engineering News Report* estimates global construction at $4.8 trillion and U.S. construction at $1.288 trillion. With more than 50 percent of that cost attributed to waste, we reach more than $500 billion.
2. "The industry we work in is estimated at $4.5 trillion and some estimates identify the waste in the industry at over 50 percent," said Dianne Davis, Economic Programs Leader for the BuildingSmart Alliance (http://www .buildingsmartalliance.org/programs/).

3. Kyle Davy's book *Value Redesigned* traces the history of shifting business models in the architecture, engineering, and construction industry.
4. Barry Lepatner, (2008). *Broken Buildings, Busted Budgets: How to Fix America's Trillion-Dollar Construction Industry*. Chicago: University of Chicago Press.
5. Scope is another variable sometimes included in the discussion of trade-offs. Scope refers to the size and features of the project.
6. Jim Long, Jennifer Magnolfi, Lois Massen, (2008). *Always Building: The Programmable Environment*. Zeeland: Herman Miller, Inc.
7. "Non-value added effort or waste is a significant problem in the construction industry. Much of the waste comes from inaccurate or untrusted information causing the information to have to be regathered multiple times throughout the life of the project," Dianne Davis, Economic Programs Leader for the BuildingSmart Alliance (http://www.buildingsmartalliance.org/programs/).
8. Finith E. Jernigan, (2008). *BIG BIM little bim, Second Edition*. Salisbury, MD: 4site Press.
9. New tools like Gensler's Workplace Assessment, Haworth's "Competing Values" survey, and Strategic Dimensions "rules-based" pro forma modeling software now allow companies to quickly collect, synthesize, and analyze input from the multiple stakeholders.
10. Kyle Davy, co-author of *Value Redesigned*, calls this "whole systems awareness." This is one critical skill for project success. Kyle spends a day and a half delving deeply into this skill during the Senior Executive Institute.
11. This is an exercise of developing "causal loops."
12. Building Information Modeling (BIM) is explored in detail in the third part of the book. BIM shifts design from linear drawing to 3D modeling. Virtual modeling behaves like physical construction and therefore requires multidisciplinary coordination.
13. Steve Fridsma, architect at ProgressiveAE.
14. The back-story is that the general contractor and subs had not yet been selected for the project. They would still have to bid the project along with five other general contractors. The developer felt strongly enough that he asked these firms to invest three weeks into an experiment to "prove the system wrong." When the project was bid and the results were in, the team then learned that the preplanning had paid off.
15. Clive Thomas Cain, *Profitable Partnering for Lean Construction*, (Malden, MA: Wiley-Blackwell, 2004).
16. Too much information can work to a bidder's disadvantage. If they have worked with the client or the GC in the past they may factor in to their price contingencies encountered in the past and increase their price for the bid.
17. Energy Information Administration Statistics and Pew Climate Report.
18. John, Prescott, (1998). Rethinking Construction. London: Department of Trade and Industry.
19. Ibid.
20. Great Britain, (2000). *Modernising Construction* (House of Commons Papers). London: Stationery Office Books.

21. U.S. Dept. of Commerce Bureau of Labor Statistics from 1964 to 2003.

22. Greg Wilkinson, president of the regional firm Hill & Wilkinson, shared in 2008 at a gathering of several industry firms the challenges within the contracting industry. Louise Jurkowski, president of BJAC architects, shared similar concerns; at the same event that the architecture lost approximately 4,200 architects retiring and gained only 3,700 who graduated.

23. Clive Thomas Cain, *Profitable Partnering for Lean Construction*, (Malden, MA: Wiley-Blackwell, 2004).

24. Clive Thomas Cain, *Profitable Partnering for Lean Construction*, (Malden, MA: Wiley-Blackwell, 2004).

25. According to KPMG's Construction Tax Planning practice, up to 6 perent of the cost for a ground-up building qualifies for accelerated depreciation and up to 17 percent for an interior build-out.

26. Barry Lepatner, (2008). *Broken Buildings, Busted Budgets: How to Fix America's Trillion-Dollar Construction Industry*. Chicago: University of Chicago Press.

27. Rebecca R. Merrill and Stephen M.R. Covey, *The Speed of Trust* (New York: Simon & Schuster, 2006).

28. Lean refers to a process that Toyota adopted and refined that creates a more efficient and flexible approach to making cars. Many of the same ideas are being applied to construction with similar positive results.

29. Interoperability enables different software tools to easily exchange data.

30. Trade silos include: The Construction User's Round Table, The American Institute of Architects, United States Green Building Council, Open Source Consortium for Real Estate, Associated General Contractors, BuildingSmart Alliance, National Building Information Model Standard, and many others.

CHAPTER 2

1. John Paul Newport, (2008, September 27). *Team USA's Management Victory*. *Wall Street Journal*. Retrieved September 30, 2008. The article provides a timeless example of the value of crafting a team with disciplined forethought. The U.S. Ryder Cup team had lost the last five out of six competitions with the Europeans. Azinger left off most of the marquee players and instead selected six rookies and changed all of the previous protocols for team selection. The story is very instructive for team selection in construction.

2. U.S. team managing director Jerry Colangelo said that simply throwing together a collection of NBA stars doesn't cut it anymore. He noted that the nucleus of this team was assembled in 2006. "The core players have been together for the last three years," he said. "In the past, all-star teams were selected. That was good enough, but that's not the case any more." http:// www.nydailynews.com/sports/more_sports/2008/07/28/2008-07-28_confident_team_usa_arrives_in_china_lebr.html.

3. Paul Hawken, Amory Lovins, and L. Hunter Lovins. *Natural Capitalism: Creating the Next Industrial Revolution*. New York: Back Bay Books, 2000, p. 275.

4. Barry Lepatner, (2008). *Broken Buildings, Busted Budgets: How to Fix America's Trillion-Dollar Construction Industry.* Chicago: University of Chicago Press.

5. McGraw-Hill Survey 2008. The *AIA Integrated Project Delivery Guidelines* list additional delivery methods, pp. 44–49.

6. Reed Business Data told us that the actual numbers were far higher than our estimates. The average number of general contractors involved in a bid is 15. The number of product manufacturers—air compressors, lighting, security, etc.—will double the total number of contractors and subcontractors.

7. One architect told us that the cost for developing a bid response for a $350 million project was $500,000. If they lose, that cost will need to be made up somewhere in the future. The design partner had already spent more than $1 million to make it to the shortlist stage.

8. Buying out the contracts is a process that most owners are unaware of. When the contractor submits their quote, it is a number without reference to any particular subcontractor. Once contracts are awarded, the general contractor will often use that leverage and renegotiate to see if any of the subs will lower their quote. The contractor also has to make sure that the sub is still available to do the work. It is possible that the sub was selected for another project that came in before this one.

9. Clive Thomas Cain, *Profitable Partnering for Lean Construction*, (Malden, MA: Wiley-Blackwell, 2004).

10. Successful efforts to rein in cost seem to be the outcome of well-formed, highly competent teams that display "above and beyond" behavior. The success comes in spite of the system. One executive for a national real estate firm commented on a chip fabrication facility that started late due to the fragmented decision process. Each hour the facility was late cost the company $1 million. The facility was completed on schedule due to individual heroics, a large financial incentive, and some high-level red-tape cutting with the local government. In this case, speed and quality were accomplished with a high premium and the political muscle of several executives.

11. LePatner points out that "fixed price" contracts are not truly fixed price and allow for change orders. He points to the design-build model as strategy for controlling costs, but with several other trade-offs giving the contractor virtually total control over design, quality, and schedule.

12. Owners have a hard time making the connection that paying more up front actually lowers the overall cost of the project and shortens the schedule. Many projects in their initial phases are speculative (planned before there are identified tenants). Developers will ask architects for "free" concept drawings to secure contractor quotes and then seek funding, with the promise of using their firm if the project gets funded. In this case developers walk the fine line of not including enough cost to properly build the project hoping to secure funding or building in too much buffer so that there is enough to build what is needed and pricing themselves out of the market. Owners also minimize front-end planning

to respond to pro formas that minimize early cash outlay and then demand faster delivery to get the building operational and producing as quickly as possible.

13. Steven Levy, "We Should Build Our Own," *Wired,* October 2008, 150.

14. Arizona State has developed a vendor assessment process called "Performance Based Procurement" that offers institutions and public entities an alternative due diligence process for selecting a best value supplier. Companies like Nortel and institutions like Harvard have used it with successful results.

15. Great Britain, (2000). *Modernising Construction* (House of Commons Papers). London: Stationery Office Books.

16. As part of the background on John McCain's use of "Joe the Plumber," several media outlets researched his professional plumbing credentials. One Toledo Blade article stated, "Mr. Wurzelbacher said he works under Al Newell's license, but according to Ohio building regulations, he must maintain his own license to do plumbing work. He is also not registered to operate as a plumber in Ohio, which means he's not a plumber." Wikipedia, http://en.wikipedia.org/wiki/Samuel_Joseph_Wurzelbacher.

17. Once a contractor sets their Guatanteed Maximum Price (GMP), they now take on the risk for keeping costs below that level or eat into their profits. They will use the buy-out process and change orders to protect that GMP.

18. Mike Wolff, Principal for Project Solutions Group.

19. Several different stakeholders in the industry, including project and construction managers, expressed these opinions.

20. CCM Consulting Group was organized in January 1992 for the purpose of providing construction project auditing and consulting services for construction project owners. Since 1992, it has reviewed more than $16 billion in construction contracts.

CHAPTER 3

1. George Elvin, (2007). *Integrated Practice in Architecture: Mastering Design-Build, Fast-Track, and Building Information Modeling.* New York, NY: Wiley.

2. Trammel Crow merged with CB Richard Ellis, Staubach merged with Jones Lang LaSalle and firms like Jacobs Engineering are absorbing others to create greater vertical integration.

3. Charles O'Reilly and Michael Tushman. "The Ambidextrous Organization," *Harvard Business Review*: 1–8.

4. *Blue Ocean Strategy* is a business strategy book that promotes a systematic approach, not to outperform the competition in an existing industry, but to create new market space or "blue ocean," thereby making the competition irrelevant (http://en.wikipedia.org/wiki/Blue_Ocean).

5. Charles O'Reilly and Michael Tushman. "The Ambidextrous Organization," *Harvard Business Review*: 1–8.

6. Michael Schrage, *Serious Play: How the World's Best Companies Simulate to Innovate* (New York: Harvard Business School Press, 1999).

CHAPTER 4

1. Additional attendees include Jim Oswald with Gensler; Jabir Al-Hilal with KPMG; Ric Nelson with Transwestern; Mabel Casey, Lydia Knowles, and Bill Black with Haworth; and Paul Beitler and Terri Stewart with the AIA. Those who could not join this meeting came to a Chicago gathering in June and an October session in Calgary.

2. Ed Mazria, (n.d.). *Climate Change, Global Warming, and the Built Environment—Architecture 2030.* Retrieved December 10, 2008, from http://www.architecture2030.org/home.html.

3. The others who joined the effort include Mark Iammarino, vice president with Turner; Ray Lucchesi, principal with Lucchesi Galati; Markku Allison, resource architect with the AIA; Les Shepherd, chief architect for GSA; Mark Charette, president of Solidus; Kyle Davy, architect and industry consultant; Ben Weeks, principal for Aardex; George Zettel, Lean champion for Turner; Gary Hamor, president of Lean Practices Inc.; and Kurt Young, principal at Walter P. Moore.

4. Clayton M. Christensen, "The Innovator's Dilemma: When New Technologies Cause Great Firms to Fail," (New York: Harvard Business School Press, 1997).

5. VBR's core members were Dean Reed and Atul Khanzode with DPR Construction; Dan Gonzales, now with Swinerton Builders; Chris Raftery, who at the time was a project executive for Magnusson Klemencic in Seattle; Martin Fischer at Stanford's Center for Integrated Facility Engineering (CIFE); Andy Fuhrman, who at the time owned a company providing computer-aided facility management services (CAFM); Kathleen Liston, a PhD student in the engineering program through CIFE; and Gregory Luth, who led a structural engineering firm.

6. Jerry Laiserin, "The LaiserinLetter (tm)," http://www.laiserin.com.

7. Jerry Laiserin, "The LaiserinLetter (tm)," http://www.laiserin.com.

8. Jerry Laiserin, "The LaiserinLetter (tm)," http://www.laiserin.com.

9. Sharon Simonson, "Sutter builds 'lean' to pre-empt Kaiser," *East Bay Business Times*, August 9, 2004, National Business News.

10. Michael Shaw, "Building a better contract" *Sacramento Business Journal*, September 15, 2008, National Business News.

11. And these changes have already rippled outward:

    Will Lichtig's groundbreaking IFOA contract has become a key building block to both the AIA's and AGC's integrated project team contracts, as well as a key component to LCI's team formation process.

    Kathleen Liston has her own consulting firm specializing in Virtual Design and Construction and construction software integration, and she recently co-authored the *BIM Handbook: A Guide to Building Information Modeling for Owners, Managers, Designers.*

    Andy Fuhrman is CEO of Open Standards Consortium for Real Estate (OSCRE), a non-profit focusing on developing standards to better exchange information across the many software platforms used through the entire real estate process.

    Dan Gonzales heads Swinerton's Virtual Design and Construction and is active with the AGC's BIMForum.

    Martin Fischer is still with CIFE and a leading change agent.

CHAPTER 5

1. Nadine Post, "Sutter Health Unlocks the Door to A New Process," *Engineering News Record* November 26, 2007.
2. Project Management Director in Sutter Health's Facility Planning & Development Department.
3. AEC stands for architecture, engineering, and construction.
4. Director of Sustainable Construction
5. Hard-bidding (lump sum) means that suppliers provide a fixed and certain price. Hard bidding requires that the design intent is clear and there is enough detail for suppliers to provide a firm and fixed price for doing the work.
6. The proposed solution included Haworth's TecCrete raised floor tiles. The tiles are made of concrete and sit on adjustable pylons. This solution provided a three-inch chase to distribute the power and data. Placing the power and data under the floor allows future reconfiguration without expensive labor or new materials.
7. Clive Thomas Cain, *Profitable Partnering for Lean Construction*, (Malden, MA: Wiley-Blackwell, 2004).
8. Some may claim that design-build provides a single point of contact and is, therefore, a solution. Design-build can be adapted to provide an integrated solution, but it does so only if the firms adopt a collaborative philosophy and bring in their sub-trades early. It has to overcome its built-in bias toward sacrificing quality and design to cost.
9. Mike Foley, "St Helen's Council," *The Beacon Scheme* January 29, 2007.
10. Arol Worlford was the founder of Construction Market Data, which was sold to Reed Business, and an original investor in Revit, which was sold to Autodesk.
11. 80 percent of projects are up to $6 million.
12. The definition of Class A office space; http://en.wikipedia.org/wiki/Class_A_Office_Space.
13. Cain lists other criteria as well:

   - How often have final settlements matched the contract price?
   - What final settlements exceeded their contract and by how much?
   - How often is the effective use of labor and materials measured?
   - What is the average level of effective use of labor and materials?
   - What evidence is available for the durability of the work over time?

   These are some examples. Cain's point is to develop an evidenced-based evaluation process that shows performance and reliability.

CHAPTER 6

1. John Paul Newport, "Team USA's Management Victory," *Wall Street Journal,* September 27, 2008.
2. Ibid.
3. Rebecca R. Merrill and Stephen M.R. Covey, *The Speed of Trust* (New York: Simon & Schuster, 2006).
4. Rebecca R. Merrill and Stephen M.R. Covey, *The Speed of Trust* (New York: Simon & Schuster, 2006).

5. Clive Thomas Cain, *Profitable Partnering for Lean Construction*, (Malden, MA: Wiley-Blackwell, 2004).

6. Rebecca R. Merrill and Stephen M.R. Covey, *The Speed of Trust* (New York: Simon & Schuster, 2006).

7. Amy Lyman, "Great Place to Work® Institute," Best Practices from the Best Companies. (White Paper) December 21, 2008.

8. Christian Sarkar, "The SPEED of Trust: Trust, Branding & Competitive Advantage: An Interview with Stephen M.R. Covey by Christian Sarkar," Emory Marketing Institute: Goizueta Business School, Emory University.

9. Isabell Horvath, "CEOs who fail to actively manage outsourcing relationships miss out on 'trust dividend' worth up 40 percent of contract value," *Logica*, November 24, 2005.

10. Adapted from Covey's chapter, "One Thing That Changes Everything." Rebecca R. Merrill and Stephen M.R. Covey, *The Speed of Trust* (New York: Simon & Schuster, 2006).

11. "Collaboration, Integrated Information, and the Project Lifecycle in Building Design, Construction and Operation," CURT, WP-1202 (White Paper) August 2004.

12. DiscProfile™; http://www.discprofile.com.

13. The Bartlett Group; http://www.profilexpert.com/.

14. The Strengthsfinder assessment is included as part of the purchase of one of the books in their series, like *Now Discover Your Strengths* and *Strengthsfinder. 2.0*. The book contains an access code that allows you to go online and take the assessment. The Strengthsfinder assessment can be a good place for a team with a variety of companies to start. It is inexpensive and easy for each person to go to a bookstore and buy a copy of the book. It also avoids the problem of trying to get everyone using the same profiles. DISC and IPM are both good tools, but not every company is subscribed to their service.

15. www.coreclarity.net: CoreClarity offers a more defined process when it comes to team formation and team development.

CHAPTER 7

1. Michael Schrage, "No More Teams!: Mastering the Dynamics of Creative Collaboration," (New York: Currency Doubleday, 1995).

2. In the previous chapter we shared some of the tools available to identify and blend individual strengths.

3. The definition of project management—Wikipedia, the free encyclopedia. http://en.wikipedia.org/wiki/Project_management.

4. Which in the old system is neither guaranteed or the maximum price for the project.

5. Arol Wolford was an original investor with Revit and the founder of Construction Business Data, which sold to Reed Business.

6. Thomas Mcduffie, "BIM: Transforming a Traditional Practice Model into a Technology-Enabled Integrated Practice Model," Architects, AIA, Green Architecture—The American Institute of Architects.

7. Maryanne Wolf, *Proust and the Squid: The Story and Science of the Reading Brain*, (New York: Harper, 2007).

8. Michael Schrage, "No More Teams!: Mastering the Dynamics of Creative Collaboration," (New York: Currency Doubleday, 1995).

9. 5 Whys—Wikipedia, the free encyclopedia. "The 5 Whys is a question-asking method used to explore the cause/effect relationships underlying a particular problem. Ultimately, the goal of applying the 5 Whys method is to determine a root cause of a defect or problem." http://en.wikipedia.org/wiki/5_Whys.

10. Tim Brown, (June 1, 2005). Strategy by Design, Fast Company, from http://www.fastcompany.com/magazine/95/design-strategy.html?page=0%2C1.

11. One technique to consider is Edward DeBono's *6 Hat Thinking*, which labels the various roles as different colored "hats": http://en.wikipedia.org/wiki/DeBono_Hats.

12. Jack Hallman, Alex Ivanikiw, and Robert Mauck, "3D Enabled Lean, Collaborative Design-Build Delivery General Motors Flint V6 Engine Assembly Plant," *Design-Build*, December 1, 2006.

CHAPTER 8

1. James Cramer and Jane Gaboury, "Creativity, Leadership, and the New Green Standard," *Design Intelligence*, 2008, 5–18.

2. "Cost Benefits of Going Green—Davis Langdon," AIA, www.aiadc.com/architectureDC/spring2007/costbenefit.pdf.

3. If you want to sound like you know what you are talking about, talk about LEED(s) as plural. The proper use of the word "LEED" is like a fraternal handshake.

4. Rebecca Bell, "Q&A on green buildings with Rick Fedrizzi," The Green Blog, a *Boston Globe* blog on living Green in Boston, comment posted September 19, 2008, www.Boston.com.

5. "Green Buildings and the Bottom Line," BDC Network, www.bdcnetwork.com/article/CA6390371.html.

6. Jim Collins, (n.d.). Jim Collins.com I Library., from http://jimcollins.com/lib/articles/01_01_e.html.

7. Public records supplied by the USGBC on December 3, 2008.

8. More than 20,000 professionals were accredited since the August update of 2008.

9. "Cost Benefits of Going Green—Davis Langdon," AIA, www.aiadc.com/architectureDC/spring2007/costbenefit.pdf.

10. The project was managed by Cushman Wakefield.

11. George Denise, "Adobe System's big payback," CSE Live Reed Business Information, December 1, 2007.

12. "BUILDING MOMENTUM," USGBC: U.S. Green Building Council, https://www.usgbc.org/Docs/Resources/043003_hpgb_whitepaper.pdf.

13. "3328 Brengel Tech Center," Green Facilities, www.greenerfacilities.org/admin/data/case_studies/Brengel_Technology_Center.pdf.

14. Preston Koerner, "Skyscraper Sunday: LEED Platinum Banner Bank Building," Green Building Blog—Jetson Green, comment posted April 8, 2007.

15. "Sustainability Case Study: Banner Bank—A LEED Platinum, High-Performance Facility," Facilities Management: Professional Resources for Facility Managers from FMLink, April 2004. http://www.fmlink.com/ProfResources/Sustainability/Articles/article.cgi?USGBC:200703-19.html.

16. "Aardex Signature Center—LEED Platinum," USGBC: U.S. Green Building Council. April 21, 2008. (Project Profile) www.usgbc.org/ShowFile.aspx? DocumentID=.

17. Andrew Burr, "CoStar Study Finds Energy Star, LEED Bldgs. Outperform Peers—CoStar Group," CoStar # 1 Commercial Real Estate Information Company, http://www.costar.com/News/Article.aspx? id=D968F1E0D.

18. Andrew Burr, "CoStar Study Finds Energy Star, LEED Bldgs. Outperform Peers—CoStar Group," CoStar # 1 Commercial Real Estate Information Company, http://www.costar.com/News/Article.aspx?id=D968F1E0D

19. Christopher Hawthorne, "Turning Down the Global Thermostat," *Metropolis Magazine*, October 1, 2003.

20. The Pew Center on Climate Change attribute up to 53.5 percent of the emissions to commercial and industrial buildings.

21. "Commercial Buildings Fact Sheet," Center for Sustainable Systems—University of Michigan, css.snre.umich.edu/css_doc/CSS05-05.pdf.

22. Arthur Nelson, "City Mayors: Built environment—USA." City Mayors: Mayors running the world's cities, http://www.citymayors.com/development/built_environment_usa.html.

23. "U.S. Energy System," Center for Sustainable Systems—University of Michigan, http://css.snre.umich.edu/.

24. "HYBRID SYNERGY DRIVE: Prius Low Emissions." HYBRID SYNERGY DRIVE, http://www.hybridsynergydrive.com/en/prius_emissions.html.

25. http://en.wikipedia.org/wiki/Absorption_refrigerator

26. David Thurm, "Master of the House: Why a Company Should Take Control of Its Building Projects," *Harvard Business Review*: 1–9.

27. In 2006, Gallup found the cost of disengagement to companies exceeded $300 billion, http://gmj.gallup.com/content/24880/Gallup-Study-Engaged-Employees-Inspire-Company.aspx.

28. Paul Hawken, *Blessed Unrest: How the Largest Movement in the World Came into Being and Why No One Saw It Coming* (New York: Viking, 2007).

29. We pulled together reports from many sources:
    Green Buildings and the Bottom Line—United States
    A Business Case for Green Buildings—Canada
    The Cost of Green Revisited—United States
    The Economics of LEED® for Existing Buildings—United States
    The Dollars and Sense of Building Green—Australia
    National Trends and Prospects for High-Performance Green Buildings—United States
    What Does Green Really Cost?—United States
    The Greening of Corporate America—United States
    Sustainability Roadmap—Australia
    Aligning Industry—United States

CHAPTER 9

1. Larry is retired and runs a consulting firm called the Great Lakes Renaissance Group, http://www.glrg.biz/.
2. "DALI stands for Digital Addressable Lighting Interface and is a protocol set out in the technical standard IEC 62386." http://www.dali-ag.org/.
3. Joe Laur, Sara Schley, Peter M. Senge, and Bryan Smith, *The Necessary Revolution: How Individuals And Organizations Are Working Together to Create a Sustainable World* (New York: Currency, 2008).
4. Discovery AE; http://discoveryae.com/.
5. Clayton Christensen; http://en.wikipedia.org/wiki/Clayton_M._Christensen.
6. Ronald Heifetz; http://en.wikipedia.org/wiki/Ronald_Heifetz.

CHAPTER 10

1. Big BIM refers to the distinction that Frinith Jernigan makes in his book *BIG BIM little bim* between BIM as tool and BIM as a paradigm change for design and integrated project delivery.
2. http://en.wikipedia.org/wiki/Boeing_777.
3. We like Virtual Building^{TM} because it is descriptive and simple. Graphisoft has trademarked its use. The name selection may come down to which manufacturer leads in market share. Revit has chosen BIM as its label. Virtual Design and Construction originates out of the Virtual Building Roundtable.
4. The title of EDS Fellow is awarded to the company's most innovative thought leaders in recognition of their exceptional achievements. Each Fellow has a proven track record of creating world-class solutions for our clients. In addition to their academic achievements and invention history, the EDS Fellows average 25 years of industry experience and innovative technology implementations.
5. There was a significant innovation phase for BIM that is worth mentioning. "Development started in 1982 for the original Apple Macintosh, and it became a popular product for that platform. It is recognized as the first CAD product on a personal computer able to create both 2D and 3D drawings. Today more than 100,000 architects are using it in the building design industry." —Wikipedia
6. Some of these organizations include Open Standards Consortium for Real Estate (OSCRE), The buildingSMART Alliance, National Building Information Model Standard (NBIMS), and the International Alliance for Interoperability (IAI).
7. Haworth's Global Ideation team uses an assessment tool to profile the cultural dynamic of an organization and its different work groups. This profile links to different archetypical designs that best support that cultural dynamic.

CHAPTER 11

1. The Lean Construction Institute, the Center for Integrated Facility Engineering (CIFE), Texas A&M, and the Egan Report out of the United Kingdom.
2. Glenn Ballard and Gregory Howell, "Competing Construction Management Paradigms," *Lean Construction Journal 1.1* (2003): 38–45.

3. http://en.wikipedia.org/wiki/Frederick_Winslow_Taylor.
4. Derrick Story, "Swarm Intelligence: An Interview with Eric Bonabeau | O'Reilly Media," OpenP2P.com – p2p development, open source development.
5. "Integrated Project Delivery: First Principles for Owners and Teams."
6. Matthew E. May, *The Elegant Solution: Toyota's Formula for Mastering Innovation* (New York City: Free Press, 2006).
7. Some of those games include The Post-it Note Game, The Parade of Trades, Silent Squares, The Tarp Exercise, and The Broomstick Exercise.
8. Alan Mossman, "Last Planner: Collaborative Production Planning, Collaborative Programme Coordination," *Lean Construction Institute UK* 26 (November 2007): 1–6.

CHAPTER 12
1. Michael Malone, "Washington Is Killing Silicon Valley," WSJ.com, December 21, 2008, Business News, Finance News, World, Political & Sports News from the *Wall Street Journal*.
2. "Typically, a merger of this size would take several months to complete and cost several million dollars to pay for accountants, auditors, and attorneys to verify and validate all kinds of information. But in this instance, because both parties operated with high trust, the deal was made with one two-hour meeting and a handshake." Rebecca R. Merrill. and Stephen M.R. Covey, *The Speed of Trust* (New York: Simon & Schuster, 2006).
3. Scott, Bob, "Partnering Alliance Contracts; a Company Viewpoint" (1994).
4. Mindshift Wiki Site; http://omswiki.pbwiki.com/Trust-Based+Agreements.
5. Cohos Evamy Integrated Design; http://www.cohos-evamy.com/index.cfm?pagepath=Integrated_design/Advantages_of_integrated_design&id=619.
6. Will Lichtig, "The Integrated Agreement for Lean Project Delivery," McDonough Holland & Allen PC, June 1, 2006.
7. Integrated Project Delivery is a trademark of Westbrook Air Conditioning and Plumbing.
8. Westbrook Heating and Air Conditioning; http://www.westbrookfl.com/offerIPD.html.

CHAPTER 13
1. Visit the Center's website at http://www.kimmelcenter.org/building/ for a virtual tour of the project.
2. Manufactured by Haworth Inc.
3. http://en.wikipedia.org/wiki/Construction_Specifications_Institute.
4. Weinberger, David. *Everything is Miscellaneous: The Power of the New Digital Disorder.* New York: Times Books, 2007.
5. Kieran, Stephen, and James Timberlake. Refabricating Architecture: How Manufacturing Methodologies are Poised to Transform Building Construction. New York: McGraw-Hill Professional, 2003.

CHAPTER 14
1. Jim Long, Jennifer Magnolfi, Lois Massen, (2008). *Always Building: The Programmable Environment.* Zeeland: Herman Miller, Inc.

2. Gallup Consulting's research has identified 12 questions that measure employee engagement and link powerfully to relevant business outcomes, including retention, productivity, profitability, customer engagement, and safety.

3. We will also draw from some of the top experts in this field like Tim Springer and Vivian Loftness. Vivian Loftness— University Professor of Architecture at the Carnegie Mellon University and a LEED AP. Vivian is an internationally renowned researcher, author, and educator with over thirty years of focus on environmental design and sustainability.

4. *Minds at Work*. Jasper: Kimball Office (2008).

5. PhD. Senior Lecturer in Psychology, Victoria University, New Zealand.

6. Small, G., & Vorgan, G. (2008). *iBrain: Surviving the Technological Alteration of the Modern Mind*. New York: Collins Living.

7. Maryanne, W. (2007). *Proust and the Squid: The Story and Science of the Reading Brain*. New York: Harper.

8. Jim Long, Jennifer Magnolfi, Lois Massen, (2008). *Always Building: The Programmable Environment*. Zeeland: Herman Miller, Inc.

9. *Minds at Work*. Jasper: Kimball Office (2008).

10. Excerpts from: Miller, M. Rex. The Millennium Matrix: Reclaiming the Past, Reframing the Future of the Church (J-B Leadership Network Series). San Francisco: Jossey-Bass, 2004.

11. Three examples taken from: The Integrated Workplace: A Comprehensive Approach to Developing Workspace. Washington, DC: GSA, 1999.

12. Aardex Corporation. User Effective Buildings. St. Paul, MN: Aardex Corporation, 2004. The book is available as a free download at http://www.aardex.com/projects_office.shtm.

13. Sick building causes are frequently pinned down to flaws in the heating, ventilation, and air conditioning (HVAC) systems. Other causes have been attributed to contaminants produced by outgassing of some types of building materials, volatile organic compounds, molds (see mold health issues), improper exhaust ventilation of light industrial chemicals used within, or fresh-air intake location / lack of adequate air filtration (see Minimum Efficiency Reporting Value).

References

3328 Brengel Tech Center. (n.d.). www.greenerfacilities.org/admin/data/case_
studies/Brengel_Technology_Center.pdf.

5 Whys—Wikipedia, the free encyclopedia. (n.d.). http://en.wikipedia.org/wiki/
5_Whys.

ACEC: Education—ACEC Senior Executives Institute. (n.d.). http://www.acec
.org/education/sei.cfm.

Aardex Signature Center—LEED Platinum. (April 21, 2008). www.usgbc.org/
ShowFile.aspx?DocumentID=5111.

Anderson, R. (1998). *Mid-Course Correction: Toward a Sustainable Enterprise:
The Interface Model.* White River Junction: Peregrinzilla Press.

Archetypes—Interaction Structures of the Universe. (n.d.). http://www.systems-
thinking.org/arch/arch.htm#archaa.

BEA: News Release: Gross Domestic Product. (n.d.). http://www.bea.gov/news
releases/national/gdp/2008/gdp407p.htm.

BUILDING MOMENTUM. (n.d.). http://www.usgbc.org/Docs/Resources/043003_
hpgb_whitepaper.pdf.

Ballard, G., and Howell, G. (2003). Competing Construction Management Paradigms. *Lean Construction Journal, 1(1),* 38–45.

Bell, R. (September 19, 2008). *Q&A on green buildings with Rick Fedrizzi, The Green Blog, A. Boston Globe blog on living Green in Boston.* http://www .boston.com/lifestyle/green/greenblog/2008/09/qa_on_green_buildings_with_ ric.html.

Bonabeau, E., Dorigo, M., and Theraulaz, G. (1999). *Swarm Intelligence: From Natural to Artificial Systems (Santa Fe Institute Studies in the Sciences of Complexity Proceedings).* New York: Oxford University Press, USA.

Brinkley, I. (July 3, 2006). *Defining the knowledge economy: knowledge economy programme report.* http://www.theworkfoundation.com/research/publications/ publicationdetail.aspx?oItemId=65&parentPageI.

Brown, K. (November 29, 2007). *Justice in the Context of Environmental Sustainability.* www.informedesign.umn.edu/_news/nov_v05r-p.pdf.

Brown, T. (December 8, 2008). *New Economic Orientation for the 21st Century.*

Brown, T. *Design Thinking. Harvard Business Review,* 84–92.

Brown, T. (June 1, 2005). *Strategy by Design | Page 2 | Fast Company* http://www .fastcompany.com/magazine/95/design-strategy.html?page=0%2C1.

Buckingham, M., and Clifton, D. (2001). *Now, Discover Your Strengths.* New York City: Free Press.

Burr, A. (April 26, 2008). *CoStar Study Finds Energy Star, LEED Bldgs. Outperform Peers—CoStar Group.* http://www.costar.com/News/Article .aspx?id=D968F1E0DCF73712B03A099E0E99C679.

CEOs who fail to actively manage outsourcing relationships miss out on, Äòtrust dividendchar(39) worth up 40 per cent of contract value. (November 24, 2005). http://www.logica.co.uk/r/350233169/CEOs+who+fail+to+actively+manage+ outsourcing+relationships+miss+out+on+%E2%80%98trust+dividendchar (39)+worth+up+40+per+cent+of+contract+value/400002957.

Cain, C. (2004). *Profitable Partnering for Lean Construction.* Malden, MA: Wiley-Blackwell.

Cameron, K., Degraff, J., Quinn, R., and Thakor, A. (2007). *Competing Values Leadership: Creating Value in Organizations (New Horizons in Management).* London: Edward Elgar Publishers.

Christensen, C. (1997). *The Innovator's Dilemma: When New Technologies Cause Great Firms to Fail (The Management of Innovation and Change Ser.).* Boston: Harvard Business School Press.

Churchill, E. (March 4, 2008). *IT Conversations | O'Reilly Media Emerging Technology Conference | Elizabeth Churchill (Free Podcast).* http://itc.conversations network.org/shows/detail3775.html.

Commercial Buildings Fact Sheet. (May 1, 2007). css.snre.umich.edu/css_doc/ CSS05-05.pdf.

Confident Team USA arrives in China, LeBron James practices. (July 28, 2008). http://www.nydailynews.com/sports/more_sports/2008/07/28/2008-07-28_ confident_team_usa_arrives_in_china_lebr.html.

Construction. (December 18, 2007). http://www.bls.gov/oco/cg/cgs003.htm.

Corporation, A. (2004). *User Effective Buildings.* St. Paul, MN: Aardex Corporation.

Cost Benefits of Going Green—Davis Langdon. (April 1, 2007) www.aiadc.com/ architectureDC/spring2007/costbenefit.pdf.

Cramer, J., and Simpson, S. (2006). *The Next Architect: A New Twist on the Future of Design.* Atlanta: Greenway Communications.

Cramer, J., and Gaboury, J. (2008). Creativity, Leadership, and the New Green Standard. *DesignIntelligence, 14*(4), 5–18.

Davis, H. (2006). *The Culture of Building.* New York: Oxford University Press, USA.

Davy, K., and Harris, S. (2005). *Value Redesigned: New Models for Professional Practice.* Atlanta: Greenway Communications.

Daylighting the New York Times Headquarters Building. (n.d.). http://windows .lbl.gov/comm_perf/newyorktimes.htm.

Dekker, S. (2004). *Ten Questions About Human Error: A New View of Human Factors and System Safety (Human Factors in Transportation).* Boca Raton: CRC.

Demountable Partitions—CSI Wiki. (n.d.). http://wiki.csinet.org/index.php?title= Demountable_Partitions.

Denise, G. (December 1, 2007). *Adobe System's big payback.* www.csemag.com/ article/CA6512579.html.

Ditz, S. (January 25, 1999). *Permit process gets 'smart' with use of technology - Silicon Valley/San Jose Business Journal:* http://sanjose.bizjournals.com/sanjose/stories/ 1999/01/25/focus2.html.

Elvin, G. (2007). *Integrated Practice in Architecture: Mastering Design-Build, Fast-Track, and Building Information Modeling.* New York, NY: John Wiley & Sons.

Engineering News-Record (ENR) The Top 400 Contractors—2007 Electronic Edition. (May 21, 2007). enr.ecnext.com/coms2/summary_0271-40086_ITM.

Fabozzi, F. (2002). *The Handbook of Financial Instruments.* New York, NY: John Wiley & Sons.

Fallon, K. (n.d.). *Interoperability: Critical to Achieving BIM Benefits.* http://www .aia.org/nwsltr_tap.cfm?pagename=tap_a_0704_interop.

Foley, M. (January 29, 2007). *St Helens Council.* http://www.beacons.idea.gov .uk/idk/core/page.do?pageId=72131.

GSA - Design Excellence Program. (n.d.). http://www.gsa.gov/Portal/gsa/ep/ channelView.do?pageTypeId=8195&channelId=-12885.

Garrison, T. (June 7, 2007). *Lean Construction: Maximize Value and Eliminate—Construction Business Management for Contractors/Construction Business Owner Magazine.* http://www.constructionbusinessowner.com/topics/general-management/lean-construction-maximize-value-and-eliminate-waste.html.

Gladstone, B. (December 6, 2008). *Brand China.* www.onthemedia.org/transcripts/ 2008/06/20/01.

Godin, S. (2008). *Tribes: We Need You to Lead Us.* Ottawa: Portfolio Hardcover.

Gray, J. (2004). *Men Are from Mars, Women Are from Venus: The Classic Guide to Understanding the Opposite Sex.* Brattleboro: Harper Paperbacks.

Green Building Smart Market Report 2006. (n.d.). http://www.construction.com/ SmartMarket/greenbuilding/default.asp.

Green Buildings and the Bottom Line. (November 1, 2006) www.bdcnetwork .com/article/CA6390371.html.

Greenleaf, R. (1998). *The Power of Servant Leadership.* San Francisco, CA: Berrett-Koehler Publishers.

HYBRID SYNERGY DRIVE: Prius Low Emissions. (n.d.). http://www.hybrid synergydrive.com/en/prius_emissions.html.

Hallman, J., Ivanikiw, A., and Mauck, R. (December 1, 2006). 3D Enabled Lean, Collaborative Design-Build Delivery General Motors Flint V6 Engine Assembly Plant. *Design-Build,* 17–23.

Hawken, P., Lovins, A., and Lovins, L. (2000). *Natural Capitalism: Creating the Next Industrial Revolution.* New York: Back Bay Books.

Hawken, P. (2007). *Blessed Unrest: How the Largest Movement in the World Came into Being and Why No One Saw It Coming.* New York: Viking.

Hawthorne, C. (October 1, 2003). *Turning Down the Global Thermostat.* http://www.metropolismag.com/story/20031001/turning-down-the-global-thermostat.

Heerwagen, J. (2000). Green Buildings, Organizational Success, and Occupant Productivity. *Building Research and Information, 28(2000: 353–367),* 1–25. www.wbdg.org/pdfs/grn_bldgs_org_success.pdf.

Holtzman, C. (April 27, 2007). *B-school's 40% shocker.* seattle.bizjournals.com/seattle/stories/2007/04/30/story1.html?f=et178&b=1177905600^1453633& hbx=e_vert.

Horgen, T., Joroff, M., Porter, W., and Schoren, D. (1998). *Excellence By Design: Transforming Workplace and Work Practice.* New York, NY: John Wiley & Sons.

Horvath, I. (November 24, 2005). *CEOs who fail to actively manage outsourcing relationships miss out on, Àòtrust dividendchar(39) worth up 40 per cent of contract value.* http://www.logica.co.uk/r/350233169/CEOs+who+fail+to+actively+manage+outsourcing+relationships+miss+out+on+%E2%80% 98trust+dividendchar(39)+worth+up+40+per+cent+of+contract+value/ 400002957.

Irving, W., and Wallechinsky, D. (n.d.). *Most Powerful Groups in the World - The Business Roundtable Part 1—Trivia-Library.com.* http://www.trivia-library. com/c/most-powerful-groups-in-the-world-the-business-roundtable-part-1. htm.

Jernigan, F. (2008). *BIG BIM little bim Second Edition.* Salisbury, MD: 4site Press.

Jones, S. *Introduction to BIM. SmartMarket Report Design and Construction Intelligence,* 1–45.

Kaspoir, D. (n.d.). *The Maze Corporation.* http://www.themaze.org/opensource .html.

Kats, G. *Cost and Benefits of Green Buildings. A Report to California's Sustainable Buildings Task Force,* 1–134.

Kennedy, D., and Charles, L. (n.d.). *Healthy Communities Movement.* www .bibalex.org/supercourse/supercoursePPT/4011-5001/4261.ppt.

Kennedy, M. (2008). *Product Development for the Lean Enterprise: Why Toyota's System Is Four Times More Productive and How You Can Implement It.* Richmond: Oaklea Press.

Kieran, S., and Timberlake, J. (2003). *Refabricating Architecture: How Manufacturing Methodologies are Poised to Transform Building Construction.* New York: McGraw-Hill Professional.

Kim, W., and Mauborgne, R. (2005). *Blue Ocean Strategy: How to Create Uncontested Market Space and Make Competition Irrelevant.* New York: Harvard Business School Press.

Koerner, P. (April 8, 2007). *Skyscraper Sunday: LEED Platinum Banner Bank Building - Green Building Blog—Jetson Green.* http://www.jetsongreen.com/2007/04/skyscraper_sund_1.html.

Kuhn, T. (1996). *The Structure of Scientific Revolutions.* Chicago: University of Chicago Press.

Laiserin, J. (July 1, 2002). *The LaiserinLetter (tm).* http://www.laiserin.com/features/issue05/feature01.php.

Laur, J., Schley, S., Senge, P., and Smith, B. (2008). *The Necessary Revolution: How Individuals And Organizations Are Working Together to Create a Sustainable World.* New York: Currency.

Lepatner, B. (2008). *Broken Buildings, Busted Budgets: How to Fix America's Trillion-Dollar Construction Industry.* Chicago: University of Chicago Press.

Lepatner, B. (October 1, 2008). *Fixed-Price Contracts.* http://www.aia.org/nwsltr_pm.cfm?pagename=pm_a_112007_fixedpricecontracts.

Levy, S. (October 10, 2008). We Should Build Our Own. *Wired, 16.10,* 150.

Lichtig, W. (June 1, 2006). *The Integrated Agreement for Lean Project Delivery.* www.mhalaw.com/mha/newsroom/articles/ABA_IntegratedAgmt.pdf.

Loftness, V., Hartkopf, V., and Gurtekin, B. Cost-Benefit Tool to Promote High Performance Components, Flexible Infrastructures and Systems Integration for Sustainable Commercial Buildings and Productive Organizations. *Building Investment Decision Support (BIDS),* 1–30.

Long, J., Magnolfi, J., and Massen, L. (2008). *Always Building: The Programmable Environment.* Zeeland: Herman Miller, Inc.

Lyman, A. (n.d.). *Great Place to Work Æ Institute.* http://www.greatplacetowork.com/.

M. Civitello, Jr., A. (1987). *Contractor's Guide to Change Orders: The Art of Finding, Pricing, and Getting Paid for Contract Changes and the Damages They Cause.* Alexandria, VA: Prentice-Hall.

Malone, M. (December 21, 2008). *Washington Is Killing Silicon Valley—WSJ.com.* http://online.wsj.com/article/SB122990472028925207.html.

Manfra, L. (October 5, 2004). *Report Disputes Extra Cost of Building Green.* http://www.metropolismag.com/story/20041005/report-disputes-extra-cost-of-building-green.

Manning, J. (June 30, 2006). *Museum building work 36 percent over budget. ORian (Portland, OR).* http://www.accessmylibrary.com/coms2/summary_0286–15806235_ITM.

Maryanne, W. (2007). *Proust and the Squid: The Story and Science of the Reading Brain.* New York: Harper.

May, M. (2006). *The Elegant Solution: Toyota's Formula for Mastering Innovation.* New York City: Free Press.

Mazria, E. (n.d.). *Climate Change, Global Warming, and the Built Environment - Architecture 2030.* http://www.architecture2030.org/home.html.

Mcduffie, T. (September 1, 2008). *BIM: Transforming a Traditional Practice Model into a Technology-Enabled Integrated Practice Model.* http://www.aia.org/nwsltr_pa.cfm?pagename=pa_a_200610_bim.

Merrill, R., and Covey, S. (2006). *The Speed of Trust*. New York, NY: Simon & Schuster.

Michael Schrage Home Page. (n.d.). http://ebusiness.mit.edu/Schrage/.

Miller, M. (2004). *The Millennium Matrix: Reclaiming the Past, Reframing the Future of the Church (J-B Leadership Network Series)*. San Francisco: Jossey-Bass.

Mossman, A. (November 16, 2007). Last Planner: Collaborative Production Planning, Collaborative Programme Coordination. *Lean Construction Institute UK*, pp. 1–6.

NCBG: Public Works:. (n.d.). http://ncbg.org/public_works/millennium_park .htm.

National Builders Alliance. (n.d.). http://www.nationalbuildersalliance.com/.

Nelson, A. (December 19, 2004). *City Mayors: Built environment—USA*. http:// www.citymayors.com/development/built_environment_usa.html.

Newport, J. (September 27, 2008). Team USA's Management Victory. *Wall Street Journal*. http://online.wsj.com/article_email/SB122246633744980277-lMyQjAxMDI4MjIyOTQyNjk2Wj.html.

Office, G.B. (2000). Modernising Construction (House of Commons Papers). London: Stationery Office Books.

O'Reilly, C., & Tushman, M. The Ambidextrous Organization. *Harvard Business Review*, 1–8.

Orr, D. (2008). *Design on the Edge: The Making of a High-Performance Building (Cooperative Information System)*. London: The MIT Press.

Palfrey, J. (2008). *Born Digital: Understanding the First Generation of Digital Natives*. New York: Basic Books.

Post, N. (November 26, 2007). Sutter Health Unlocks the Door to A New Process. *engineering news record*. http://enr.ecnext.com/coms2/article_febiar071121a-1.

Prescott, J. (1998). Rethinking Construction. London: Department of Trade and Industry.

Products and Players' Trends—Outlook 2009—Research—Analytics—McGraw-Hill Construction. (October 23, 2008). http://construction.ecnext.com/coms2/ summary_0249-295662_ITM_analytics.

Project management—Wikipedia, the free encyclopedia. (n.d.). http://en.wikipedia. org/wiki/Project_management.

Ray Anderson, sustainable biz pioneer, answers questions | Grist | InterActivist | Nov 8 2004. (November 4, 2004). http://www.grist.org/comments/ interactivist/2004/11/08/anderson/.

Real Estate Developer.com. (n.d.). http://www.realestatedeveloper.com/.

Revit Provides Parametric Design for Architects. (April 1, 2000). http://aecnews. com/articles/619.aspx.

Roger's Roundtable—TIME. (August 29, 1969). http://www.time.com/time/mag-azine/article/0,9171,901319-1,00.html.

Rogers, E., and Rogers, E. (2003). *Diffusion of Innovations, 5th Edition*. New York City: Free Press.

Sarkar, C. (n.d.). *The SPEED of Trust: Trust, Branding & Competitive Advantage: An Interview with Stephen M.R. Covey by Christian Sarkar*. http://www .emorymi.com/covey.html.

Schrage, M. (1995). *No More Teams!: Mastering the Dynamics of Creative Collaboration.* New York, NY: Currency Doubleday.

Schrage, M. (1999). *Serious Play: How the World's Best Companies Simulate to Innovate.* New York: Harvard Business School Press.

Schultz, S. (December 21, 2007). *Hopkins Project Delayed, Over Budget.* baltimore.bizjournals.com/baltimore/stories/2007/12/24/story1.html?b= 1198472400^1566928.

Shaw, M. (September 15, 2008). *Building a better contract, Sacramento Business Journal.* http://www.bizjournals.com/sacramento/stories/2008/09/15/focus1 .html.

Simons, T. (2008). *The Integrity Dividend: Leading by the Power of Your Word.* San Francisco: Jossey-Bass.

Simonson, S. (August 9, 2004). *Sutter builds 'lean' to pre-empt Kaiser, East Bay Business Times* http://www.bizjournals.com/eastbay/stories/2004/08/09/ focus3.html.

Small, G., and Vorgan, G. (2008). *iBrain: Surviving the Technological Alteration of the Modern Mind.* New York: Collins Living.

Smith, D., and Tardif, M. (2009). *Building Information Modeling: A Strategic Implementation Guide for Architects, Engineers, Constructors, and Real Estate Asset Managers.* New York, NY: John Wiley & Sons.

Smith, D., and Edgar, A. (July 24, 2008). *Building Information Modeling (BIM) | Whole Building Design Guide.* http://www.wbdg.org/bim/bim.php.

Smith, D., and Edgar, A. (July 24, 2008). *Building Information Modeling (BIM) | Whole Building Design Guide.* http://www.wbdg.org/bim/bim.php.

Sowards, D. (May 5, 2008). *IndustryWeek: Manufacturers Need to Look at Lean Construction.* http://www.industryweek.com/ReadArticle.aspx?ArticleID= 16241.

Stewart, J. (May 6, 2008). *Worldchanging: BIMstorm: Honing Bureaucracy, Giving Urbanism an Edge.* http://www.worldchanging.com/archives/008010.html.

Story, D. (February 21, 2003). *Swarm Intelligence: An Interview with Eric Bonabeau | O'Reilly Media.* http://www.openp2p.com/pub/a/p2p/2003/02/ 21/bonabeau.html.

Sustainability Case Study: Banner Bank—A LEED Platinum, High-Performance Facility. (April 4, 2007). http://www.fmlink.com/ProfResources/Sustainability/ Articles/article.cgi?USGBC:200703-19.html.

TOYOTA: Non-Automotive > Housing. (n.d.). http://www.toyota.co.jp/en/ more_than_cars/housing/index.html.

Tapscott, D. (2008). *Grown Up Digital: How the Net Generation is Changing the World.* New York: McGraw-Hill.

Thaler, R. (1994). *The Winner's Curse.* Princeton: Princeton University Press.

The Federal Government's Financial Health. (n.d.). www.whitehouse.gov/omb/ financial/reports/citizens_guide.pdf.

The Top 25 Newsmakers of 2007—McGraw-Hill Construction | ENR. (n.d.). http://enr.construction.com/people/AOE-Gallery/newsmakers/080114/ 080114-15.asp.

Thomas Kuhn (Stanford Encyclopedia of Philosophy). (August 13, 2004). http:// plato.stanford.edu/entries/thomas-kuhn/.

Thomsen, C. (2006). *Project Delivery Processes*. Washington, DC: AIA.

Thurm, D. Master of the House: Why a Company Should Take Control of Its Building Projects. *Harvard Business Review*, 1–9.

Trammell Crow Company—Office. (n.d.). http://www.trammellcrow.com/default.aspx?ServiceId=26&TabId=172.

U.S. Energy System. (May 1, 2007). http://css.snre.umich.edu/.

Vellequette, L., and Troy, T. (October 16, 2008). *Joe the plumber' isn't licensed*. www.toledoblade.com/apps/pbcs.dll/article?AID=/20081016/NEWS09/810160418.

Wallace, I., and Wallechinsky, D. (1981). *The People's Almanac #3*. New York: Bantam Books.

Weinberger, D. (2007). *Everything Is Miscellaneous: The Power of the New Digital Disorder*. New York: Times Books.

What the Bleep Do We Know!? & What the Bleep!?—Down the Rabbit Hole. (n.d.). http://www.whatthebleep.com/.

Wood, S. (January 1, 2008). *Toyota enters housing market*. http://www.mysanantonio.com/business/MYSA012006_01C_toyota_1c3428d0_html.html.

Zeiger, M. (January 11, 2008). *Technology: BIM Streamlines, and Blurs Lines*. http://www.architectmagazine.com/industry-news.asp?articleID=809080.

Zeleny, J. (November 9, 2008). *Obama Weighs Quick Undoing of Bush Policy*. *NYTimes.com*. http://www.nytimes.com/2008/11/10/us/politics/10obama.html?ref=politics.

(2007). *Integrated Project Delivery Guide*. Washington, DC: American Institute of Architects.

(2008). *Minds at Work*. Jasper: Kimball Office.

(1999). *The Integrated Workplace: A Comprehensive Approach to Developing Workspace*. Washington, DC: GSA.

Index